play in CREATIVE PROBLEM-SOLVING
for planners and architects

Creative problem-solving requires an appreciation for ambiguity, uncertainty of outcome, complexity that leads to the discovery of novelty and innovation. In *Play in Creative Problem-solving for Planners and Architects*, "play" is defined, explored and demonstrated as a critical catalyst in creative problem-solving processes.

This book defines the current psychological research into play and creative problem-solving, explores the necessary integration of the two, and exemplifies the use of play in creative endeavors and the role that play serves in separating linear from creative problem-solving approaches. With a focus on urban design, planning, architecture, and landscape architecture, the book re-establishes the whole mind–body thinking process of play as a means of object-learning to provide readers with alternative ways of design-thinking.

It incorporates examples and exercises in play activities related to the design and planning fields, and exercises related to play-tools and skills for students and professionals. It also defines terms used in play and creativity psychology, provides examples and structure for play and creative problem-solving activities, and describes the type and use of appropriate play-tools. Richly illustrated, *Play in Creative Problem-solving for Planners and Architects* is fundamental reading for students and professionals in urban design and planning fields.

Ron Kasprisin is an architect, urban planner and watercolor artist, and Professor Emeritus, Urban Design and Planning, College of Built Environments, University of Washington, Seattle. Ron has practiced as Kasprisin Pettinari Design (Seattle and Portland) since 1975 and taught urban design since 1989. His books include: *Urban Design: The composition of complexity*, *Design Media*, *Visual Thinking for Architects and Designers*, and *Watercolor in Architectural Design*.

"Design is a serendipitous conversation between the sketching hand and the critical eye. This iterative process is dull and incomplete without some playful speculation and explorative fun, which loosen the senses and shuffle preconceptions. This agile book privileges the physical hand over the electronic hand."—**Doug Kelbaugh, University of Michigan**

"This book is visually stunning for the quality of the images, and academically for elucidating the role of creative problem-solving in art, design and planning. The principles of Friedrich Froebel's Kindergarten are vividly exemplified in contemporary terms through object-learning and PLAY, guiding the reader to the discovery of where ideas come from."—**John Gilbert Luebtow, Artist, www.luebtow.com**

play in **CREATIVE PROBLEM-SOLVING**
for planners and architects

Ron Kasprisin

Routledge
Taylor & Francis Group

NEW YORK AND LONDON

First published 2016
by Routledge
711 Third Avenue, New York, NY 10017

and by Routledge
2 Park Square, Milton Park, Abingdon, Oxon OX14 4RN

Routledge is an imprint of the Taylor & Francis Group, an informa business

Library of Congress Cataloging in Publication Data
Names: Kasprisin, Ronald J., author.
Title: Play in creative problem-solving for planners and architects /
By Ron Kasprisin.
Description: New York : Routledge, 2016. | Includes bibliographical
references and index.
Identifiers: LCCN 2015049667| ISBN 9781138120044 (hardcover) | ISBN
9781138120051 (pbk.) | ISBN 9781315651965 (ebook)
Subjects: LCSH: City planning--Decision making. | Architectural design--
Decision making. | Creative thinking. | Play.
Classification: LCC HT166 .K3585 2016 | DDC 307.1/216--dc23
LC record available at http://lccn.loc.gov/2015049667

ISBN: 978-1-138-12004-4 (hbk)
ISBN: 978-1-138-12005-1 (pbk)
ISBN: 978-1-315-65196-5 (ebk)

Typeset in Adobe Garamond
by Florence Production Ltd, Stoodleigh, Devon, UK

Printed and bound in the United States of America by Sheridan

CONTENTS

List of figures   *viii*

Dedication   *xiii*

Acknowledgments   *xv*

Foreword   *xvi*

Introduction   **1**

Major Elements of the Book   2

The Integration of Creative Problem-solving and Object-learning through Play   2

CPS: Why is it Different from Normative Problem-solving?   2

Creativity in CPS   3

What Activates the Creative Aspect of CPS: Play in Object-learning as a
    Sensory Process   5

Challenges   5

Definition of Terms   6

1   Creative Problem-solving (CPS) for Design and Planning   **9**

Creative Problem-solving (CPS)   9

The Creativity Path: Whole Mind–Body Thinking   10

The CPS Process   13

What Makes CPS Different from Conventional Problem-solving?   14

An Example of CPS in the Design/Planning Context   20

**2   Object-learning through Play: Object-learning, Constructivism, and
    Self-learning through Symbolic Play**   **23**

Object-learning   23

Constructivism and Play   24

Object-play: The Activity-vehicle for Object-learning   26

Play   27

Motivational Aspects of Play and Creativity   31

3   The Gifts of Friedrich Froebel   **41**

Kindergarten: The Children's Garden   41

Kindergarten: Playtime and the Froebel "Gifts"   42

The Twenty Gifts of Froebel   42

CONTENTS

The Froebel Kindergarten's Impact on Art and Design   46
The Importance of Froebel's Gifts to Contemporary Designers and Planners   48

4 How do Designers Play?   **49**

How Do Architects and Artists Play?   49
Interviews with Regional Architects, Designers, and Artists   52
An Enjoyable Experiment   53

5 Setting the Stage—Play Environment   **59**

Advantages of the Studio Process   59
Studio Principles and Methodologies: Environment, Process, Culture   60

6 Object-learning with Play-tools/Skills   **71**

Skill Development   71
Learning with Symbolic Objects   72
Let's Play: Exercises in Meta-play   74
Symbolic Object-play   75
Symbolic Objects   76
Symbolic (Spatial) Reference Guides: The Grid   78
Paper   79
Cardboard   85
Wood Blocks   91
Playskool and other Wood Blocks   97
String and Yarn Materials   100
Plastic Blocks   100
Clay (Modeling) and Wax   102
Metal   103
Sculpture   103
Drawing   104
Painting and Pastels   110
Watercolor   111
Pastels, Pastel Pencils, and Crayons   117
Models   118
Spatial Movement as Play   122
Games and Gaming   123

7 Object-learning Applications in Design and Planning   **127**

CPS Object-learning and Play Applications   127
The Semiotic Diagram   129
Techniques for the Semiotic Diagramming Process   132
Play Applications for Brainstorming   146
Internal Team Brainstorming   147
Public Interactive Brainstorming   147

Design Intensives or Charrettes   150

Case Study One: Sechelt Vision Plan, Sechelt, BC, Canada   152

Case Study Two: Project Safe Haven—Tsunami Vertical Evacuation on the
        Washington Coast   155

Development and Building Typologies   160

Object-learning Activators for Play-activities   168

Experiments in Object-learning Play   172

Mixed Symbolic Object Compositions   188

Drawing as Object-learning   198

8   Integration of Digital Technologies and Crafting Processes   **203**

Divergent Thinking   204

Convergent Thinking   204

Some Final Thoughts . . .   208

Appendix: Suggested Exercises in Object-learning Play   *209*

Notes   *214*

Bibliography   *215*

Index   *219*

FIGURES

1.1	The CPS Process	9
1.2	The CST Matrix and Context	14
2.1	Object-learning	23
3.1	Froebel and Object-learning through Symbolic Objects	43
4.1	The Conceptual Drawing—the Prima Drawing	54
4.2	The Progressive Drawing	54
4.3	The Final Piece	55
4.4	The Final Piece Activated	55
4.5	Architects at Play (A)	56
4.6	Architects at Play (B)	56
4.7	Architects at Play (C)	57
4.8	Architects at Play (D)	57
4.9	Architects at Play (E)	57
5.1	Studio Environment	68
5.2	Studio Duality	68
5.3	Studio Discovery Model 1	69
5.4	Studio Discovery Model 2	69
6.1	CPS Diagram	73
6.2	Symbolic Objects as Tools	76
6.3	The Grid and Grid-derivatives	78
6.4	Student Construction Paper Experiment	80
6.5	Construction Paper Volumetric Studies	80
6.6	Craft Paper Process Model	81
6.7	Abstract Collage	82
6.8	"Let's Play Spaceship"	83
6.9	Repetition with Variety	84
6.10	Vertical Planes in Motion	85
6.11a	Cardboard Play	86
6.11b	Group Cardboard Interaction	87
6.12	Cardboard Compositions	88
6.13	Chipboard as Context and Process Models	89
6.14	Poster Board Constructions	90
6.15	Halsam's American Wood Building Bricks	92
6.16	Two-dimensional Combinations of Line and Square	93
6.17a/b	Setting the Directional Movement	94

6.18	Compaction	95
6.19	Compaction Cluster	95
6.20	Brick Mass A	96
6.21	Brick Mass B	96
6.22	Brick Mass C	96
6.23	Brick Mass D	96
6.24	Brick Mass Additives	96
6.25	Wood Blocks	97
6.26	Cylinders	98
6.27	Pyramids and Triangles	98
6.28	Wood Slat Pattern	99
6.29	Pick-up Sticks	100
6.30	String and Yarn	100
6.31	Manipulating Primary Shapes with Legos	101
6.32	Legos as Circular Compositional Structure	101
6.33	Clay Blocks or Bricks	102
6.34	The Doodle Sketch	105
6.35	The Playful Perspective Sketch	106
6.36	The Axonometric Drawing	107
6.37	Color Marker Diagrams	108
6.38a	Color Pencil Example	109
6.38b	St. Paul Connection (Color Pencil)	110
6.39	The Roman Forest God	115
6.40	Bruno	115
6.41	Red Rider	116
6.42	Blue Boy	116
6.43	Pastels: Haines, Alaska	117
6.44	Semi-abstract Models: Everett Voids A	119
6.45	Everett Voids B	120
6.46	Everett Civic Center	120
6.47	Gaming Model	121
6.48	Gaming	124
7.1	CPS Diagram: Play Diagrams	128
7.2	Line Weight and Type	135
7.3a	Line Values, Weights and Arrangements	137
7.3b	Symbol Types	138
7.4	Movement, Direction, Spatial Characteristics	139
7.5a	Portland Waterfront Historic Patterning	140
7.5b	Ketchikan Historic Patterning	140
7.6	Existing Context Diagram Series	141
7.7	Scale Ladder (Planet to Room)	142
7.8	Natural Environmental Structures	143
7.9	Downtown Ketchikan District Diagram	144
7.10	Roosevelt Commercial District: Emerging Reality	144

Dedicated to my beloved "Whidbey"
2001–2013

Thank you from my heart to your heart

and

For your continuance, young "Bacchus"

and

To my granddaughter Margot, who at one year
discovered how to connect her Legos as well as take
them apart!

*Why dedicate a book to a Labrador Retriever, two in fact?
To me, they are play. One friend passes on with the others,
always in memory for his pure joy of living and his play;
and the next is born and embraced and is embracing in
that same joy.*

ACKNOWLEDGMENTS

This book began in discussions with my friend and colleague John Luebtow, glass sculptor and recently retired Director of Arts at Harvard Academy (Los Angeles). We are both in admiration for the contributions of Friedrich Froebel, educator and developer of the kindergarten system in Germany in the early 1800s—the children's garden; and with kindergarten's later impact on the artists and architects of the Bauhaus; and later including Frank Lloyd Wright through his mother's introduction to the Froebel system at the Philadelphia Exposition (1897), and Froebel's contribution to early learning worldwide. I also want to thank friend and colleague Greg "Fish" Salmon for his assistance on lighting for the photography in this book. Fish was the sound and sometime lighting specialist for Neil Young, Joni Mitchel, Carli Simon and others in his prime—what fun. I will take responsibility for the "flubs." To my long-time business partner and friend, Professor Emeritus James Pettinari, Director (retired) of the Urban Architecture Program, University of Oregon, Portland, Oregon for letting me highlight his beautiful pen-and-ink drawings and for his sage advice during this process—of course, over a little red wine. And lastly, to the various graduate students at the University of Washington who provided comment, examples and sage advice for their professor in this endeavor. This includes the many students who have tolerated my constant reminders to play and craft along with their digital technologies, as I appreciate their feedback and support. Of course, to young Bacchus, my lab, I thank him for his patience as I worked on the book instead of throwing his sticks. And, if names of former graduate students have been omitted, please accept our apologies.

FOREWORD

Kindergarten for Adults

Okay, this is about *kindergarten—for adults, especially in the design and planning fields,* including architecture, landscape architecture, urban design and planning and the graphic arts. And the principles in the book apply to most other fields where creativity can be a desired and integral part of the problem-solving process. Why kindergarten? Because the original *children's garden* embodied the key components and activities of creative actions through object-teaching (and object-learning), as developed by Friedrich Froebel, as we shall discuss.

There is a serious message in this book based on a significant and contemporary body of literature and research. I want that message to come across to students and young professionals in a direct, personal and enjoyable manner. I have interjected some personal experiences hopefully with an element of humor to facilitate the message, along with playful experiments and exercises.

There are many experiments and exercises that are possible given the idea of object-learning and play. I was limited in time as I wanted to do most of the work myself—to learn for myself more about creative problem-solving that can apply to the design and planning professions. I kept the experiments limited to or focused on conceptual compositions rather than sophisticated design solutions with detailed case studies and contextual background. That may be a weakness but the emphasis here is on object-learning through play. I hope the reader enjoys reviewing the work as much as I enjoyed doing the work. The lessons contained within that work can extend into the classroom, studio and office—next to the computer.

Most of the exercises and experiments in the book may be done on a computer with three-dimensional modeling programs. Consequently, the principles embodied in the experiments can apply to both computational design and hand-crafting with the senses. How they are done, with specific skills and tools, what is discovered along the way and why, constitute the significant difference between computational design methods and crafting methods. The *how* affects creative outcomes in problem-solving—this difference represents the basics of the mission of the book. This is not an anti-technology work. I address the necessary integration of processing/evaluation and generation represented by convergent and divergent thinking, respectively in the final chapter. They are different and are both needed in the complex design process.

Older designers and planners will recognize many of the materials, objects, skills and means highlighted in the work. They may be considered "out-of-date," childish or even historic. I beg to differ. I have found through hands-on play that they are classic and relevant in creative problem-solving today more than ever.

Many younger students and professionals may simply view them as "old-fashioned," obsolete, time-consuming and clumsy. Many contemporary students that I observe in design and planning curricula have never done any design-related problem-solving except on a computer; a significant shortcoming, I argue, in their education and design capacities. I have observed enough clip-art and simulations replacing design visualizations and outcomes that I think a restart is needed in what we teach and how we teach in these spatially oriented fields.

Is this book simply justifying my training as an architect and urban designer beginning in the 1960s? Is it nostalgic for skills that are fast disappearing? In some measure, of course those factors are always present. But don't I wish that I had had much of this background and training in architecture! In part, this work is my way of teaching myself important skills that I did not learn or were loosely provided by well-intentioned instructors. They were talented and dedicated but the explanations of the elements and principles of design composition were lacking, limited to "good work," "try this," etc. This is not a criticism of their energy and knowledge but simply a reflection on the missing links of "why," "based on what principles," and on the retention of an order in the design of community complexity. Design composition is a language that requires "nouns" (objects and shapes) and "verbs" (activators) and real objects to manipulate into cohesive form. Consequently the book picks up where *Urban Design: The Composition of Complexity* (Kasprisin, 2011) left off in pursuing this compositional language and process.

Design and planning require a dedicated and earnest responsiveness to the key factors of urbanism: need (the users), program (what and how much to meet that need), and context (the reality factors of "where")—in other words, meaning and functionality. It is not about form versus function or form follows function or conversely. It is a process of compositional integration which requires sound information and analysis that is translated into community relationships and spatial metaphors; integrated with creative experimentation to spatially manifest those relationships; embracing an openness to diversity, a tolerance for uncertainty, an appreciation for ambiguity and discovery that can lead to novel solutions that just may lead to innovation; and may even lead to a definition of a *creative urbanism*.

The Umbrella of Creative Problem-solving

This is why the book begins with the overall umbrella of creative problem-solving (CPS)—a term not to be taken lightly, as it is significantly different in every way from normative and linear problem-solving. And this CPS, when overlaid with the culture/space/time trialectics of community (Soja, 1996), requires a plurality of design/planning thinking processes and skills—not one, whether technology based or hand-crafted, but many. In addition, this process requires a return to the inclusion of sensory thinking with manual dexterity skills along with more disconnected (from the senses) technological means and methods in the larger problem-solving process.

In my watercolor classes, I marvel at the initial reticence (a form of fear) of architecture and landscape architecture students as they engage brush, water, pigment, palette and paper in a sensory dance (and wrestling match)—about as sensory as one can get in art/design. This initial fear or trepidation is always followed by exhilaration as they improve skills, gain confidence and progress as "painters." And they look in wonder at their final academic quarter paintings and reflect on what they produced in relation to where they started—that is exciting. I get the same reaction and growth in my urban design composition courses from urban planning students—a discovery of a new language with new abilities that can lead to compositional creativity. I hope I can pass that exhilaration on to many readers.

All cultures have creative capacities and the ability to play. Some are fortunate in that they have the time to dedicate to creative endeavors. Others have integrated those endeavors into everyday life activities, and others are so busy surviving the world that play is minimized and creativity is limited to survival means and methods. I cannot address all cultures in regard to play, and am of the opinion based on years of teaching, practice and travel that many of the basic principles of play cross most cultural boundaries. The work in this book is certainly oriented toward Western cultures in its examples; time and resources are limited; and the principles within CPS, object-learning and play can apply universally. For a discussion on play in other cultures, refer to Luciano L'Abate's *The Praeger Handbook of Play across the Life Cycle: From Infancy to Old Age* (2009).

Consequently, is this work about old-fashioned means and methods? You decide. All materials, objects, methods and skills will not appeal to everyone, as the market for the book may range from high school to postgraduate school to professional offices. Find your comfort zone. I hope it leads to a lively discussion on the need for an integration of sensory and technological thinking and processing in design and planning—and a return to the elemental principles of the spirit of kindergarten. And they are all founded in the principles of art, a subject, considered trivial by many school boards, that is rapidly becoming obsolete in many school systems.

INTRODUCTION

Creativity exists not only where it creates great historical works, but also everywhere human imagination combines, changes, and creates anything new.

(Vygotsky, 1978, p. 14)

Creative problem-solving (CPS) is a process that is often taken for granted, assumed to be a natural or inherent part of the design and planning processes. It certainly has a recognized history as a part of architecture and related domains. It also represents a significant difference in cultural approaches to problem-solving, between divergent and convergent thinking and their related methods, but more on that later. The design and planning processes are being challenged and altered by new approaches, skills and tools, mainly associated with digital technology. The ways and means by which information and ideas are processed has reached a tipping point. Is it time for some reflection on where we are, where we are going and how—as professions?

An early reviewer of this manuscript appreciated the discussion of "old-fashioned" skills and tools. The question then emerges that if these are "old-fashioned," what indeed are the new and contemporary design and planning skills and tools? If the answer is essentially digital technologies, then I argue that a reassessment of our design/planning approaches is in order. One shoe does not fit all feet. And let me state clearly upfront: this is *not* an anti-technology book; moreover, it is an argument for an integral pluralistic approach to design and planning through creative problem-solving that focuses on object-learning/object-teaching through play in association with digital technologies: divergent and convergent thinking processes.

The book's discussion of creative problem-solving defines a process that is not linear, not goal-oriented, is oriented toward sensory thinking and cognitive perception; and goes beyond competence in the search or, better yet, the discovery of novelty that can lead to innovation in the design/planning domains. Those professionals in middle age and beyond will find familiar processes, skills and tools described and exemplified in the book. In my teaching experience I am now challenged by students who have never engaged problem-solving except with digital technologies. I hope they will find the book's material to be a significant expansion of their problem-solving efforts, not a replacement for the new technologies.

As a young boy I was fortunate to have had parents who, without any education beyond the eighth grade, understood the positive joy that play brought to my growth—they accepted and affirmed my desire to play, provided the space and patience for that play to occur, and encouraged rather than constrained my play-activities. And they had no idea of why but understood the reason for . . . I had a spare room on the second floor of our family's house in Cleveland, Ohio that was partially finished with floor and insulation. The room had wooden planks across the floor, insulation in the ceiling, places that were off-limits (my dad actually put his leg through the dining room ceiling walking around upstairs), a large double bed, blankets, cushions and other available objects that became for me mountains, hills and valleys that accepted my wooden blocks, rubber toy soldiers, trucks and cardboard concoctions—constantly undergoing changes in form as the stories I played out changed in their evolutions. Calls to dinner were often ignored due to my rapture and often resulted in a semi-stern mother standing at the door insisting I join everyone for dinner. "You can always go back to your play," she often said. And, of course, I did with her support and encouragement. I was in a place that had no fear, no failure; a safe and familiar environment, a "playroom" that provided years of pleasure and joy as opposed to the fun and rewards of sandlot baseball (which I also did with gusto!) . . . and my mother understood that feeling of safe discovery through play.

My father was on board to a degree. One summer day he was walking through the back yard coming home from work when he stopped, rolled his eyes and yelled: "Annie, come get your son—he is ruining my yard!" In my revelry I had removed a 15-foot-long 6-inch-wide swathe of his carefully groomed grass in a large area for a "road" for my bulldozers, trucks, tanks and wood blocks in some imaginary world. I thought my outdoor playroom was neat! Dad was not so convinced. The ability to transform one place into a fantasy world was exhilarating and, of course, the grass grew back.

Major Elements of the Book

This book addresses five major elements with associated materials, skills, means and methods and experiments and examples:

1.   CPS
2.   Creativity
3.   Object-learning/Object-teaching
4.   Play and Playfulness
5.   Object-learning Activators.

The Integration of Creative Problem-solving and Object-learning through Play

Problem-solving is a daily challenge, an activity that confronts us both in our occupations and personal lives. It is commonly based on goal-oriented processes and conventions, with established rules and programs resulting in a formalized approach. CPS is significantly different in that the process is open with an uncertain outcome; where rules emerge and change during the process; with a product that evolves in the same fashion. The challenge in CPS is to maintain the integrity of creativity during the process. And as we shall explore, CPS requires a mind–body, intellect and sensory-based process. That sensory aspect requires engagement with real objects, materials and all their characteristics, and is referred to in the book as object-learning (primarily with symbolic objects). Object-learning is activated through play-activities that reduce and even eliminate fear and failure. Froebel referred to the process as object-teaching in kindergarten.

CPS: Why is it Different from Normative Problem-solving?

CPS is differentiated from *normative* or goal-oriented problem-solving with four essential characteristics:

- The problem is not specified exactly, especially at the onset of the process;
- The nature of the solution is largely open during the process;
- The pathway to the solution is not specified, is complex, can be ambiguous, and
- The criteria for recognizing a solution are open.

(Cropley and Cropley, 2009)

Creativity in CPS

Creativity is essential to CPS; *creativity: the ability to imagine what has never existed* (Lehrer, 2012). Creativity as a process includes sensory exploration, play, imagination and fantasy in a transformative activity that synthesizes emotion, meaning and cognitive symbols (Vygotsky, 1978). Later I discuss the importance of those cognitive symbols in design and planning as expressed through semiotics, the language of signs and symbols.

CPS is critical to the design and planning design fields in particular; and offers both processes and products that can better our lives, reduce compromise and further creative discoveries. Within this creative process are actions and activities that foster openness and lead to novel solutions which in turn can lead to innovation. These activities consist of "play" and "playful behavior" with objects during the process. Design and art are the most recognized processes associated with CPS; and their principles can apply to any field of endeavor. In my explorations I find that play can be applied within almost every aspect of divergent and convergent thinking. I narrow its focus later in the book to the imaginal, symbolic and conceptual phase of problem-solving due to time constraints.

The possibility that a *playful* orientation promotes insight into problem-solving or that a playful orientation is characteristic of creativity has motivated significant research regarding creativity, object-learning and play. The inclusion of play in the design process challenges current design theories that claim or pursue a universality of application; or formulize problem-solving methods, skill and tools into set applications. Meta-play and meta-determinancy, the uncertain path to creativity that generates an emerging awareness of involvement, is at the heart of this work guided by play.

Snodgrass and Coyne (2006, p. 65) capture the principles of play:

> It is not possible to play a game without rules; yet the rules only take actual shape when the game is played; and outside the particular specific instance of its playing, neither the game nor its rules have concrete shape or existence. The rules provide a framework for the playing of the game and determine the range of appropriate actions the players can take, but they do not account for the way the game is played or the way it turns out each time it is played. Like the game itself, the rules only really exist in the actual playing of the game. The game is not the rules but its playing . . . design rules govern the design process but only "come to life" when they are applied in a particular concrete design instance . . . in playing the game, the rules never take the same shape or are realized in the same way on two occasions . . . the rules of the game change in their application.

Later in the book I make a distinction between "gaming" and "playing," as they are different in their rules, characteristics and motives. A game is usually competitive with a winner/loser and a set of overall rules that are less flexible or changeable, whereas play is a free activity, beginning with rules that change as the play progresses with no winner/loser.

As opposed to the concept of gaming, the "why" in play is replaced by the unknown "discovery," following its own lead in the "wandering nature of play" (Eberle, 2014), and revealing new potentials as the play progresses, fueled by a joy at the engagement. And we shall explore in the definitions of play that it is not possible to remove the play from the viewpoints or intentions of the player, i.e., the play cannot be taken from where and when and with whom it involves (Eberle, 2014). This is truly distinct from "gaming."

In order to explore object-learning and play for adults in the design and planning professions, this book builds on the work of Friedrich Froebel (1898), the founder of Kindergarten in Germany in the early 1800s (Froebel, *The Education of Man* (republished in 1926)). Many discussions of Froebel's work with my friend and colleague John Luebtow, internationally renowned glass artist, cemented my motivation to explore Froebel's *classic* object-teaching, assess its viability and transferability to contemporary problem-solving and integrate its principles into a pluralistic approach. Both John and I agree on the need to reinsert the concept of "play" into the art, design and urban studies fields. Froebel's work provides a guide and a dialogue on the role of object-learning/object-teaching and play in CPS, and serves as the foundation of this book.

> There must be an inner connection between the pupil's mind and the objects which he studies, and this shall determine what to study. There must be an inner connection in those objects among themselves which determines the succession and the order in which they are to be taken up in the course of instruction . . . there is an inner connection within the soul that unites the faculties of feeling, perception, phantasy, thought, and volition, and determines the law of their unfolding. Inner connection is in fact the law of development, the principle of evolution . . . Froebel's aim is to educate the pupil through self-activity . . . unfold[ing] his will-power quite as much as his sense-perception . . . [and] . . . he must begin with that which is attractive to him.
>
> (Froebel, 1926, pp. v–vi)

Froebel introduced "play" as a self-activity, enjoyable, sensory, wondrous and thoughtful—not frivolous or "childish."

> In play the child ascertains what he can do, and discovers the possibilities of will and thought by exerting his power spontaneously. In work he follows a task prescribed for him by another, and does not reveal his own proclivities and inclinations, but another's. In play he reveals his own original power. But there are two selves in the child—one is peculiar, arbitrary, capricious, different from all others, and hostile to them, and is founded on short-sighted egotism. The other self is reason, common to all humanity, unselfish and universal, feeding on truth and beauty and holiness. Both of these selves are manifested in play.
>
> (Froebel, 1926, pp. vi–vii)

John and I also agree on the seriousness of play; on the value of play in our everyday lives and in the "work" we engage in as a pursuit of creativity. Play is the glue, the interconnection among the activities of CPS, and we agree that play is fun, a journey of arousal and discovery. Hopefully this work initiates a dialogue on the return (or initiation) of play into CPS in planning and design academia and professions.

One important lesson learned by experimenting with play activities through object-learning is that the principles of CPS and play are interchangeable among specific domains, but in most cases the specific skills and objects/tools are not. In hindsight this is logical and a challenge in addressing a larger audience. Consequently, I focus the experiments and activities of the book within the domains related to the spatial aspects of human settlement CPS: architecture, landscape architecture, urban design, urban planning and urban geography.

Melinda Wenner (2009) writes in *Scientific American* that "play has to be reframed and not seen as an opposite to work, but rather as a compliment . . . curiosity, imagination, and creativity are like muscles. If you don't use them, you lose them." And play can transform even the most mundane task into a potentially creative activity.

What Activates the Creative Aspect of CPS: Play in Object-learning as a Sensory Process

Based on the definition of "play" and its relationship to the creative process, I argue that it is a sensory process, thinking and working with the senses, based on research in psychology and psychiatry. The book defines the relationships among play, object-learning, creativity, CPS, meaning-making, crafting—thinking with the senses through manual dexterity and emotions. This distinguishes the creative process from most digital technologies, thus the distinction in the book between "play" and "gaming." Key components of play and CPS are discussed and explored regarding environment, motivation and skill development. This is followed by experiments, examples and suggested exercises and activities for academic and professional applications.

Too often in non-design fields there exists a common criticism of "design," particularly in the academic area (urban planning, urban studies, public affairs, etc.), that design has minimal value, it is frivolous, subjective; that the methods and skills of design (i.e., drawing, model-building and other simulations) all have little relevance in critical thinking and are just play . . . Why? Possibly the criticisms are from a utilitarian and rational viewpoint where activity without a worthwhile end is inconsequential, where a non-deterministic and uncertain process is irrational (Lieberman, 1977). The "players" are playing and enjoying themselves, and are consequently not relevant. I argue that play and playfulness have immense value as the creative catalysts in CPS in all fields. Hopefully the book can contribute to a clear distinction between normative or linear and CPS.

There is a developmental continuity in playfulness that makes adult play necessary to CPS, gifting play with great value:

> [with] artists like Leonardo da Vinci or Michelangelo, a clear-cut distinction becomes evident between the frivolous and the playful, the latter helping to produce the kind of art forms (designs) that are novel yet allow their continuity to be traced from earlier forms, forms that are unfettered in their imagination yet disciplined in their execution.
>
> (Lieberman, 1977, p. 11)

All of this contributes renewed energy to a plurality of design methods and tools.

Adult play in CPS: is it possible and, if so, what is it and how can it be taught? Can we provide the guidance for a *Kindergarten for Adults: Friedrich Froebel—A Foundation for Play*?

Challenges

I actually reached a barrier or impasse for a while when I began the section on experiments and guidelines for object-learning and play. I did not want to formulate the play-activity into a restrictive and controlled process. I experimented with a number of approaches that were connected to a design process and soon realized that I was forcing the play-activity into "boxes"—just what I wanted to avoid. During this intellectual wrestling match, along with a "time-out" to watercolor, I came to the conclusion that I had to let play take the reins and the planning-of-play be put aside. I just started to play and describe the process and results after the activity ended. I stopped thinking about my end point.

I must acknowledge that my background as an architect, urban designer/planner and painter influenced the nature and conduct of that play; something that reinforced the principle that we are all creative and the specifics of creativity are not necessarily transferable as models to other domains. So be it: I allowed the nature of my domains (applied design fields) to be a part of the process; and this aided in dissolving the barrier that prevented me from moving on into the second half of the book.

Again, some readers of the book may perceive an anti-digital technology undercurrent based on the discussions of creativity and play. That is not the case, and I argue that there is an appropriate use for certain methodologies and tools and they are not universal. Being on the cutting edge of digital technologies does not equate with being on the cutting edge of creative endeavors.

Definition of Terms

This section defines key terms used in the book as a way to demystify concepts and perceptions of creativity, play, gaming, personality and other factors. They provide a guide and foundation for the experiments and exercises in later chapters.

Meaning-making and Spatial Metaphors

Creativity, CPS, play, etc. are meaningful endeavors and not superficial activities. They have meaning and purpose. I utilize the work of Edward Soja (1996), Henri Lefebvre (1991), Vygotsky (1978) and others in the exploration of meaning-making in design and planning—the CST Matrix (culture, space and time). Specifically, meaning-making is the construction of knowledge (history) combined with emergent realities into an understanding with others (consensus without compromise) within and across a variety of cultural, spatial and historic/time contexts, using semiotics in the process of learning and comprehending these understandings. In this exploration, play becomes a binding agent in the integration of meaning and functionality. It does not isolate forms of thinking into separate specialized skills or categories—viewing them as a complex synthesis of interdependent processes, appropriating thought and signs together—making meaning (Vygotsky, 1978).

Play

"Play is an ancient, voluntary, 'emergent' process driven by pleasure that yet strengthens our muscles, instructs our social skills, tempers and deepens our positive emotions, and enables a state of balance that leaves us poised to play some more" (Brown, 2009, p. 12). Play is a dynamic activity that is always changing; an uncertain, complex activity that represents an interactive form (social and individual) of imagination which leads to the making of something—an embodiment, a novel product, symbolic constructions. This embodiment is accompanied by collaborative protocols, emotional arousal and control, and the potential production of group cultural lore (Vygotsky, 1978, p. 11). Can this be learned/relearned in adulthood? That is part of the exploration. Vygotsky distinguishes play in children from other activities based on the following:

1. A player creates imaginary situations in play.
2. Play is always based on rules.
3. Personal development calls for the capacity to be able to act in a situation "which is only conceived on an imagined level" and is independent of reality.

Why? Play disables fear, failure, and creates voluntary intentions as opposed to simple reactions to physical stimulation.

Play-objects

I discuss the significant differences between playing with symbolic objects and playing with toys. One is an abstraction that can be anything based on the emergent rules of the play; the other is a typed and categorized specificity with built-in predetermined rules not emergent from the play: the cardboard box vs. the doll's house vs. the digital game?

Play-skills

Play as an activity has a dual mission regarding skills. First, a skill base is necessary to engage creatively in play. Second, play as a process teaches skill development. Subsequently, play is an evolutionary process of skill development, requiring basic skill levels to engage it and acquiring more and in-depth skills during the process.

Play as Cathartic Function

Play can be a purifying or emotional cleansing process. This catharsis involves an association among feeling, imagination and the symbols of meaning or sign systems.

Play as Emergent Systems

Play is a process of emergent systems with two major halves: adaptive variability and self-organization.

Emotion

"[A]rt is the social technique of emotion, a tool of society which brings the most intimate and personal aspects of our being into the circle of social life" (Vygotsky, 1978, p. 249). Design traditionally and historically was a function of art—not so much in contemporary society. Bringing the art (through play) as that social technique into design and planning (and many other fields), as extensions of the CST Matrix, is a major objective of this work.

There are major connections between emotion and play, and this book explores the *arousal modification theory* where arousal from play leads to innovation and the innovation leads to additional arousal. There is no separation between player and product. The architect (team) designs a building based on a needs/desire program and in essence constructs a spatial metaphor—a physical story with "their" emotions (positive and negative) as inherent aspects of the final design.

Vygotsky referred to form as an action or verb, "[an] artistic arrangement of the given material, made with the purpose of generating a specific aesthetic effect" (1978, pp. 53, 19). Emotion begetting new emotion.

Environment

A creative problem-solving process is dependent on the environment within which it occurs. The concept of "studio," "workshop," "den" and "playroom," etc. is explored regarding atmosphere, attitude, supplies and materials, a place that provides flexibility, individual and group interactions, and a plurality of tools.

Insight

An unhindered flow of associations: phase one—impasse (there must first be a block); phase two—seeing hidden connections (remote associations); phase three—relaxing, unfocusing (letting the flow begin); phase four—feeling of certainty that comes with a new idea (aha!).

Neoteny

The evolutionary process where a species growth slows down to the point where adults retain many of the features previously seen in juveniles: "a slower rate of development . . . that may even have shaped our vaunted intelligence, by stretching out the time when we are most receptive to new skills and knowledge."

Charles Mudede observes succinctly that we are the animal that never really grows up . . . never stops doing two things: playing and wondering.

> If one sees humankind from the perspective of neoteny, from wonder and play, then art begins to assume a very central role in the development of our species.

Object-learning (and Teaching)

Object-learning is the transference of information and perceptions to the brain for processing through the senses, the physical manipulation of objects (reality)—cognitive perception.

Panpsychism

This is the idea that there is memory and anticipation everywhere . . . that nature is alive with feeling and playfulness.

Proprioception

This is the awareness of our bodies in space, the dynamic sense of the relation of the parts as players controlling the parts and bringing them in close relationship to the whole. It provides feedback.

Chapter 1

CREATIVE PROBLEM-SOLVING (CPS) FOR DESIGN AND PLANNING

Creative Problem-solving (CPS)

Creative problem-solving (CPS) is the heart and distinguishing process in art, design, engineering and scientific applications; and provides the base foundation for the creativity-related experiments and exercises in this book. CPS is distinguished from conventional problem-solving processes in significant ways: it is a non-linear process characterized by open-ended experimentation and discovery process with

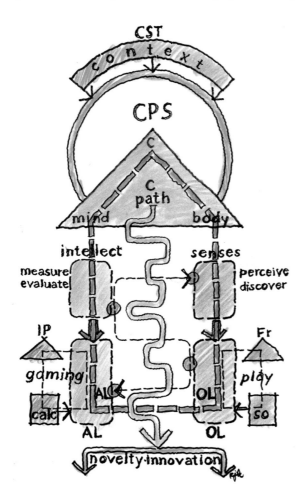

Figure 1.1
The CPS Process

As a guide to the major components of the book and the CPS process, this diagram highlights its major elements in relationship and is used throughout the book as a guide to a discussion of those elements. **CST (Culture, Space, Time)—CPS—Cpath (creativity path)—Mind—(intellect), AL—analytical learning, Calc—The "Calculator," Gaming, Body—(senses), Fr—Froebel, OL—object-learning, so—Symbolic Objects, Play.** *Creative Problem-solving requires both mind and body in an integral thought process. In recent years, in the design and planning fields, the mind/intellect aspect has gained prominence in methods and tools at the expense of the senses: cognitive perception.*

an uncertain outcome—one that is novel and potentially innovative, not merely competent. CPS is also the arena for object-learning through play; entering into the unknown, using a majority of the senses to discover novelty and innovation in product development. And there is always a product (policy and strategy are considered products in this arena). This exploration of CPS forms the basis for the incorporation of play as a catalyst in information evaluation, idea generation and product evaluation.

In the spatially focused fields of architecture, landscape architecture, urban design, planning and graphic design, CPS drives the design process. All fields of endeavor are spatially related but not necessarily focused on that aspect of reality. Let us begin by describing the aspects of creativity.

This chapter is divided into three sections:

1. The Creativity Path
2. The CPS Process
3. An Example of CPS in the Design/Planning Context.

The Creativity Path: Whole Mind–Body Thinking

Creativity: The Inherent Energy in CPS

Creativity is the distinguishing element in CPS and is often viewed as an abstract term representing an accidental occurrence or an aspect limited to "talented" people. Creativity is essential to CPS and can be taught and incorporated into the problem-solving process. It is not a "talent" or an innate ability. People who seemingly have a "natural" propensity for creative endeavors may have more openness resulting from a reduction in fear factors.

Creativity

> Creativity involves a deliberate challenge to the status quo. It involves an intention to bring about change so that it differs from introduction of novelty that results simply from natural evolution with the passage of time, by accident, or through misunderstandings—it is revolutionary, rather than simply evolutionary . . . it is important because it is the basis of the ability to generate and implement useful (i.e., relevant and effective) novelty.
>
> (Cropley and Cropley, 2009, pp. 24–25)

> From a cognitive point of view, creativity is typically described as a process of combination, one that blends seemingly incompatible concepts together to produce surprising new meanings and one through which "properties often emerge in a combination that were not evident in any of its constituents.
>
> (Prager, 2014, p. 29)

This point is critical: the aha! moment in design as uncovered as an emergent notion not before present in the data. It actually does not exist until discovered through experimentation—emerging, evolving and becoming reality—then changing again.

Let us view aspects of creativity that relate to the design and planning fields, and academic and professional environments.

Learning Creativity

Creativity can be learned and/or trained using two common-sense approaches:

1. Focusing on the creative potentials that already exist in a person and eliminating blockers that inhibit the expression of these potentials. This also falls in line with Johnston (1991) and creative differences, discussed later, in that creative capacitance varies in intensity, viewpoint, method and personality traits from person to person, requiring an analysis of individual capacitance—not an easy task and a necessary one for educators in particular.
2. Focusing on what people do not possess such as certain knowledge, experimentation skills (especially for play), positive attitudes and related values; and assisting them in acquiring these components through exercises that go beyond the mental/intellectual and that involve play/work (play and sweat). These exercises can be loose and conceptual, similar to quick sketches in a drawing class to advanced systemic training in the investigation of the organization and structure of a task or problem. This can involve sequences of approach and process, special materials and methods of creative experimentation, special skill development and practice (Cropley and Cropley, 2009). The exercises and experiments in Chapter 7 focus on creative play-skills useful in CPS.

Training for Creativity

In academic and professional settings, creativity training can have significant benefits for individuals, teams, institutions and firms when that training addresses at least five requirements:

1. The training is based on general cognitive principles such as problem recognition as defined through a culture, space and time (CST) lens.
2. The training is prolonged and demanding in presentation, demonstration, practice and critique of means and methods.
3. The training involves case studies and other real-life examples so that students can make the connection between theory and application.
4. The training includes practice exercises that are domain-specific (architecture, urban design, etc.). They can build from conceptual and abstract exercises that lead to the real-life exercises (see Kasprisin, 2011).
5. The training includes practice (of process and skills) that is simultaneous and specific, promoting the integration of elements as opposed to a linear step-by-step application. Creativity training deals with relationships, not simply objects or elements.

Guidelines for Assessing Creativity in a Solution

These guidelines provide a basis for assessing creativity in solutions to a given problem: relevance and effectiveness, novelty, aesthetics, and general application and transferability, based on work by Cropley and Cropley (2009). Creative capacity can be increased in a design process by the way in which the problem is defined—or not. If problems are defined in degrees, less rigid, more open-ended, leaving the solution pathway variable and ambiguous with clear criteria for identification of a solution, this capacitance is greatly expanded. Part of the evolutionary definition of the problem, from variable degree to specific degree, is a part of the creative process. There exist aspects of the problem that are neither understood nor discovered until the process is engaged and explored. This creative capacitance needs to be present in both the player(s) and the community, as the community is eventually the author of its own story.

1. *Relevance and effectiveness* (correct, effective, appropriate): these are the beginning and fundamental criteria for competent solutions, not creative solutions. These must be present as a starting point of evaluation.

2. *Beyond competence* (generation, reformulation, originality, relevancy, hedonics, play, complexity, condensation, synthesis):

    •   *generation* (giving rise to new directions—so important in (urban) design fields)
    •   *reformulation* (improving by alteration or correction)
    •   *originality* (fresh and unusual)
    •   *relevancy* (having meaning and functionality)
    •   *hedonics* (the arousal factor, receiving pleasure from the process)
    •   *play* (the free activity of experimentation within the process)
    •   *complexity* (having intricacy, interdependence, interwoven parts, systems within systems)
    •   *condensation* (making compact or dense)
    •   *elaboration* (developing thoroughly with more detail and care)
    •   *synthesis* (bringing together disparate elements into a coherent whole—the "composition of complexity").

    Does the solution satisfy the requirements in the problem statement; does the solution accurately reflect the conventional knowledge and/or techniques for arriving at a correct solution? Design solutions require competence as a base; they need to fulfill the challenges of the problem at a minimum with meaning and functionality. Once a competency is acknowledged, the assessment can evaluate the solution based on its creativity content.

3. *Novelty*

    •   *Understanding the problem* (diagnosis, prescription, prognosis): has the problem been critically analyzed as to its nature and extent; does the solution draw attention to shortcomings and weaknesses in what already exists? Does the solution indicate how to improve what already exists? Does the solution indicate the likely effects of changes brought about by the solution? Novelty goes beyond competence in this guideline, demonstrating not only that the problem has been resolved but that it advances what exists and anticipates the impacts and changes of the solution; arriving at something new and unusual.
    •   *Adds to existing knowledge* (replication, redefinition, combination, incrementalization, reconstruction): does the solution add to existing knowledge by transferring the known to a new setting? Does the solution use the known in a new way? Does the solution exhibit new combinations of existing elements? Does the solution extend what is known in existing directions or in alignment with what is working, what is coherent? Does the solution reconstruct approaches previously considered or abandoned?
    •   *Develops new knowledge* (redirection, re-initiation, generation): does the solution extend what is known in new directions? Does the solution indicate a radically new solution? And does the solution achieve "thirdspace" (Soja, 1996) by constructing a fundamentally new and

potentially effective solution that embodies principles of past polarities with little or no compromise? In physics this is the aha! moment, a fundamentally new discovery; a *thirdspace* that incorporates the essences of the known and is a fundamentally different outcome.

4. *Aesthetic*

   - *The effect on other people* (recognition, convincingness, pleasingness): is the solution meaningful, does the observer perceive value in the solution? Is the observer convinced that the solution has relevance and value? And does the observer perceive an aesthetic to the solution? This is an underlying principle and mission of design—to positively affect the behavior of people and positively affect their environments—place-making.
   - *The integrity of the solution* (completeness and harmony): is the solution a whole system, not fragmentary? Does the solution have strong and meaningful relationships exhibited by the design? Are the components of the design composition consistent and integrated? Does the final composition relate to and exhibit complexity without being complicated?

5. *General usability* (foundationality, transferability, germinality, seminality): does the solution provide a foundation or framework for future work? Can its principles be transferred to other applications or problems? Does it provide new ways of looking at existing issues or problems? And does it draw attention to previously unnoticed or undiscovered problems? All design solutions have this responsibility in that they are emergent resolutions, not finalized static products. A creative design is a catalytic influence on its surrounding context, encouraging creative actions beyond its own scope.

Creativity may be differentiated into verbal, mathematical and spatial processes. Important to this focus is the observation (Dow and Mayer, 2004) that training in solving spatial insight problems was the *only form* (emphasis in original) that consistently fostered creativity and clearly improved the solving of spatial problems. This again leads to the principle that not all approaches to training creativity and play are equally effective and that the effects of training are domain-specific (Cropley and Cropley, 2009).

The CPS Process

The Reality of Community: CST Matrix and Context

CPS is by its definition uniquely designed to engage complex problems in complex contexts—the realities of most human communities.

As discussed at length in *Urban Design: The Composition of Complexity* (Kasprisin, 2011), the definition of context is multi-faceted, encompassing culture (socio-economic-political), space and time/history based on the works of Soja (1996), Lefebvre (1991) and others. This CST trialectic is essential and integral to any problem-solving process in design and planning, and cannot be limited to one or two of the basic components of CST. As is discussed later in the book, creativity methods and skills may be applied to the understanding of relationships within the CST Matrix, the underlying meaning and functionality or stories of community.

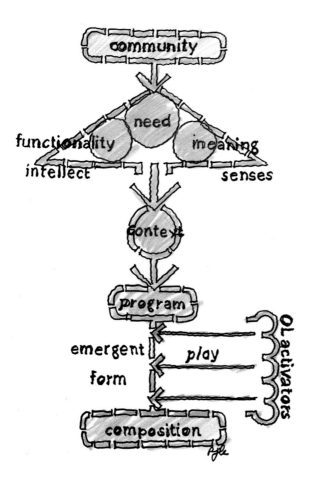

Figure 1.2
The CST Matrix and Context

The CST Matrix contains the essence of community context. Understanding the relationships within the matrix is inherent to the identification of need and problems in context. OL refers to object learning in the diagram.

What Makes CPS Different from Conventional Problem-solving?

Component Elements of CPS

In CPS, there can be eight or more components expanded from the basic six outlined by Cropley and Cropley (2009).

1. *The Process*

    There is a thought process that occurs using whole mind–body thinking, both mental/ intellectual processing and thinking with the senses, or cognitive perception (Arnheim, 1969). It is within this whole mind–body cognitive process that object-learning through play has the strongest application and benefit. Play may be viewed as a secret garden that one enters at varying times of the journey—safe, fearless, motivating without failure or the pressure of accomplishment; experienced with the senses.

2. *The Problem*

    There is an identified task to be solved with a product as an outcome (product can be a design, an art form, a policy or strategy, etc.). The definition and description of the product is something which the player(s) must have a direct role in developing.

Problem Identification Set-up. Setting up a problem for resolution either in a professional design office or academic design studio sets the tone and pathway for the entire creative process. If too rigid and controlled it can hinder the creative play-activity and even imply a predetermined outcome. Thus, the need for initial ambiguity and a tolerance for complexity and uncertainty in problem definition are required. This enables creative action.

Problem identification:

- Keep the problem specifications somewhat ambiguous as open issues, such as conflicts in client/community groups, gaps or missing components of meaning and functionality in a problem; involve team members and client/community in the problem-identification process without overstatement.
- Be aware of the problem context in that there is a nesting of problems like watersheds—not one singular problem—locally specific and globally connected..
- Introduce varying and even conflicting source materials, community input and its polarities, and conflicting space program needs that result from those polarities—embrace complexity.
- Introduce the guidelines for assessing creativity and novel solutions at the outset of a project (effectiveness/appropriateness, novelty, generalizability—discussed below).
- Have players discuss the mission or larger aspiration of the problem regarding its meaning and functionality for the client/community—avoiding goal definition; focusing on intent and principles, not detail.
- Do not specify or even allude to a solution; set tasks that are not associated with predetermined outcomes. This involves avoidance of "models" or "ideals" of design approaches such as new urbanism, landscape urbanism, thematic or traditional design approaches. Aspects of these model approaches have value in later stages when assessing typologies that may meet certain program requirements. They can channel creative energy prematurely if used as guides at the onset of the process.

3. *The Person or Player*

There is a point of view that affects the process, whether it be an individual or team; the observer is a part of the observation and affects directly the result of experimentation. Your personality as a designer/planner is an integral part of the CPS process. You as the key player are also the motivator for engagement in the process, a factor that affects the level and intensity of engagement with creative potential.

4. *Object-learning and Play*

Object-learning or constructivism is a form of learning (gaining awareness and perception) through the senses, using symbolic objects with manual dexterity in open and playful ways. This is a key aspect of CPS that is at the heart of this argument for a return to and integration of crafting processes in the emerging design and planning paradigms dominated by new digital technologies.

"Play" and "playfulness" are integral to object-learning and are also key foci of this book, and are discussed in consort with CPS—the vehicle of design-play.

5. *Analytical Learning Through Gaming*

Analytical learning through the intellect is a key component of CPS as the evaluation factor in assessing ideas and concepts as they emerge from the larger process. This component consists of information processing (IP), evaluation and calculation, often using gaming means and methods. The difference between gaming and playing is discussed later in this chapter.

6. *Product*

   In CPS there is always a product whether it is two- or three-dimensional art, a novel or poem, a building, master plan, even policy and planning strategy. In the end, there is a resolution that hopefully is devoid of significant compromise so that problems are actually resolved as opposed to reinvented and continued in different forms. Product is something made. As discussed by Johnston (1994), the product is also emergent not static. It requires insertion into reality and life-context to complete its creative cycle—it reveals the status at that point of both history and emerging relationships and begins to change again—and it is real and physical (or has significant physical ramifications).

7. *Environment*

   There are two aspects of environment here: the larger environment or context that the problem is immersed in and bounded by, and the actual space for creative activity in solving the problem. The larger environment for CPS entails an analysis of the CST Matrix (culture, space and time/history context) that is demanding and requires time. No analysis can result from an investigation of one or two aspects of the matrix. It is an interactive environment with time frames and periodicities discussed below that if engaged thoroughly can lead to the discovery of *thirdspace* (Soja, 1996), novelty and innovation. The environment for CPS enables both object-learning and play—i.e. the "studio".

8. *Phases and Timing*

   These are the time periods within which problems occur, are resolved and implemented. This involves historical context and trends, emergent realities and trends, and future probabilities. "Current" time frames relate to what is coherent, remaining useful and therefore carried forward as a part of the larger problem resolution. "Current" is not a static situation, but simply a transition from one change sequence to another, using what is still working as the transitional vehicle.

The aspiration of CPS is to achieve or conceive an effective novel product (used broadly) that may lead to innovative outcome(s).

Principles of CPS

Based on the work of Cropley and Cropley, Soja, Lefebvre and others, CPS (being creative) exhibits a number of major principles that guide it:

1. CPS generates ideas based on the construction of theories rather than the testing of a given theory; avoiding established "models," "beliefs," clichés and conventions.
2. CPS has available and employs the analytical tools for the handling of masses of raw data from the Culture-Space-Time (CST) awareness matrix using both qualitative and quantitative methodologies with both crafting and digital methods, skills and tools.
3. CPS evaluates those ideas that include the consideration of alternative meanings and phenomena, and exhibits an awareness of emergent realities and phenomena.
4. CPS is systemic and creative simultaneously, and utilizes visual thinking processes to organize and structure relationships and emergent ideas.
5. CPS identifies, develops and relates the concepts that are the building blocks of (new) theory.
6. CPS exploits the novelty resulting from those ideas and/or theories—leading to innovation.

These are a combination of CPS principles or basic rules for both product generation (making something) and for use in grounded theory research. A CPS process requires different approaches and methods from those now practiced in most educational institutions and design offices to deal with complex, multi-layered sets of information and idea discovery. This path toward creativity applies to all fields and not just those of traditional (urban) design. CPS also requires a solid foundation of knowledge or historical information assembled as relationships of meaning and functionality in order for that idea discovery to emerge. All information is viewed as emergent or descending, based on the cultural, spatial and time/historic forces (CST Matrix) at the heart of those relationships (Soja, 1996).

Essential Characteristics of CPS

Key characteristics or descriptions of CPS include the following:

1. Cognition (gaining knowledge through awareness, reasoning and judgment) that utilizes an integration of analytical and symbolic/imaginal processes through a whole mind–body thought process of intellectual and sensory thought or perception (thinking with the senses)
2. A recognition of *problem-in-context* that is evolutionary and emergent, not predetermined
3. A process that is prolonged and demanding
4. A process that combines abstract thinking with real-life experiences and case studies
5. A process that requires developed skills which are usually domain specific, i.e., architecture and urban design, with special materials, tools and techniques
6. A process that requires practice in skill and methodology
7. A process that contains object-learning through "play" as an energizer and experimentation activity, activated by compositional principles
8. A process that has a definitive product, something that is made, i.e., fashioned, composed, strategized, etc.

In research, a similar process takes place using *grounded theory*. The researcher begins with an area of study (general problem identification) and allows the theory to emerge from the data. Grounded theories, because they are drawn from data, are likely to offer insight, enhance understanding and provide a meaningful guide to action (Strauss and Corbin, 1998, p. 12). As we will see in the CPS process, grounded theory and qualitative evaluation inquiry draw on critical and creative thinking—both in science and the art of analysis (Strauss and Corbin, 1998, p. 13). In grounded theory research, certain behavior traits are also helpful in the promotion of creative thinking:

1. Being open to multiple possibilities
2. Generating a list of options (not settling on one outcome)
3. Exploring various possibilities before choosing one
4. Making use of multiple avenues of expression such as art, music and metaphors to stimulate thinking
5. Using non-linear forms of thinking such as going back and forth and circumventing around a subject to get a fresh perspective
6. Diverging from one's usual ways of thinking and working to get a fresh perspective
7. Trusting the process and not holding back (uncertainty principle)

8. Not taking short cuts but rather putting energy and effort into the work
9. Having fun while doing it (the arousal factor).

(Strauss and Corbin, 1998, p. 13)

CPS Guidelines

This outline is repeated in discussions of creative studio environments later in the book. It forms the basis for the creative atmosphere of problem-solving.

1. The problem is not specified exactly.
2. Students, team members, community and stakeholders are expected to participate in problem identification and adequate context description.
3. The nature of the solution is largely open.
4. The pathway to the solution is not specified.
5. The criteria for recognizing a solution are open.
6. Embraces complexity: context is more than a "setting" (CST Matrix).
7. Embraces and tolerates ambiguity.
8. Discovers and explores relationships not objects: meaning and functionality.
9. Works through a system of scale-based relationships, a scale ladder (Kasprisin and Pettinari, 1995) defining their boundaries and redefining them as those boundaries dissolve.
10. Avoids compromise fallacies.
11. Encourages awareness of "thirdspace," a third and distinctly different outcome.
12. Develops necessary skills and knowledge to participate in a process.
13. Defines a specific outcome.

Yes! Over-structure is frowned upon in CPS. In an academic studio process, the faculty member frames the problem in a way that students are required to redefine the problem and approach for themselves. This does not mean haphazard or helter-skelter thinking, and requires demanding effort in the organization and structure of the problem. CPS requires openness not an adherence to established ideas or models (closedness); it requires divergent thinking, and again an appreciation for ambiguity and complexity.

CPS Environment

As discussed earlier, a creative environment for CPS is essential and a part of the process, since it provides the atmosphere, space, tools and attitudes for creative behavior. "Studio" is the historic term for this environment and may be adapted to many fields. Comfort, familiarity and territorial occupation are all critical to engaging creative actions. It is not a games room but a playroom—a significant difference.

Studio environments vary according to the type of information processing, play-tools and product required for resolution. They can be traditional studio workrooms, temporary set-ups for a specific product resolution, or an on-site charrette workspace. A contemporary studio can contain a plurality of facilities in a comfortable environment, with crafting and digital tools as appropriate and not exclusive, and space for interactive group activities.

The studio environment provides a place and opportunity to display context information and physical conditions for constant observation, play and experimentation. The traditional hand-crafted three-dimensional models of project and/or district sites remain valid and critical to the CPS process. Restricting context information to individual stations and computers is neither useful nor interactive beyond the individual. In addition, the "reality representation" of a three-dimensional model provides the ability to constantly be aware of physical conditions related to the analytical process. The same issue applies to the wall poster or visual display of information and analysis—it has little value if not shared and made available for constant observation. View the wall poster assembly as an opportunity to construct a "story board" sequence as information is compressed into diagrams and analysis is summarized in an emerging visual pattern.

Game boards are often a part of the experimentation and play process in CPS and require access and visibility for effective operation. They can be separate from the context display models (representing a portion of a model—block, sector, etc.) or incorporated into their construction.

Play-tools for CPS

Play-tools are skill-based objects used to experiment and discover ideas, emerging realities and concepts. These are discussed in detail in Chapter 6 and they have their formal foundation in the educational work of Pestalozzi and Froebel. They require skill competence in order to be effective, and require repetition, preparation and practice. Reliance on *packaged* skill mechanisms can disconnect the designer/player from the CPS process, making them an observer rather than a player.

CPS Rules and Guides (The Principles of Engagement)

Prior to directly engaging the CPS process, initial rules and guides are identified as a beginning path to discovery. They can always be altered or hybridized as they are applied and understood. The rules can be on skill application; application of elements and principles of composition; guides for facilitation with the community/client; rules on how to compress and/or filter out information without loss of relational associations; gaming rules, etc.

These rules are important for the clarity of the process, the quality of team and community interactions, and as a visual recording of the process and relationship identification.

CPS Observation/Reflection/Compression/Response/Recording

Information and analysis are often lost in the mass and process of assembled data. Using play in CPS as a means of compressing information as it is collected and assessed, constructing a visual summary of that information and its implications and relationships enables the designer to build the storyline, at least its beginning stages, without being overcome by detail. This is added to the semiotic diagrams that convey the emergent relationships in the existing context, any obvious polarities and associations.

How the information and analysis of a process are observed, reflected upon, compressed, responded to and recorded directly affect the dynamics of the creative process and at a minimum require discussion and preparation prior to further engagement with the process.

An Example of CPS in the Design/Planning Context

Problem to be Solved (Community/Client Need, Aspirations, Desires)

Creative problem-solving begins with issues, concerns, problems, aspirations, needs and wants as put forth by a specific body (community, client, etc.). It ends in a product, a resolution and a new beginning. The urban design and planning fields in particular have been at the forefront of interacting with community members to address need and design/planning solutions. As is discussed below in the Cultural-Spatial-Time (CST) Matrix, all aspects of the community, including spatial, cultural and time/historic factors, are a part of problem definition, analysis and resolution. It is not spatial, spatial-cultural or time-cultural but all three (CST). This in-depth approach to need assessment requires methods and techniques beyond data gathering and linear analysis.

Context Defined: The CST Matrix

Context is not a set or a location. Context is the reality of the situation as defined by the CST Matrix as relationships—subsiding, coherent and emergent. Context is similar to a multi-dimensional game board and requires in-depth construction. This is not an easy task and requires time, an appreciation for complexity, and new creative methodologies and techniques for analysis and resolution. In context, multiple boundaries influence its analysis and understanding, from project or site boundaries, to surrounding areas to cultural and community boundaries. I refer to this cluster of boundaries as "adequate" boundaries, suitable to identify as many influencing forces as possible regarding the "problem" to be resolved. Boundaries are temporary, subject to dissolution and expansion or redefinition. Keep in mind the concept of a "scale ladder" (Kasprisin and Pettinari, 1995)—places within places in defining adequate context.

Information processing and working memory come into play in defining context. Working memory is essentially the amount of memory and information we can process within a specific time period. Consequently it is important to establish methods which process information within containers that may be expanded and collapsed as necessary; and that always identify connections to adjacent containers. Playful techniques can assist the designer in compressing complex information into relational statements and diagrams. This is explored in the use of semiotic analytical diagrams, telling stories via symbols, as a means of compression.

Examples abound about students gathering information for design studios in three ring binders and being at a complete loss as to what is included in the mass of data. The data require compression into clear and understandable stories with meaning and functionality defined and visualized. As demonstrated in Chapter 7, the semiotic diagrams, semi-abstract compositions related to a context, are vehicles for this meaning.

Identification and Specification of Need and Wants

The CPS process is designed to solve problems and arrive at a novel and innovative product (solution). Product/design/"something made" are essential outcomes in creative processes. With most clients and communities, this requires an in-depth investigation of their profiles, directions, polarities or conflicts, and stated needs and wants. Within a client/community statement of need and want lies other layers of issues: conflicts within the client regarding certain needs and wants as a starter. A community may wish to "Redevelop the Downtown Waterfront" as a want and need due to deterioration or changing economies. What is wanted by whom and for what purpose can be an embedded and contentious issue.

Understanding the range, extent and conflicts within a client/community's wants and needs is crucial to proceeding with the CPS process. Most conflicts cannot be resolved prior to start-up, and identifying as many as possible at the outset expands the rules of engagement. In a CPS process, all ideas are valid options and are vetted through the process, not via debate.

Addressing the CST Matrix

The cultural, spatial, time/historic matrix contains the information and resultant relationships of a given community/client/stakeholder group, etc. The matrix requires structuring (data identification, collection and categorization) which begins in and of itself to define problems, opportunities and constraints. As is discussed under Semiotic Diagrams (Chapter 7), these relationships require a clear and meaningful visual portrayal—looking beyond the data and beyond packaged analytical tools. This is no small task and engages the conventional and innovative means and methods of planning and design processes.

Assessing Information as Relationships: Meaning and Functionality

The relationships (connections and associations among the data) that result from the CST analytical process are the basis for design, not the information alone. A land-use map, for example, indicates spatial location, extent and economic generalities (uses). To uncover the meaning and functionality of that "map" requires further investigation into cultural issues, market forces, spatial structure, conflicts and unworkable situations, to name a few aspects. A series of "stories" or emerging patterns and realities is the result of this phase, providing a basis for design programming.

Phase One Programming: What and How Much?

Given a set or series of relational patterns emerging from the information, certain wants and needs can be specified in terms of what is required to meet the need and how much. For example, a need may be improved recreational facilities in neighborhoods. This is translated into what type of facility and how much for each specific neighborhood—and they are not the same specification.

Identifying and Describing Emergent Polarities: The "Color Wheel"

Within these relationships and *programmed need* there exist numerous conflicts and/or polarities—the outer extent of opposing preferences and ideas: tot lot versus soccer field, for example. Here is where the design process begins to heat up and have an impact. Identifying and describing these polarities sets the temporary boundaries for dialogue and design testing. Imagine a color wheel with primary, secondary and tertiary colors and their complementary or opposite colors. Each set of polarities defines a set of temporary boundaries regarding an issue or idea. A process to accommodate these polarities (and not compromise them, as, for example, a gray color on the color wheel) is referred to as bridging polarities without compromise—seeking thirdspace in reality (see below).

Bridging Polarities

Bridging polarities can be a part of the initial generation of notions and concepts. The path to resolution as a new and distinctly different aspect, avoiding compromise, generates new ideas that can expand the CPS process. Without engaging the polarities, these ideas can remain hidden, abstract. The polarities establish the temporary boundaries of the discussion and the pursuit of the bridging principles open the door to creative actions.

Generating Notions and Concepts

From the preceding steps, notions and concepts emerge for experimentation and testing through a play process of experimentation. Experience with play-skills is critical to this step, as design is a spatial metaphor-making process. Consequently, the experimentation of composition and form through visual tools is essential. This is the role of divergent thinking, seeking novel and innovative ideas through object-learning and play, pushing the boundaries toward creative solutions. The more ideas the better at this stage. At this stage there are no bad ideas, simply notions that are later vetted by the process itself, not argument.

Testing Product in Context

This is the place for convergent thinking, the processing and analysis of ideas generated above. This level is served by an integration of digital technology and hand-crafted methods, especially in community/client interactions regarding the testing of product. Gaming can serve a valuable process in the evaluation of notions and concepts, adding the qualitative aspect of analysis.

Periodicities of Implementation

Strategizing for implementation of design and planning product requires a recognition and analysis of time-event periods, time frames within which certain actions can have a higher probability to occur.

New Beginnings

Creative solutions require testing in context as a part of the larger process. In many ways, the solutions are viewed as emergent realities already subject to change as soon as they are developed and placed in context—new beginnings. Creativity is a dynamic process, and the principle of emergent reality is fundamental.

Chapter 2

OBJECT-LEARNING THROUGH PLAY

OBJECT-LEARNING, CONSTRUCTIVISM, AND SELF-LEARNING THROUGH SYMBOLIC PLAY

Object-learning

The sensory sibling of the mind–body creative thinking process, the body—sensual experience— cognitive perception—is at the heart of the design process. As discussed in the Introduction, this aspect of CPS has been overshadowed by digital technologies in recent times and remains a necessary ingredient in creative thought, not an "old-fashioned" methodology. The roots of creative thinking have

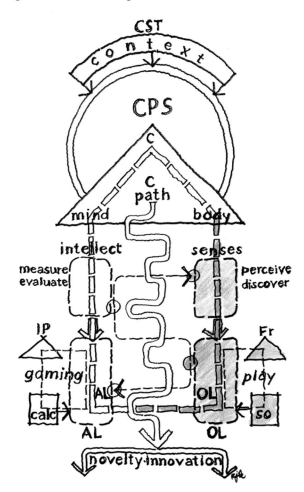

Figure 2.1
Object-learning

Cognitive perception and thinking with the senses increase the potential for perceptions, concepts and discovery in design and planning processes through manual or hands-on activities of symbolic objects. Friedrich Froebel assembled symbolic objects as "gifts" for students in their object-learning exercises in his Kindergarten Model.

undergone a tortuous track of acceptability in education, dominated by formality and rigidity, the "bottom-line," goal-oriented processes. The work of Johann Pestalozzi and Friedrich Froebel form the foundation for revolutionary changes in education with object-teaching, thinking with the senses, cognitive perception (Arnheim, 1969), being connected to reality through manual dexterity actions.

Object-teaching and object-learning represented a revolutionary change in European education in the late 1700s and early 1800s with the work of Swiss Pedagogue Johann Heinrich Pestalozzi (1746–1827). Enter *object-learning—Anschaung: object lessons—hands-on activities—direct, concrete observation.* Pestalozzi's work was revolutionary regarding the education of children, especially the poorest children excluded from any education and opportunity. He advocated active hands-on activities—thinking with the senses. This set the stage for Friedrich Froebel who passed up an opportunity to study architecture and instead joined the Frankfurt Model School circa 1805 to teach, leading to his eventual expansion of Pestalozzi's object-learning in the format of "kindergarten." (Do not confuse contemporary kindergarten formats and experiences with Froebel's work, as the original framework has been diluted and distorted in many cases, essentially being early childhood education rather than a creative and sensory activity. The introduction of computers into the "kindergarten" environment is a key example of that dilution.)

> Froebel made *objective work,* or object teaching, central to his pedagogy, recognizing that the handling of material things aided children in the development of their creative faculties and provided varied and complex experiences through simple means. By examining real things, kindergarten pupils developed originality in thinking and problem solving.
>
> (Brosterman, 1997, p. 34)

As the experiments in this book demonstrate, the direct handling and manipulation of materials can benefit adults, especially those involved in spatial-oriented fields, in engaging complexity that can lead to creative thinking.

> [T]he use of something tangible to enhance the understanding of something conceptual—may be categorized as *symbolic education.*
>
> (Brosterman, 1997, p. 34)

The next chapter reviews Froebel's Kindergarten format and the "gifts" or symbolic objects he developed as a part of an active exploration process of learning. A contemporary off-shoot of object-teaching and -learning is constructivism.

Constructivism and Play

Constructivism is a theory of knowledge where learning is "a self-regulated process of resolving inner cognitive conflicts [and challenges] that often become apparent through concrete experience, collaborative discourse, and reflection" (Brooks and Brooks, 1993, p. vii). I make the argument here that the "concrete experience, collaborative discourse, and reflection" aspects of constructivism are enhanced and strengthened by play activities in the CPS process. This "concrete experience" relies significantly on object-learning or object-play—experimenting with symbolic and real objects through manual dexterity—trying, failing, trying again, discovering. And what is discovered? Something that was not conceived of at the outset and awakened during the play activity.

Constructivism has a set of principles for instructors that mirror key principles in creative problem-solving. They focus on flexibility and provide an atmosphere suitable for creative experimentation and not simply competent resolutions. Criticisms of constructivism focus on the benefit of guided discovery within a domain-specific framework versus pure discovery. This section focuses more on guided discovery with play as the primary activity.

Principles of Constructivism from an Instructor's Perspective

1. Pose relevant problems (where relevance is anchored in the CST Matrix of a particular community) with the interaction of other players and the community.
2. Structure learning around primary concepts (immediate, direct, original).
3. Seek and value the ideas of students (inclusion, appreciation for creative differences and diversity).
4. Adapt the curriculum to address these ideas (flexibility, ability to adapt and change).
5. Assess student learning in context (where context is reality, again as described through a CST Matrix, not franchised), guided by case studies.

Characteristics of Constructivism

1. Students are freed from fast-driven curricula, where reflection and introspection are diluted, replaced by preprogrammed rules and conditions and goal-driven processes.
2. Students can focus on larger ideas by not being immersed in preprogrammed detail.
3. Opens the pathway for students to discover unique and novel conclusions.
4. Encourages students to appreciate the world as a complex place with multiple perspectives and realities.
5. Underscores that students are responsible for their own learning—the instructor is a guide and the student engages in self-discipline, i.e., self-learning.

Learning Environment for Constructivism

1. Student-generated ideas: this can be stimulated by a larger instructor-initiated notion or issue.
2. Student self-selection of focus areas.
3. Creative environment: studio, on-site insertions, i.e., intensives and charrettes, "playroom" (can have many variations and interpretations and is not a game or recreation room or other "break-time" space. A playroom is a flexible space large enough for individual and group explorations with various symbolic objects large and small. In a corporate office or the new "non-office" set-ups, the playroom is critical for creative interactions that go beyond the mobile computer).
4. Encouragement of student interaction as well as self-guided experimentation; and student interaction with the relevant community-cultural-context issues.
5. Use of critical thinking as opposed to fragmented, narrow and disjointed or cliché-driven thinking.
6. Students personally construct "meaning" from the CST Matrix, again as opposed to an overreliance on typology, model, cliché or convention.
7. Utilize content-area learning tasks that assimilate real-world experiences through on-site insertions or gaming situations.
8. Provide a purpose for learning: solving a problem, seeking a new direction, contributing understanding of community, increasing the capacity of a community to heal itself. In a visual

communication course I taught for years, many students wanted to learn how to draw and failed to make the connection of the "why" and "what for," as drawing is a language and not simply a presentation device.

9. Encourage students to take ownership of the learning process, becoming less dependent upon rigidity and conventional learning tools.

Object-play: The Activity-vehicle for Object-learning

Play is described in more detail at the end of this chapter.

"The symbolic mode of representation . . . enables [one] to use one object to represent another object. Thus the advent of symbolization ushers in the possibility of playing in a qualitatively different way" (Sylvia et al., 1976, p. 42). Studies suggest that learning with symbolic play and symbolic objects progresses from simple, single transformations to multiple and more complex ones. Initially, realistic replicas (even toys) can assist in making progress toward more complex and imaginative play. "[L]ess realistic objects appear to facilitate make-believe play, affording more scope for inventiveness and imagination" (Sylvia et al., 1976, p. 45). This permits the player to transform the objects to suit the occasion. For a skilled player/pretender, a cardboard box can be transformed into a house, a space station, an office building, etc. Many of the exercises using discovery models later in the book follow these principles.

Play also assists in the progression from experimentation to discovery to simple manipulation of basic compositions to the imaginative use of objects by freeing the player from goal-driven tendencies. Object-play increases familiarization with the experience, and fosters the manipulation of initial compositions through practice and repetition, building confidence and skill. Increased visual/sensory play contact with the tools can result in more complex conceptualizations and in-depth results. This is referred to as "incidental learning" in that the term "play" describes an activity that lacks an intrinsic goal and thus facilitates creativity and divergent thinking (Cropley and Cropley, 2009).

> Throughout life, play with objects undergoes many changes. As [one] becomes more skilled and experienced, the playful treatment of objects becomes more diverse and sophisticated. Both imagination and intellectual curiosity begin to contribute to one's play. More and more, meaningful associations accrue to objects, and play with objects is combined with other aspects of play. Often objects are incorporated as props in dramatic play, or governed by complex rules in games. All through these changes, objects continue to arouse curiosity and the desire to learn. They provide enjoyment in mastering their use in understanding the properties of things, and they also continue to facilitate social contacts and to assist in the expression of ideas and feelings.
>
> (Sylvia et al., 1976, p. 57)

Where to Start?

Begin with some simple and fun exercises where completeness is not as important as process, method, tool use and skill development (repetition and practice); in "Urban Design Composition," a graduate studio preparation class I teach at the University of Washington, students start out with simple construction paper designs working with circles and squares. They are asked to manipulate the primary shapes without losing their characteristics. This is simple, thoughtful and requires manual dexterity—and they enjoy the introduction to form, shape and manipulation; and the introduction of complexity in basic shapes.

- Identify the appropriate tools and skills for the domain-specific situation.
- Repetition and practice: there is no replacement for skill competence and demanding work is the only way to achieve that competence through imitation, practice and constructive guidance.
- Explain tool use through discussion, demonstration and individual critiques (not criticisms).
- Repetition and practice again.
- Encourage imitation as opposed to copying (identify and explain principles and techniques used effectively by others).
- Emphasize accuracy with looseness; the skill use is not about drudgery—it is about visual thinking.
- Identify the arousal factor and encourage focus at that point.
- Identify strengths and build on those to increase proficiency and confidence.
- Downplay failure—focus on failure as a positive outcome of experimentation.

Play

> Play is an ancient, voluntary, "emergent" process driven by pleasure that yet strengthens our muscles, instructs our social skills, tempers and deepens our positive emotions, and enables a state of balance that leaves us poised to play some more.
>
> (Eberle, 2014, p. 231)

Play is defined in the *American Heritage Dictionary* (5th Edition) as the occupation of oneself in an activity for amusement or recreation; and to take part in a sport or game [usually with rewards]. These definitions indicate a misconception of and confusion in our culture regarding the important role of play as a learning experience—a way of creative thinking, and, as is explored in this book, a necessary ingredient or agent in creative problem-solving.

Many psychologists support the idea that play is participation in an imaginary situation with rules, where the rules emerge from the play-action, not necessarily predetermined. Play occurs in all cultures with significant differences in play-skills, objects and environments. The connecting principle among cultural play is a recognition of the multiple possibilities of the *free activity* understood as play (Shepard, 2011). Aside from play as a learning endeavor for survival, play provides a space for joy (distinguished from fun), experimentation and discovery, make-believe, cultural interaction, an exchange of ideas and the removal or reduction of fear—no winner or loser.

Definitions and characteristics vary among psychologists on what constitutes play. An accepted definition is as follows:

> A voluntary activity pursued without ulterior purpose and on the whole with enjoyment or expectation of enjoyment; a process whereby the player incorporates external objects to his/her own thought schemata in a joyful manner . . . amorphous and open ended.
>
> (Lieberman, 1977, pp. 23, 19)

This is significant for the design/art professions: can we as adults play with some ulterior purpose, i.e., a design assignment? What are external objects? Are they games, computer programs, toys or symbolic objects? Do their uses imply manual dexterity manipulations and crafting methods and skills? Is open-endedness the same as the "uncertainty" principle? When play is inserted into the CPS process, I argue that these challenges are positively resolved.

Let me reinforce and expand the above definition from others compiled from numerous psychology study sources that have direct application to the design/art fields:

- Play is a free activity with free (not constrained) movements within prescribed limits (not bound by goals and immediate material interests) occurring temporarily outside of the real world, initially non-directed and fluid, always subject to change, abrupt turns, etc.
- Play is an activity with no (direct) profit gain and contains no (immediate) material interest with rules determined by and emergent from the play-activity—this is a critical principle; integrated with motivation, possible rapture/joy, performed in a "playground" or environment that together insulates the player(s) from failure—thus no (or greatly reduced) fear.
- Play is a process of discovery and experimentation as opposed to simple exploration (where a determined outcome is investigated). Exploration can accompany play at various stages as discoveries are "evaluated" or reflected upon. A novel or innovative outcome does not exist at the outset of play and is only discovered in a thirdspace within the play-activity.
- Play is a process of mind–body activities, mental processing and cognitive perception (thinking with the senses) that requires manual dexterity and skill acquisition in order to engage in a consistent and quality performance of play-activity—another critical principle that may cause some consternation among die-hard technologists.
- Play both requires skills and is a learning process for those skills.
- Play is an integral catalytic agent in CPS. For me and through my experiences, play is play-work where a carefree activity is also committed and serious.
- Play by itself is not the sole conductor of creativity in the design/art processes. Its insertion in CPS enables periods of play-activities that can be less directed, experimental, with fewer rules, and be reinserted into the larger CPS process.

Major elements of play, according to Eberle, include: anticipation, surprise, pleasure, understanding, strength and poise. Eberle states that play may seem purposeless to many but holds an abiding utility or deeper motive and contingent objectives. As a part of the play process, he states that rule-making also includes rule-breaking; subversion and mischief often become part of the experience and fun; and play can go back and forth between regulation and abandon, order and disorder, or contain both forces at once. This is why it is considered a free activity, with initial rules that change as play evolves and changes play as the rules evolve.

Playfulness is an attitude on how we play that helps us relax and engage in the joy of the activities. Play combines or forms associations and relationships from among known things, motivation, skill, environment/context and freedom (from fear) that are essential to imagination and creativity (Lieberman, 1977). Playfulness can be the catalyst for *thirdspace* experimentations leading to the aha! moment whether in architecture or physics. Playfulness is characterized by humor, joy and spontaneity, enabling the designer to manipulate and contort that knowledge into something unique, novel and creative.

Familiarity, clarity, simplicity and congruity are stimulation characteristics that can trigger or encourage play; and novelty, ambiguity, incongruity, uncertainty, surprise and complexity can trigger experimental and exploratory behaviors that provide the fundamentals for play (Dewey, 1933).

In design and art processes there can be hesitation, fear or reticence about starting or engaging the tasks at hand. The designer or player is best served by increasing his or her confidence or self-centeredness through evolutionary exercises. This increases their feeling of confidence regarding their competence to achieve success in the task. Buhler (1930) refers to this as the "function pleasure" and is the point where playfulness enters into play. Once the novel or difficult becomes familiar, behavior can be altered from cautious to exploratory or experimental.

Here are some consensus descriptions of play:

- Play is a voluntary action.
- Play is enjoyable.
- Play can be deferred or suspended at any time.
- Play is free.
- Play is a stepping out of real life into a temporary area of activity; it stands outside of the satisfaction of wants and appetites.
- Play is a cultural function, necessary for the individual and society.
- Play contains its own course and meaning, beyond "local time."
- Higher forms of play contain elements of repetition and alternation.
- Play occurs in a "playground," emergent through initial notions and rules, and changing as the play-activity advances, thus changing the "playground."
- Play is pretend and engaged with seriousness.
- Play is uncertain, open to chance and discovery.
- Play is a time to discharge energy (from surplus to tensions to driven passions).
- Play is a time to recharge energy from negative (tensions) to positive (arousal).
- Play is a time to practice skill development and the competence necessary to apply them in CPS.
- Play is a time for growth (the design charrette/competitions example).

Attributes of Play

Attributes associated with play as opposed to work include humor, joy and spontaneity.

- *Humor:* Humor is often seen in play as riddles or puns. Humor is a state of amusement. The cognitive variables of humor that relate to play and design include: (1) incongruity where the attitude is not in keeping with what is correct or is out of place; (2) the humor involves or engages novelty, surprise; (3) humor can assist in arriving at a mediating process; (4) humor can assist the player in arriving at arousal; (5) holding reality in abeyance and letting the fantasy elements play out further on a temporary basis; and (6) the importance of visual imagery as a cognitive function for the observer and player to appreciate the humor.
- *Joy:* An uplifting response, a form of arousal distinguished from fun; joy is the motivating attribute that contributes to the desire to continue playing.
- *Spontaneity:* An activity that occurs in familiar surroundings, has flexibility, unexpectedness, and enables the player to engage new situations and changes in direction that may also be unconventional. In Chapter 7 I explore the use of spontaneity in the production of ever-different products from the same components in design composition exercises. And as in "intuitiveness," spontaneity depends on informational input, a body of knowledge, information and contextual understanding as combinatorial play to produce a creative product. In play, cognitive spontaneity can transform a symbolic object into an entity, a given thing that can be played with (Lieberman, 1977, p. 84).

These attributes can enable creative discoveries in design by removing or reducing the pressures of accomplishment, over-focus and deadlines. Play contains these attributes, freeing the player to engage the play-activity without fear.

The Functions of Play

Play has key vital functions that relate to most cultures, including the following:

- Play is related to the acquisition of skills, a fundamental function of life and survival.
- Play enables the observation and retention of environmental information beyond memory through sensual contact—whole mind–body contact.
- Play encourages the development of normative social behavior (and healthy non-conventional or experimental behavior—there is no criticism or fear of failure; and this healthy non-conventional behavior needs to be recognized as healthy and possibly creative by instructors and managers alike.
- Play enables the discovery and release of previously unformed emergent notions.

Play enables the processing and flow of information insulated from "failure" or fear because in part it embraces failure. Play also introduces the *simulative mode* of thinking where play assists in uncoupling a process output from its normal relations to other systems at multiple levels, enabling experimentation without failure. Feedback is maintained, fear is not a factor, there is no finality, and the decrease in fear enables an increase in confidence and quality of engagement.

Psychologists agree that play is crucial for normal social, emotional and cognitive development. Play is a mechanism to cultivate creativity, solve problems and generate ideas (Brown, 2009). One key function of play is the opportunity it offers to reassemble behavioral sequences for skilled action (Bruner, 1966), reconfiguring convention sequences into creative experimentation. This underscores the need to reduce goal-directed actions that can be predetermined or so structure the process that the outcome is predictable or limited in possible outcomes. The push or pressures to successfully accomplish something can lead to fear or pressured manifestations, raising barriers to creativity. Play can reduce excessive drive and related frustrations (Bruner, 1966).

The Flexibility Complex: Meta-play

Reynolds states that "play must be viewed as part of an adaptive complex involving ontogenetic plasticity in behavior, an (inexperienced or undeveloped) dependency, a capacity for learning from previous action, and (leadership/instructor/guide) care" (Glover et al., 1989, p. 622).

For Reynolds, this is the "flexibility complex" and it provides a range of evolutionary options in creativity. The following is an application of that complex using play in the design process:

- An increased delay in the maturation of decision-making by the designer by extending the time for learning through joy and arousal—avoiding a rush to cliché and naivety—a positive development.
- A greater reliance on pre-play social developments (with colleagues, the community, etc.).
- An increased ability to manipulate objects and incorporate them into instrumental behavior and constructive creative products; playing with objects requires ample time to successfully engage play in a creative way.

- An increased reliance on observational learning for the acquisition of both behavior patterns and environmental information.
- A progressive increase in complexity of the subculture of the play group (team, studio-mates).
- The acquisition of functions that enable the continued existence and usability of the play group functions, one-day sketch problems, internal design charrettes or intensives.

[W]ith the advent of observational learning (object lessons), new behavior patterns and their environmental consequences are learned in play, organized, and made available to non-lay control.

(Glover et al., 1989, p. 627)

As play is explored for adults in the design fields, rules must not dominate as in video games, sports, etc., reducing the essence of play. The state of design education and the professional office, immersed as it is in a digital-technological fascination, can bifurcate learning and playing, trivializing play in the process. Design education and practice can "transform not knowing into a deficit; creative imitation into individualized accomplishments, rote learning and testing, and completion into correction and competitiveness" (Connery et al., 2010, p. 36). *Imitation* is necessary in creative problem-solving as a starting point at a minimum, since it is critical in skill development. In adults, continued imitation can give way to copying or clip-art; losing the creative edge. *Imitation* is explored in the suggested exercises in Chapter 7.

Combinatory Play

Combinatory play is the conscious and unconscious cognitive playful manipulation of two or more ideas, feelings, sensory experiences, images, objects, sounds or words. Players experiment with hypotheses, possible outcomes, and even "failures"; they then compare, contrast, synthesize and break apart disparate elements or constructs in re-envisioning a larger whole (Stevens, 2014). I remember an exercise from undergraduate school where the instructor placed disparate ideas and concepts in a hat and had each student pick out three and begin a design process with those three ideas—quite challenging to say the least. It aided in eliminating clichés and set patterns in the design process.

Motivational Aspects of Play and Creativity

Is There a Play Personality?

There are, according to many psychologists, personalities and behavior patterns that increase the creative capacity in individuals. The good news is that most people can develop or increase this capacity given an identification of the barriers or weaknesses that inhibit creative-potential behavior. Assessing behavior patterns for functional and aesthetic creativity traits and deficiencies can lead to exercises to reduce those deficiencies and strengthen key traits. This is less about teaching them the missing traits identified by psychologies and more about "encouraging people to change the way they give expression to what they already have" (Cropley and Cropley, 2009, p. 216).

The following are traits summarized from *Fostering Creativity* (2009).

Personality traits that support creativity

- Nonconformity in attitudes and behavior
- Autonomy and inner directedness
- Intuitiveness (based on information input)
- Tolerance of ambiguity and a preference for complexity
- Flexibility
- Openness to stimulation and fantasy based on a breadth of interests
- Ability to take risks
- Androgyny or the possession of both male and female characteristics
- An acceptance of being different, i.e., a self-acceptance and the ability to tolerate contradictory aspects of oneself
- A positive attitude to work and play and a high evaluation of aesthetic qualities.

(Cropley and Cropley, 2009, p. 103)

We are remarkably different from one another, yet the profundity of this diversity most often goes unnoticed—living in different worlds we pass barely seeing one another. Or we recognize differences but we don't understand them. People who are different become "others", acknowledged, but known ultimately less for who they are than as reflections of what we find strange and other in ourselves.

(Johnston, 1994, p. 1)

To become aware of personality diversity is a beginning step to understanding the creative differences in ourselves, our colleagues and community members, leading to more open-mindedness and increased creative capacity. Johnston identifies three major personality typologies that each exhibit a creative capacity and creative difference. That is the key: all types can be creative and are creative in different ways.

Personality Patterns

- *Early Axis Personality Patterns.* This is the "inspiration" personality, imaginal and symbolic, motivating, conceptual, and not necessarily finished and polished.
- *Middle Axis Personality Patterns.* This is the "perspiration" personality, emotional and moral, the implementation people, managers.
- *Late Axis Personality Patterns.* This is the "finished and polished" personality, the rational and material, the administrator, principal.

Many architects fall into the early and late categories in their behavior patterns. The early axis patterns are conceptual, imaginal and symbolic, probably cluttered and less organized. The late axis patterns are complete, polished, organized. The many architects who write specifications, prepare construction documents and work hard to make sure buildings do not leak may have strong middle axis patterns in their behaviors. All are creative and creative in different ways with different means and methods and approaches. This is an important point for educators in particular. This does not mean that people are typed—simply that their creative difference is critical to be aware of regarding the individual's learning process and his or her contribution to a team or community in design. There is significantly more to the creative difference discussion; hopefully the point is made: creative *difference*. Refer to two works by Charles Johnston: *The Creative Imperative* (1984/1986) and *Necessary Wisdom* (1991).

Other key personality traits that better enable creativity are autonomy, flexibility, preference for complexity, self-confidence and ego-strength or self-centeredness. These can be taught/learned with the appropriate time, guidance, exercises and environment.

"Many people cannot tolerate discrepancies, weaknesses, gaps in knowledge, and the like: they are closed. Open people, by contrast, seek novelty" (Cropley and Cropley, 2009, p. 105). Cautiousness versus openness: are they set in stone? Of course not, and guided learning is required to bridge the gap. The cautiousness to openness scale is to me the fear–joy scale. Play can reduce that fear and enable the creative capacities to reach fruition. Play and humor are linked to openness because play is not anchored in the strict rules of reality and is free from many social pressures. In the description of my course work in watercolor painting, failure with work or through work was celebrated, not condemned or criticized. In play, novel situations can be tried without fear of failure or risk (Cropley and Cropley, 2009, p. 106).

When I taught watercolor painting (as art as opposed to descriptive rendering) in the Architecture Department at the University of Washington, each quarter I was confronted with twenty-five or more different personalities, ranging from "tell me what to do, I need structure" to "let me do it by myself, I want to play," and those in between. Environment, fear reduction (lots of bad jokes on my part), work, and a strong sense of play (it is okay to experiment, let go, be free, don't treat your work as something precious—and work!).

Autonomy and flexibility are emphasized for each student with individual assignments that stress means, methods and different approaches. For example, one student may be comfortable painting wet brush/pigment onto wet paper (wet on wet); another enjoys painting wet brush/pigment onto dry paper, while a third wants to paint watercolor as if it is oil—drier and very detailed. Understanding all approaches is important and understanding individual preference patterns is also critical to guiding the student through a complex art process. Watercolor painting definitely requires an appreciation for complexity. Self-confidence is gained through step-by-step skill development that leads to confidence that leads to increased skill adaptation that leads to a feeling of "I can do this . . . ," ego-strength. These traits are not learned through a solely mental or intellectual process. One can read a hundred books on watercolor painting and not be able to understand one technique in reality. The environmental aspect is also key and is discussed at length in Chapter 5. In summary, there is a place for every creative difference in the creative problem-solving process. Positive traits can be learned and/or strengthened through guidance and an awareness on the part of the instructor-guide of those differences.

Play as a Social Unit

Play has the potential to change and alter relationships between players, providing new and novel points of reference and enabling them to experience themselves and others as co-authors of the creative situation. Play can create meanings for the community of players in an immediate situation, i.e., not rehearsed through drama, story-telling, intensives and other group interactions (Connery et al., 2010). I discuss this principle in the discussion of play in community (public and private) involvement processes (Chapter 7).

Play as a Cathartic Function

Catharsis is a purifying or cleansing of the emotions (*American Heritage Dictionary*). There is a cathartic function of art and design as it is stimulated by and through play, related to the joy of the activity. Play stimulates a need or desire to engage in the creative process that then leads to an emotional purification by providing an association among feeling, imagination, play-context and sign systems—the symbols of meaning used by the players and the essence of creative skill application. This connection is inseparable and fundamental to creative problem-solving. The loss or dilution of one weakens the others and the connection fails. In point, if your skill development related to play becomes corrupted through clip-art, copying, cliché usage and packaged preprogrammed "skills," the association or relationship of the cathartic function is lost. This happens every day and can result in completion that is competent, efficient, and lacking in passion, creativity and innovation.

The artist and designer utilize a conglomerate of symbolic patterns and rhythms related to the context content, the category or style of artistic composition and materials (objects of play) to intentionally draw out an aesthetic response on the part of a given audience by means of the resultant or emergent and creative composition, event or artifact (Connery et al., 2010, p. 23). Thus, in play as a cathartic function, there is a reciprocity of creative production and aesthetic response. Is this not in part what art and design are about? And are we losing that in the building of our cities?

Semiotic mediation and the mediation of meaning interconnect the way we receive and absorb information to make sense of reality dominated by a spatial dimension of CST. Critical to play is the employment of both physical and psychological tools that enable the processing of information in the CST Matrix, particularly the cultural aspects of reality. The physical tools comprise the symbolic objects of play and the tools of free play such as drawing, model-making, sculpting, etc.—the tools used with manual dexterity. The psychological tools are encapsulated in principles such as a tolerance for diversity, and an appreciation for ambiguity and complexity—aspects of creative thought processes.

Communities and groups of people contain a cognitive pluralism that is a signature composed of visual, aural, verbal, kinesthetic, tactile and olfactory ways of making meaning out of cultural and historic forces in their realities. The contemporary mobile culture in many ways has deviated from this pluralism with an embrace of efficiency in verbal, written and mathematical symbols because they are easily packaged into fast-paced electronic tools and processes—diluting this critical cognitive pluralism that defines each community (Connery et al., 2010).

Why is this critical to the design and creative problem-solving process? Play and play-skills provide a means of making sense of cultural identity, in the use of signs (symbols) and symbolic objects (as signs) to provide a way of mediating generalizations and patterns in cultural forces.

In the discussion of play-based skill development, the principles of sign/symbol systems and their tools are linked to playful methods of capturing the meaning of cultural, spatial and historic forces in communities—play as a basic means of composing the building blocks of signs that tell the stories of community.

All aspects of CPS contain play potential as both a catalyst for learning and as a motivating stimulus for engagement. Play may be viewed as the invisible page between the CPS phases; or a tandem process being inserted into the CPS process at critical points.

The obvious example in the design fields is a pause in the intellectual process, marked by the doodle-diagram over lunch, the napkin sketch, the collage semi-abstraction or the (hand-crafted) process model. These can be experimentation and discovery processes performed in a playful, non-pressured state that arouses the player through color, form, composition, and other visual and form stimulations—and invites creativity. This cannot be done on a computer with the same effect, as the manipulation of play-tools is missing. I have taught graduate students who insist they can do these playful processes on the computer—and the computer is the only tool they have ever worked with—who struggle with the hand-crafted process, as it requires a direct connection to most of the senses.

The less obvious and equally important role of play in CPS is in the gathering and evaluation of information into relationships and patterns. In Chapter 7 I discuss the creative potential of the graphic diagram as a play-tool for assessing the relevance and relationships in the CST Information Matrix. This process fascinates graduate students who know only the computer as a vehicle for processing information: GIS, CADD, etc. When asked to translate the graphic information system (GIS) data into relationships— a story with meaning and functionality in between the lines—they struggle, often simply regurgitating the GIS diagrams. It is a challenging visual thought process that requires skill and play to be successful. There is more on diagrams later in the book.

Play to Eliminate Creativity Blockages

Play occurs in a fearless environment, without failure and pressure to achieve. It is a free activity. In order to enable this activity to take place within the creative process, a level of awareness is required to deal with fear.

Creativity blockages are both physical/spatial (poor environment, inadequate facilities, insufficient resources, incorrect tools and lack of space to apply critical skills) and social/cultural (preconceived notions, erroneous assumptions on the possession of creativity traits ("I am not imaginative" or "I can't draw," etc.), fears and reticence to engage, ignorance of creative differences, etc.). The awareness of these blockages is a critical beginning; and a key place for intervention by the guide, facilitator and instructor. It is an effective place for the role of play to be introduced as a creativity enhancement process.

As a beginning, certain organizational blockages can be eliminated and/or confronted:

1. Over-emphasis on success (grades, promotion, income, bottom-line mentality).
2. Hard distinction made between work and play (where play is trivialized and demoted as having little value in the process; and *work* is not valuable if play is involved).
3. Intolerance for questioning, a need for authority and conventions.
4. Pressure to conform, to fit in.
5. Strict gender roles.
6. No tolerance for difference, no understanding of creative differences.
7. Inability to relax.
8. Inability to engage multiple idea flows due to skill deficiencies in processing those idea flows.
9. Fears in general (fear to be imaginative, fear of success (don't want to be noticed or recognized), fear of failure, of being wrong, of being compared to others, etc.).
10. Emphasis on speed over quality; on deadline and product over process (not product through process).
11. Reliance on non-participants exclusively for product/process evaluation.
12. Talking heads: avoidance of visual thinking/communication skills.
13. Analytical thinking versus qualitative imaginal and symbolic thinking.
14. Adherence to conformity and convention; fear of breaking out.

15. The meeting syndrome, an overreliance on verbal communication (if we don't know what to do or how to do it then a meeting is in order!).
16. Rigid ways, beliefs and methodologies.
17. Methodologies that are easy to employ rather than appropriate for complexity.
18. Unity compromise fallacy: there is only one answer if we talk through the problem enough.
19. Fifty/fifty compromise fallacy: take 50 percent of essence of one idea and combine with 50 percent essence of another, giving up 50 percent of each essence.
20. Separatist compromise fallacy: separate problem areas into insulated or disconnected components as a resolution to avoid conflict.
21. Consensus through compromise—a major misconception that leads to continued problems.

There are more blockages, and these are a good start for the introduction of play as therapy for creatively challenged situations. Some solutions to these blockages consist of common sense and direct actions such as abandoning or lessening the importance of grades, setting aside titles in play-work sessions, engaging in horizontal leadership processes, eliminating gender roles, etc. Others require more energy, practice and repetition. Skill development or the lack thereof is a critical blockage. In urban planning, intelligent and motivated students (and professionals) revert to set computer software or excessive oral communication because they do not have the skill sets to engage the creative process. This can be confronted with preparation exercises of many types (discussed in Chapter 7) that require practice with and through repetition and hard work.

Play and Fear

In both domain-specific design and art studios, the fear factor is the elephant in the room. There are means and methods to deal with fear, as suggested below, based on my experiences in urban design, architecture and painting studios.

Skill Deficiencies

One of the most obvious and fear-based blockages comes from the lack of key skill proficiencies. Students often think that they can engage in an urban design or painting studio, dependent upon manual dexterity skills, with their computer and intellectual cognitive skills only—and meet with failure and fear due to poor or deficient skill development. Years ago I walked into an "advanced" second-year graduate urban design studio and asked the students to pin up the assigned work. I was met with vacant stares and a multitude of excuses (papers due, etc.). I soon realized that they had no idea of how to accomplish the design tasks assigned and they were fearful of admitting that deficiency. I then instituted a series of preparation courses related to urban design skills and design composition with significant success in later design studios.

When I was a youngster from Ohio skiing in the Cascade Mountains of Washington State for the first time, I fell over a great deal. For a long time no one taught me how to stand up after falling over. I soon developed an aversion to skiing and later dropped it due to a lack of simple skills. I was frustrated over failing to achieve such a small skill and was afraid or embarrassed to ask a more proficient skier something seemingly so simple. The same is true for the skills required for play. Play both teaches skill and depends upon skill for successful engagement. It increases competence, and consequently increases confidence and the arousal factor.

Play as Creative Behavior

As a prelude to the actual engagement of play, the aspects of play as creative behavior are critical to review and understand as a foundation for play as a free activity, the glue for creative problem-solving.

Play is an activity (movement, cognitive perception mechanism) free of failure (uncertain outcome, flowing), performed via manual dexterity (with the senses) in a spatial context, affected by that space and affecting changes within that space.

It helps to repeat the main components of CPS as play is introduced.

CPS has three major creativity components:

1. The generation of novelty (which sets it apart from convention and conventional goal-oriented problem-solving)
2. The exploration of the novelty to identify effective aspects of seeking a product (requiring skills, abilities, values, self-confidence or centeredness, and social/cultural support)
3. The utilization of more specific approaches per domain in order to improve the quality of the creative play process.

CPS and play are components of the larger concept of *creativity*. Psychologists generally agree that creativity can be trained in individuals with two key methods:

1. Focusing on the existing creative potentials of the individual while eliminating blocks that can inhibit the expression of those potentials.
2. Focusing on what people do not possess and assisting them in acquiring the knowledge, skills, attitudes and values required to engage creative processes.

Keys to this chapter are some of the techniques to accomplish both of the above, including:

- Engagement with "loosening-up" exercises to build skill and play-tool familiarity.
- Engagement with suggested lessons in a sequence of learning, from simple to complex.
- Use of special materials or "gifts" that relate to specific domains, in this case the domains of urban studies (urban design and planning, architecture, landscape architecture, graphic design).
- Engagement in practice activities—critical to skill development for creative processes.

Recognized principles of creative problem-solving set the stage for experimentation in creativity and play, and include the following:
1. Problem recognition.
2. A prolonged and demanding process or engagement of activities.
3. Involves real-life examples such as case studies.
4. Requires practice exercises.
5. Are domain-specific.

This last principle is important in that creativity varies by discipline or field. It requires differentiated methods, tools and materials appropriate to those fields. Obviously there is some carry-over and the specific domain generates the kinds of creative methods that are most effective for that domain. According to Ludwig (1998), there are two major categories of fields of endeavor or domains: investigative and artistic. These differ significantly:

1. Impersonal vs. emotive
2. Objective vs. subjective
3. Structured vs. unstructured
4. Formal vs. informal.

Both involve creativity, and those creative processes are different according to culture and personality. In most domains, a combination of investigative and artistic types exists, with one being dominant at a particular time, a horizontal leadership process in thinking. The design and planning fields are good examples of this combination, as they require both types.

If we can "train" for creativity, I argue that we can guide individuals in ways to *play,* as the lubricant of CPS.

Play-tools as Fractal Geometries

Ludwig (1998) poses a principle that relates directly to the concept of play with manually manipulated tools: "the relationship between creativity and a field of endeavor is governed by the mathematics of fractal geometry. This is the geometry of self-similar objects that are characterized by a structure that repeats itself again and again at progressively smaller scales" (Cropley and Cropley, 2009, p. 210). The nature of the fractal determines the signature of the larger whole.

Thus when we approach the fields of "urban studies" we can articulate "urban" as spatial scale, cultural patterns, meaning and functionality—all composed of manufactured fractal geometries; and all represented by symbolic objects and toys that are in and of themselves fractal in the play process.

Preparation for Creative Actions as Play

I mentioned earlier the two main categories of creativity training as focusing on improving existing creative potential with the elimination of blocks to that potential; and focusing on what people do not possess. Eliminating blocks to creativity and the play process can be flipped into a positive pro-active learning process as a precursor for playfulness. Let us explore some blockages and view their positive aspects.

1. Exaggerated success criteria:
   - Grades and rewards! Reduce their importance and highlight the successes of process engagement and self-progress in the product
   - Competition! Eliminate the winner/loser aspect in a creative and playful process and replace it with personal growth and engagement with the process; when I teach watercolor painting, one of the main tasks is to have students focus on their own personal development and not compare themselves and their work with that of others
   - Goals! Eliminate the goal as a predetermined outcome and adopt a meta-determinancy approach (uncertain outcome derived from the process of play, not tested by it)

- Consider each idea or expression as a valid option that will eventually be confirmed, absorbed or dissolved by the process itself.

2. Strict distinctions between work and play:

- Incorporate playful techniques in tasks that are often viewed as work, "number crunching," data gathering and processing, etc. (see the "MJ" approach, Chapter 7)
- Incorporate play-tools into a "mundane" task, focusing on visual displays of information in the pursuit of relationships
- Increase the pleasurable aspects of "work"; i.e., focus on those aspects that produce satisfaction ("funktionlust")
- Avoid looking "ahead" to the finish and focus on the steps of the process, again incorporating play-tools that can be as simple as drawing diagrams or patterns on a chalkboard or paper to representing patterns in the data task, etc.

3. Intolerance of questioning:

- Not every question needs an answer! Treat questions as ideas in the buildup of broader ideas and visions
- Avoid personalizing the question as an attack or challenge by transforming it into a positive inquiry that again does not need an answer—maybe more options or hybrids through an expansion of the question.

4. The pressure of conformity:

- Embrace and celebrate diversity in colleagues as well as ideas
- Take an opposite stance to expand a dialogue and increase the boundary of the discussion
- Understand and be able to identify clichés
- Seek hybrids rather than adopt models or franchised ideas and outcomes
- Expand the dialogue by establishing temporary polarities that may enable additional ideas to emerge.

5. Intolerance of difference:

- Celebrate creative differences by never assuming that your perspective is the only perspective of a given issue or idea (is the glass half empty or half full? both, of course)
- Make the effort to understand personality differences
- Put yourself in someone else's position and try to understand their perspective.

6. Inability to handle the flow of ideas when it occurs:

- Practice recognizing when the flow begins (notion, insight, "aha")
- Don't analyze the flow activity; let it develop similar to allowing a dream to emerge and develop
- Don't over-focus on ideas as they emerge; treat them as emergent concepts, document them visually and move on
- Inability or unwillingness to relax
- Go play! with no outcome in mind
- Change what you are doing
- Read the comics.

7. Fear of . . .

   - Let imagination take over
   - Avoid negatives
   - Avoid being "precious" (Weigardt, 2002)
   - Remove yourself from being the "star" of the situation (use visual aids, play-tools, etc. to in part divert attention from you to the tools)
   - A "wrong answer" is simply a learning method of eliminating something that does not work at the moment.

8. Excessive emphasis on speed:

   - Slow down! Enjoy the ride
   - Focus on the steps, not the journey
   - Avoid excessive anticipation in the journey's end
   - Choose tools that give pleasure or are sensual (I use a fountain pen with red ink to write and draw with at times) so that the process itself is joyful, not the time it takes to complete a task.

9. Overreliance on external evaluation:

   - It is okay to be self-centered, to have the confidence in yourself to successfully complete a problem, and is quite different from being selfish
   - Utilize external evaluations as input, not criticism or correctness
   - Avoid one-sided emphasis on analytical thinking
   - Avoid heavy reliance on verbal communication, i.e., being a "talking head"
   - Develop skills in visual communications ranging from semiotic diagrams to cartoons so that there is a distillation and initial spatial interpretation of information; like any other language skill, visualizations can be learned by everyone regardless of personality or lack of drawing experience; it takes work and practice and is more than repeating what is on a GIS map
   - A reliance on verbal communication can be a sign of fear of engagement due to a lack of skills and confidence.

Chapter 3

THE GIFTS OF FRIEDRICH FROEBEL

Kindergarten: The Children's Garden

Friedrich Froebel (1782–1852) founded the Educational Institute in the small village of Keilau, Prussia in 1817. He practiced his teaching up until 1831, when he left due to political pressures from the Prussian government, and was replaced by Barop, who together with Froebel's friends continued the reduced program for a time. The initial institute population consisted of six boys and three instructors—Froebel, Wilhelm Middendorff and Heinrich Langethal—based entirely on the new educational ideas of Froebel. Froebel captures his mission and dreams in *The Education of Man* (1898), translated by W.N. Hailmann (2005) and demonstrates an earnest and practical approach to creative activity. His work is renowned for early childhood education but truly encompassed the "entire impressionable period of human life" (Froebel, 1898, p. xvii).

In his pursuit of a science, theory and application of education, Froebel identified a need for self-activity guided by educators, with training principles that are passive versus prescriptive, categorical and interfering—all leading toward a *spontaneous unfolding*. This self-activity is an early identification of whole mind–body thinking, implying that at all times the whole self is active and enlists the entire self in all phases of being. This has serious implications for the methodologies of his educational program—thinking with the senses as well as the intellect—and the introduction of *play* as a vehicle for this whole mind–body thinking; thinking through the manual manipulation of objects, from wood blocks to paints and paper—*play not gaming*.

Play is also important in that it brings joy to the student (player). This phenomenon is further expanded in *arousal motivation theory*. By bringing joy to self-activity, Froebel demonstrated that a further arousal (of joy) stimulated additional creative activities. Froebel also introduced the concept of polarities in educational methodologies, although he did not use that term. He called for education in training and instruction to be double-sided: *giving and taking, uniting and dividing, prescribing and following*, etc. (Froebel, 1898, p. 14). The introduction of polarities in play and creative problem-solving (design) opens the pathway to *bridging polarities* (Johnston, 1991) and the discovery of thirdspace (Soja, 1996).

Personality and environment contribute to creative learning in instruction whether in schools or professional offices. Through play, Froebel demonstrates how right-sided thinking can be strengthened and expanded as supported through a creative and playful surrounding. In the larger environment, Froebel addressed the importance of context: "the knowledge of things found in their local conditions and their relations" (Froebel, 1898, p. 338). He began in the natural world and progressed to the tools and objects of human beings. He then devised a set of gifts that began with the familiar, near and known to the student, and advanced to more complexity in objects, compositions and relationships. Poetry, music, drawing, story-telling/sharing, language exercise, color etc. all engage the player and help him or her to think and learn. Development and culture come from work done rather than from ideas acquired. His kindergarten gifts are at the core of this "work" and all lead to openness and an appreciation for complexity explored through play.

In short, Froebel's kindergarten taught abstraction and value relationships as much as searching for answers as achieved through "gift-play."

Kindergarten: Playtime and the Froebel "Gifts"

> The real kindergarten is long gone, the gifts have been transformed, the educational objective for what is left of the occupations has been lost or corrupted, the world today is radically different than it was at the beginning of the Industrial Revolution, and superficially at least, today's children may not be comparable to their nineteenth century peers . . . As later trainees were forced to learn from books, and from (teachers) who had themselves learned from books, important nuances of the original (Froebel) training were changed and abandoned.
>
> (Brosterman, 1997, p. 40)

Obviously this is not a negative slap at book-learning. Rather, the object-play or constructivism (*c.* 1920) has been lost. The advent of computers, digital graphics and digital games has drastically changed kindergarten, relying less on the senses and more on: what? Let us explore Froebel's object-play or "gift-play" as a prelude to inserting key principles into the creative problem-solving process.

The Twenty Gifts of Froebel

Gift One: The Ball

The ball, emanating energy equally in all directions, was for Froebel the beginning of play-learning. His initial ball gifts were essentially colored wool balls that were easily manipulated (squishy, pliable) to engage the senses with one of the primary shapes. He used six balls that represented objects such as heads, cabbages, etc. to mathematical relationships—a string of two to six objects, and of course, one or the point, dot.

> The first gift was the germ of everyone, the model for everything, and the most sublime expression of unity.
>
> (Brosterman, 1997, p. 42)

In the beginning phases of introducing students (regardless of age) to design composition, the ball (circle) represents unity and is the foundation of learning, a mathematical form with great tolerances for creative manipulation.

Gift Two: The Sphere, Cylinder, and Cube

Froebel grouped these together, as the cylinder is contained in the cube and the ball in the cylinder—simple figures in relationship. The composition of this gift entailed a sphere and a cube linked by a cylinder, his trademark of unity. In addition, this composition represents the classic polarity, as the sphere and cube, both primary volumes, are alike in their "perfections" and opposites in their physical characteristics (organization and structure). His concept of the law of opposites incorporated opportunities to express antitheses–polarities, and his cylinder was (is) the bridging device. The sphere represents motion and the cube represents absolute rest; no flat planes vs. no curves; unity vs. variety. The cylinder, with curves and flat planes, in motion and at rest, (is) a synthesis (Brosterman, 1997, p. 46). How is that for your first week in kindergarten?

Gifts Three through Six: Building Blocks

[T]he concept of relativity—of the whole in its relation to the parts and of the parts in relation to the whole.

(Brosterman, 1997, p. 51)

We take building blocks for granted. Early wooden toys were abstracted versions of reality: miniature classic components, realistic and specific models of trains, boats, even towns (Germany in the nineteenth century). These were destructive to Froebel, as they discouraged discovery and creativity. As Brosterman continues:

The open-ended nature of good building blocks provides opportunities for instruction in social studies—in mapping, the layout of cities, and people's work; socialization—in cooperation, clean-up, respect for others, and self-confidence; art and architecture—in pattern, balance, symmetry,

Figure 3.1 Froebel and Object-learning through Symbolic Objects

Froebel's "gifts" described in this chapter provide the basis for creative composition through a playful environment and behavior. The use of symbolic objects is distinguished from "toys" with themes and specific signatures as a means of increasing the range of creative exploration.

and construction; language—in function, storytelling, planning, and conceptual exchange; science—in gravity, weight, trial and error, and inductive thinking; and mathematics—in geometry, number, measurement, classification, fractions.

(Brosterman, 1997, p. 50)

Froebel developed a series of four block toys. His third gift was a two-inch-square building block divided through its center by three perpendicular planes forming eight smaller cubes. The player can take this block apart, examine the individual parts, smaller compositions with other parts, and appreciate the whole as they are reassembled. Simple and diverse. Froebel's gift to all of us: his radical (at the time) repudiation of the traditional and conventional concepts of play accompanied by a new definition of play as open-ended and symbolic.

Building blocks are further explored and experimented with in Chapter 7.

There was a progressive sequence to the gift-play in both two and three dimensions using tiles and volumes in pattern making. The increasing complexity of the gifts and their applications are the key learning processes bestowed by Froebel. It is more than playing with blocks. Infused in this play are mathematics, geometry, composition, and key principles of space including volume, direction or movement, position or location and size or dimension. Intoxicating.

Gift Seven: Parquetry

Parquetry is an inlay of a flat material, usually wood, that can be formed into a geometric pattern. Froebel used it as a means to make or form pictures of things unlike the tangible things made from blocks. This was a bridging device between two- and three-dimensional constructs. It taught composition as an assembly of abstraction and fragmentation, again the parts and the whole. Froebel's parquetry was cut into pieces that could also be assembled into the primary shapes.

Gift Eight: Sticks

The eighth gift is composed of sticks as lines. I always consider the line as one of the primary shapes (circle and square), essential to compositional structure. The original Froebel package of sticks consisted of sticks in one- to five-inch increments that enabled play with a grid and square system, interlacing, etc.

Gift Nine: Rings

Ring-laying was the addition of curved lines and circle segments to the gift set. It was composed of heavy-gauge steel wire fashioned into incrementally sized whole, half and quarter circles.

Gift Ten: Drawing

Drawing is the use of the line and dot to represent and/or study an object or composition. Historically, drawing was a language that enabled even the illiterate to communicate. It was used to study how things were made and assembled, as well as a language to express the meaning of art. Froebel based a lot of his drawing lessons on the grid, first described by Pestalozzi. The grid provided a base for the vertical, horizontal and, later, the diagonal line in pattern-making. It was (is) a framework for painters and designers to scale up designs, maintaining proportion and compositional relationships; thus it is an important compositional structure (Goldstein, 1989).

Some may be shocked to learn that drawing is not obsolete or a "dinosaur" tool. The advantage of drawing is in its connection to the player—through the senses of sight and touch with pressure, friction and tool all in play. Drawing is one of the oldest and most sensual means of communicating in human history, and remains a valued and valuable language and tool in all fields.

Gift Eleven: Pricking

Froebel used the established craft of sewing to develop pricking—using a pointed object to punch holes into paper to form patterns. It is a bridge between drawing and sewing, in that colored points can be made into a pattern and thread can be inserted through the punched holes. Pricking can be used to make patterns on planes and to assemble those planes with threads and sticks into volumetric compositions.

Gift Twelve: Sewing

Sewing is considered a "drawing" gift in that it is assembled with lines based on the tool (essentially a dot that is repeated in various linear patterns). Froebel valued sewing for color, diversity of pattern in line, and—at the time—familiarity. Again, the grid was used as a basic framework for the construction of various patterns, both realistic and abstract.

Gifts Thirteen through Eighteen

These gifts are grouped together due to their inherent relationships in the use of paper: cutting (13), weaving (14) and folding (18). Paper cutting is an historic tradition used by many cultures to create crafts, from cards to decorations. Paper weaving is derived from weaving, the intertwining of two or more strips of paper into patterns; and folding, the bending of paper into two- and three-dimensional patterns as in Japanese Origami. These require hand skills and practice to effectively achieve a successful pattern. The grid again was used as a base.

I utilize these gifts in the instruction of basic design composition. Students are asked to take the primary shapes (circle, square and line) and, using colored paper, glue and scissors, to manipulate them into as many hybrids as possible without losing their primary characteristics (Kasprisin, 2011). This is simple yet challenging in that they begin to understand the structural principles of the shapes (center, corner, diagonal, radius, etc.); how to alter and change and adapt those shapes to a given context; and to hold the shapes' principles as the basis for a compositional structure. Powerful. Froebel understood the flexibility and diversity in cutting, weaving and folding as a learning process for composition.

Gifts Fifteen through Seventeen: Slats, Jointed Slats and Interlacing

Froebel's slats are similar to the popsicle sticks (frozen juice on wood slats) and were used to teach tension and interconnections. He referred to the end products as "drawing in space," an apt title for these mobile-like wood slat constructs in various colors. Remember the "Frisbees" (flat wood slat constructions) that we constructed with interlaced popsicle sticks in our youth? Some of us still do. We worked on the construction until the tension was correct to hold all the sticks together.

Gift Nineteen: Peas-work

This is quite brilliant on Froebel's part, as he returns the student to the concept of volume with joint connectors made of softened peas, modeling clay and balls of wax. These connectors joined wire, sticks and other elements into space frames and advanced the students' appreciation and understanding of volume up another notch.

Gift Twenty: Modeling Clay

Modeling clay (clay mixed with a small amount of oil) is used throughout the art and design fields to this day. It introduces the student to sculpting a mass into an object or concept. Modeling is the opposite of drawing and other more linear gifts, and challenges the student to think in mass and volume rather than in outline and contour. The clay allows the student to utilize additive and subtractive transformation actions in play, adding to the mass or taking away, as in the examples that follow.

I underscore the necessity to place Froebel's gifts into the larger perspective of evolutionary guidance from simple cut-out constructs to complex and intricate designs. Their variety and diversity provided a flexible learning tool that facilitated their learning of "one thing and everything" (Brosterman, 1997, p. 88). How valuable was this form of education? A process of playing and making things using the hands and mind was (is) an integration of mind and body, of intellect and cognitive perception through the senses.

The Froebel Kindergarten's Impact on Art and Design

On Art

Froebel's kindergarten system in Europe influenced artists and architects across the continent. Brosterman makes the argument (1997) that the early kindergarten programs and teachers

> created an enormous international program designed specifically to alter the mental habits of the general populace, and in their capable hands nineteenth century children from Austria to Australia learned a new visual language . . . kindergarten taught abstraction . . . equating ideas, symbols, and (made) things . . . it encouraged abstract thinking, and in its repetitive use of geometric forms as the building blocks of all design, it taught children a new and highly disciplined way of making art.
>
> (Brosterman, 1997, p. 106)

He explores the impacts of this early education model on the artists' impressionist artists, from cubism (Picasso and Braque) to neo-plasticism (Mondrian) to the Bauhaus.

On the Bauhaus

In 1919, Walter Gropius (1883–1969) took over the Bauhaus (Germany's noted art school of the Weimar Republic), an interdisciplinary school for design, arts and crafts. The school's basic course, the *Vorkurs*, was based on Froebel's principles as directed by Johannes Itten (a trained Froebelian kindergarten teacher), Josef Albers, Wassily Kandinsky and Paul Klee. This basic course was focused on the Elementary Study of Form augmented by a Study of Materials in the Basic Workshop (the studio); with detailed studies in Nature, Materials, Tools, Construction and Representation, and Space, Color and Composition

Study. All of this using stone, wood, metal, textiles, color, glass and clay through manual dexterity—hands-on play.

> The Bauhaus is typically described as quintessentially modernist because of its enthusiasm for basic shapes, primary colors, and rules and theories. From the perspective of creative cognition . . . such an approach is not a matter of taste or zeitgeist, but simply sensible and intrinsically creative; its methodology instantiates the principle of categorical reduction to its core . . . for the first two semesters, students were introduced to the most basic ingredients of art and design: line, tone, color, structure, texture, surface treatment, and volume.
>
> (Prager, 2014, p. 39)

These represent sensory exploration, thinking with the senses using play, and have vastly disappeared from design and planning education, replaced by: what?

Walter Gropius brought to the USA the Bauhaus influence on modern America as new technologies and construction methods emerged.

On Frank Lloyd Wright and Le Corbusier

Frank Lloyd Wright and Le Corbusier were both children-students of the original kindergarten system and the influence can be clearly seen in their works.

> I sat at the little kindergarten table-top ruled by lines about four inches apart each way making four-inch squares; and among other things, played upon these "unit-lines" with the smooth maple blocks. Scarlet cardboard triangle (60 degrees–30 degrees) two inches on the short side, and one side white, were smooth triangular sections with which to come by pattern—design—by my own imagination. Eventually I was to construct designs in other mediums. But the smooth cardboard triangles and maple-wood blocks were most important. All are in my fingers to this day.
>
> (Wright, in Brosterman, 1997, p. 138)

Wright's mother was introduced to the Froebel Kindergarten while visiting the Centennial Exposition in Philadelphia in 1876 after observing German elementary schoolteachers giving a demonstration on kindergarten.

When you study Wright's design work, you will notice a strong pattern-making process reminiscent of the Froebel methods based on the underlying grid pattern. Wright utilized drawing, models, and painting as gift-play in his design work.

> Wright was a child of Froebel's kindergarten, and while he may still have gone on to become an architect without it, he would certainly never have developed into the one we know.
>
> (Brosterman, 1997, p. 145)

Le Corbusier (Charles Edouard-Jeannert (1887–1965))

> [H]istorian Marc Solitaire published a paper in 1993 that the architectural world was to discover what Solitaire had astutely suspected. Kindergarten first came to La-Chaux-de-Fonds (Le Corbusier's home town) in 1878, and got a tremendous boost from an academic decree of 1889 requiring

the implementation of the system cantonwide. Coincident . . . was the founding of a state-mandated Neuchatel Froebelian Normal School.

(Brosterman, 1997, p. 150)

The young Le Corbusier was enrolled at four years of age as one of the first seventy students.

On the US Public Education System

Between the Civil War and World War I, Froebelian educators sought with much resistance to establish kindergarten into a conservative Victorian and Evangelical Protestant environment within US child education. Many key principles of Froebel were lost in that battle as the kindergarten was accepted into the public educational system. In the 1830s to 1860s, Calvinism had a strong influence on early childhood education, advocating the removal of all toys from a child's environment. "No sooner does a child begin to take notice of objects so as to be placed with them," wrote one writer, "and no sooner does he covet, then he endeavors, by all means in his power, to possess them, not by gentle methods, but by force" (Shapiro, 1983, p. 9). Contrary to this attitude was the beginnings of change in early childhood education. Lydia Child in *The Mother's Book* (1831) and Theodore Dwight in *The Father's Book* (1835) began to thaw out the severity of the Calvinist influence on education. They both supported the introduction of toys and games into child education. According to Dwight, "There is room for the exercise of much ingenuity, talent and learning, (introducing toys and games) which if well exerted would produce great effects" (Shapiro, 1983, p. 9). Hartford Congregational minister Horace Bushnell went even further by identifying "play" as the highest complete state of man and a perfect activity where there is no means to an end; where play is both an end and a joy. Attitudes began to change.

Froebel's kindergarten was introduced to American readers by the liberal Unitarian paper the *Christian Examiner* in 1859. The insertion of American cultural differences into the Froebelian system altered aspects of its social and educational philosophy, shifting from political to social reforms through the kindergarten system. Gradually, the Germanic cultural influences in kindergarten processes were absorbed and replaced with a more vivacious and energized American tone. This also improved and advanced the role of women in the US educational system as they were viewed by many Froebelians as capable of a more nurturing and gentle teaching process.

The Froebel model spread quickly after 1872, with a strong foundation in St. Louis due to the many German immigrants to initially support it. The St. Louis school system matured into a more efficient and public education system.

The Importance of Froebel's Gifts to Contemporary Designers and Planners

Why is all of this significant? Froebel developed a learning process of immense impact on design and composition through the use of symbolic objects and play. The impact on many master artists and architects is well documented. Our cities have also benefited greatly from those influences based on the gifts of Friedrich Froebel.

Whole mind–body thinking is part of Froebel's gift. He provided the process and tools for creative experimentation in the integration of both the intellect and the senses (using manual dexterity manipulations in play) to discover novel and innovative concepts and solutions (more relevant today then ever).

Chapter 4

HOW DO DESIGNERS PLAY?

How Do Architects and Artists Play?

Do contemporary architects and artists play? Of course many play. How do they play and can that play be transferred to other fields, or integrated into the changing nature of contemporary design and planning fields?

The following is a smattering of play-activities from recognized architects and artists as they search for ways to be creative, novel and innovative.

Architects of course are not uniformly consistent in how they play and with what materials and tools. There are the conventions and historic tools described in the previous chapter and they are only the beginning. Not all architects and artists play. Many find an outline or methodology that works and they maintain that methodology without a great deal of adjustment or evolution. Competence does not equate with creativity. Those who do play as a part of design enjoy stepping over boundaries; in fact, they criticize those boundaries themselves. Even in architecture, the profession of visual communication, research indicates that making architecture is a practice full of contradictions between standards, conventions, and the departures and deliberate infringements that play encourages.

Krasny (2008) interviewed architects around the globe in search of their play-activities and methods. The following is a sampling of his interviews and/or observations and findings regarding these architects.

Alvar Aalto (Finland)

Alvar Aalto's Finnish culture, heritage and environment, especially the context of lakes and forests around which he grew up, were not symmetrical, but natural and related to the elements of the landscape. Aalto enjoyed drawing as a play-tool. He preferred to sketch-play with a 6b graphite pencil on paper, very soft and fluid. The concept or design took shape through the media of drawing—deliberate, sensual and immediate. The pencil and paper were tools of experimentation as he believed that the design (drawings) had to be drawn over and over again until the design emerged—learning that the design was never right the first time.

Lina Bo Bardi (Brazil)

Lina Bo Bardi (1914–1992) used symbolic objects (including spittle and cigarette ash) mixed with conventional tools (mixed media, writing, pencils and paper, and color markers) and adding watercolor and turpentine for various effects and experiments. Her deviation of established boundaries was highlighted by the collection of "goods" from the culture that she was designing within (i.e., domestic hand crafts, local building traditions), where "culture is the production of a community (design)" (Krasny, 2008).

This local collection of cultural goods and artifacts is a lesson for all designers as we become set in the ways that we approach design. Every community or neighborhood or district, even in the same portion of the same city, has unique or special cultural aspects and characteristics that are embedded in its spatial organization and structure. Finding these aspects and incorporating them into the design process is a form of instructive play that informs the design process and decisions.

Atelier bow-wow (Tokyo, Japan)

The firm Atelier bow-wow uses process models and drawings as play-tools, using the model to check the process spatially. All changes on paper are explored with new models. This is an historic play-tool process that continues to have value in the digital age. The two-dimensional nature of drawings and digital graphics (including three-dimensional digital graphics displayed on monitors) benefits from the construction of real crafted process models regarding visual evaluation and alteration.

Diller Scofidio + Renfro (New York)

Diller Scofidio + Renfro believe that almost anything can be a tool. The firm relies on extensive research augmented by an interdisciplinary visual art media-mingling, including dance movements, in order to break down the disciplinary boundaries that permeate the design process. At a minimum, these departures challenge established boundaries and assumptions, stimulating new thought and challenges. Simply changing a medium one uses frequently can alter the cognitive plurality of the designers' perspective. They are aware that the circumstances of experimentation produce the need for new tools for play. Again, just because a designer can do something with a certain tool (i.e., the computer) does not mean that it is the appropriate tool for that circumstance.

Edge Design Institute (Hong Kong)

Gary Chang of Edge Design Institute of Hong Kong stresses that tools have another life in addition to their manufacture—even multiple personalities. He has no favorite tool and uses a variety of playthings such as Lego blocks, a sketchbook and a computer to keep his creative edge. Chang also believes in a relaxed and creative environment, not just in the office but at home, the club, workshop, library and copy center (in his office), wherever the chance for creativity may occur. The entire environment is designed to stimulate creativity in a relaxed and informal manner. The concept of a contemporary and creative "playroom" applies to most fields of endeavor where the environment stimulates and challenges creative thought. The elementary schoolteacher who, when teaching science, has the students construct a drop of water (and all it contains under the microscope) within the boundaries of the classroom—as a space in and of itself—creates an educational playroom that is a drop of water constructed of cardboard, construction papers and many other play materials. And then it is gone, to be replaced by another imaginative construct.

Yona Friedman (France)

Yona Friedman believes that architecture is a serious endeavor that is neither a paper game nor a computer game. A paper model for her does not produce reality—it is a reference. Consequently, she combines series of play-tools such as process models with drawing and photomontages and simple materials as her base for play-activity. Once more we see the act of diversifying the play-tools to keep the process fresh and creative, not encumbered by clichés and predetermined outcomes that arise from established methodologies.

Steven Holl (New York)

Steven Holl relies on watercolor sketches painted on 5″ × 7″ cards to develop design notions that are then scanned as a conceptual guide. "With the advent of the computer the watercolor became supercharged," as they can then be manipulated and easily incorporated into a larger design process. The watercolors are augmented by models, drawing and other techniques that present themselves. The fast watercolor sketches filter out detail and represent broad concepts. In many watercolor sketch applications, a painter may simply represent "movement" or a certain "compositional structure" quickly and loosely with a broad brush. I will discuss watercolor in more detail in Chapter 6 as a way to break out of established limitations and boundaries of other conventional tools.

Jerde Placemaking (Venice, CA)

Jerde utilizes intensive workshops with clients, community and staff with lots of sketching. This is akin to the American Institute of Architects Regional/Urban Design Assistance Team (R/UDAT) that has been so successful since the 1970s—a design charrette with fast-paced, on-site crafted play activities working with the community; and a constant production of ideas and notions for perusal and critique by the community in an interactive manner. This intense workshop-charrette method has proven valuable in community design work as designers strive to go beyond "feel-good" exercises, instead working with community members to forge a vision for the community. Sketching ideas on paper with community members gathered around the table offering ideas and critiques is extremely powerful and beneficial to all, including the designer.

Larger Corporate Firms

Many large firms rely almost exclusively on the computer and the many and varied digital graphic programs. The design process is streamlined and made efficient based on the larger dimensions of the office (numbers of personnel, hierarchy of roles and positions, a top-down corporate structure where efficiency is highly prized). Play is minimized or discouraged and viewed as wasteful and trivial, similar to a dictionary definition. There are exceptions of course. In my youth, I spent four years at Dalton Dalton Little and Newport (Cleveland, 1968–1972) and was a part of a 300-strong office. Bob Little, a key principal in the firm, was the exception to the corporate rule. Bob established his office as a playroom, filled with large drawing tables covered in flimsy tracing paper and colored pencils, and with sketches and diagrams covering the walls.

It was always a pleasure being invited into his playroom, leaving behind the larger corporate landscape of modular partitions.

Interviews with Regional Architects, Designers, and Artists

I also sought out renowned artists and architects in the Pacific Northwest and Alaska with whom I have worked in the past for their reflections on object-learning and play. They certainly do not represent all of their colleagues and do exhibit in their work the play aspects of Froebel and the creative problem-solving principles defined by the Cropleys.

John Luebtow, Artist/Sculptor, Chairperson of the Arts Department, Harvard Academy (Los Angeles, CA and Langley, WA)

John is a glass and metal sculptor with an international reputation in large-scale urban art installations. In John's words, "I draw, I build, and I manipulate materials." His noted linear form series emerged from drawings of the female nude, demarcating a path from realism to abstraction. The playful aspect is the transference of one form and composition (the nude) to an urban art piece. His use of geometry originates from Froebel's methodology as initially taught to him in the Milwaukee, WI school system, including kindergarten, elementary and public high school.

John has an interesting beginning on many of his projects: he cleans his studio, sweeping and putting things away, repairing and organizing. As he states: "this is an element of play as it involves absolutely no predetermined ideas except to remove 'residue' . . . of what was before." This eliminates any interference from previous projects and concepts, presenting a new beginning and becoming a springboard for new ideas. He loves to scrounge the metal yards for junk, scrap and new pieces. He scours the beaches, woods for clay, wood objects—"the shapes are endless." In other words, he tries to observe his surroundings not as they are but as what they can become. In addition to enjoying the silence for its lack of distraction, John also collects and studies early educational implements and objects, including blocks and toys related to Froebel, the Bauhaus, Naef, Anchor and Milton Bradley—all of which offer unique approaches for him to form solutions.

All information-gathering for John begins with a familiarization with the parameters of the problem to be solved. "Nothing is really new! The past is continually being made the present. There are no answers or pathways . . . free the mind, empty it out, make room for the new . . . this is where the mind needs to begin, with nothing (left) to lose . . . but PLAY."

John begins a project with pen and pencil, playing with lines and shapes without a predetermined path. He enjoys the traditional pencil and its connection to his senses and intellect. "Ideas may be stimulated by anything . . . and everything . . . no doors are closed, no senses shut down." He supports the concept of the "eureka" or "aha" moments that come during the night, visiting with friends, doing something else, but designing after a lot of input has occurred during the day. John is fascinated and close to his tools of craftsmanship of all types—the tool-box. These are a form of play-tool and can be involved in making cups, bowls, toys, carpentry and repairing machinery . . . looking at one thing and seeing another. John is also open to multiple media, as understanding materials is necessary in building a technical vocabulary of media and is the base and the foundation of his art. In his play, he utilizes a visual vocabulary of materials and tools in his creative problem-solving. As he states, "artistic expression and communication are not possible without them and we must see the computer as just another tool and [he emphasizes] we must not let interface interfere with face to face" (interview with the author).

David Gignac, Artist (Langley, WA)

David Gignac is an internationally recognized artist, ranging in work from exquisite pen-and-ink drawings to three-dimensional glass and metal sculptures. As his work can exhibit strong architectural and sculptural characteristics, it provides an excellent case study for the idea of object-learning through play.

David utilizes both digital technologies and hand-crafted methods to conceive, develop and implement his artworks. Like many sculptors, for David, the material is a driving force that defines the act of design. Accompanying this appreciation for the materials he works with is an understanding that the whole process is a sum of his own experiences and his developed ability to play.

Play in his realm begins with an attitude of uncertain outcome, no goals that eliminate, at the inception of a project, the need for precision, i.e., small scale and detail. In addition, he frees himself from the notion of completeness or the finished product in order to enter the process with openness, "actually doing something but you don't think you are accomplishing something so you are free to explore." He calls this his "fidget toy." David also utilizes a form of horizontal leadership of design thinking, as I discuss in Chapter 8, which involves working at the periphery of a larger problem, allowing as many notions to develop as possible, going back and forth from divergent to convergent thinking in a process of coalescing ideas. He emphasizes the need for a freedom of failure and appreciation for failure as a learning tool.

In his play, David uses Sketchup software to establish a frame of reference for the space that will accommodate or accept the final work. He refers to this as his "scaffolding" process. He also uses a form of grid framework by working on grid paper as he begins his next phase: drawing for the same reason— providing a spatial frame of reference. As can be seen in examples of his methods, the drawings are beyond the technical shop drawing—articulated as visual expressions with meaning and sensory awareness, with an enjoyment for composition, value pattern and texture that begin to describe characteristics for the emerging work. At intermittent points in the process, David will scan the crafted drawings and manipulate them further, testing and evaluating, then move back to the drawing stage.

Figures 4.1 to 4.4 are indicative of his process, methods, play-tools and skills in this creative problem-solving process.

An Enjoyable Experiment

Bettisworth North Architects (Fairbanks/Anchorage, AK)

I asked friend and colleague Charles (CB) Bettisworth FAIA to enlist his staff in a play session with symbolic objects after learning that the staff already engaged in occasional Friday afternoon play sessions, with a few beers of course. Participants Kate Incarnato, Trent Schoenemann, Randall Rozier and Brittany Jackson worked together and individually over a couple hours of free play with variously shaped pieces of foam, cans and wire. They engaged in a free-play activity, building on one another's ideas and "moves" as they assembled various abstract design compositions in a relatively short time period.

HOME AT PLAY

Figure 4.1 The Conceptual Drawing—The Prima Drawing

Years ago David started sketching on the backs of notecards at our favorite watering hole in Langley, WA, a gathering spot for locals and visitors to our beautiful island. The proprietors began collecting his sketches and soon had a significant collection of David's work. These small, exquisite pen-and-ink sketches became a major part of his work process. Unlike many conceptual sketches, these are done with a finesse that indicates the level of particular joy in their making.

Figure 4.2 The Progressive Drawing Realized

Figure 4.3 The Final Piece in Context

Figure 4.4 Another Final Piece Activated

Figure 4.5 Architects at Play (A)

Source: Bettisworth North Architects.

Figure 4.6 Architects at Play (B)

Source: Bettisworth North Architects.

Figure 4.7 Architects at Play (C)

Source: Bettisworth North Architects.

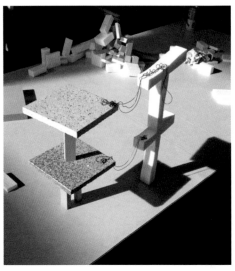

Figure 4.8 Architects at Play (D)

Source: Bettisworth North Architects.

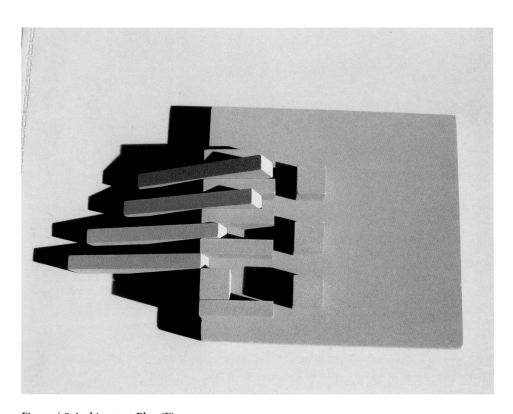

Figure 4.9 Architects at Play (E)

Source: Bettisworth North Architects.

*

Play through object-learning is still critical to the design and planning process, providing a direct contact to objects that can assume multiple personalities and characteristics. There is no one correct material or play-object and they are all important and molded by the designer/planner in his or her search for novel and innovative ideas. They help break us out of cliché and set precedents or models that are popular and easily accomplished. Play is a dynamic creative activity for all adults.

Chapter 5

SETTING THE STAGE—PLAY ENVIRONMENT

Advantages of the Studio Process

Environment is a key component in creative problem-solving (CPS) with play as a binding agent. Environment is defined as the physical place in which you are "making something"—designing or otherwise engaged in a creative process. The traditional design fields of architecture, landscape architecture and urban design, as well as those of applied and fine art, have (had) a studio culture that contains both the space and the patterned behavior ongoing in that space.

I wrote some of this work for new graduate planning students at the University of Washington. as many experienced frustration and a sense of unfamiliarity with the concept and culture of studio. Consequently, I want to make a number of clarifications regarding the traditional studio process and a studio culture:

1.   With the advent of digital technologies in the design and art fields, the physical characteristics of studio are changing. First, the drawing table or traditional place of making are reduced or replaced by computer stations. As this transition to digital technologies continues, the physical characteristics of studio environment continue to change. Presently in many design and art environments, the computer station is in a separate room (dust reduction) associated with the studio or removed to another part of the building—making interactions in the studio difficult. Work tables are still required in many but not all cases. One troubling aspect in graphic design studios is the absence of pens, paper, etc.—replaced not augmented by computers. This book argues that both are required for a CPS process; and that the key principle of studio–individual experimentation and group interactions cannot be replaced with a form of isolation or disconnection among participants.

2.   The term *studio culture* is new and potentially unsettling, unfamiliar to students and professionals new to design processes. Following is in part the memo I prepared for graduate urban planning students, most with non-design backgrounds ranging from political science, economics, sociology, etc. regarding the nature and use of both the studio environment and the culture of behavior within it.

3.   Key to a successful studio environment are motivation, cognitive and mental approaches, and skill building.

Environment for CPS in Design and Planning: Unique Educational Process

The following is intended to begin a discourse on "studio culture," especially related to the participation of first-year design and planning students; and to the design professions as offices are transformed in equipment, layout and function based on the impacts of digital/computational technologies. The "studio" is undergoing a significant shift away from crafting space to computer lab.

The term "culture" has brought raised eyebrows and signs of distress on numerous student faces both outside and within the design fields. There is a series of patterned behaviors in studio that are different from other learning formats. They are changing due to technology, and as that technology is better integrated into the studio environment, the culture will adjust.

Consequently this dialogue is worth pursuing as an introduction. Studio formats are a preferred problem-solving venue in planning and design curricula. For many students in urban planning, public affairs, real estate development and other urban studies fields, this format is new and can often cause frustration, as it requires a combination of independent work and interactive faculty and student participation. Studio space is meant to be messy, experimental, flexible, and capable of being manipulated to serve the objectives of the studio project. In the practicing design fields, computer monitors have replaced the large drawing tables, morphing into computer stations. Laser cutters have replaced the hand-crafted models; and now three-dimensional printers promise to revolutionize the "making" process.

Studio size by many college standards is fifteen students per faculty member. More than that can present additional challenges for faculty and students, and may require compromising modifications to the studio process. Environment is a key context for play and CPS processes because it contributes to (or diminishes) motivation (arousal), skill applications, flexibility, experimentation and manipulation of materials. I use the term "studio" for the basic model of environment based on its historical use in the design and art fields. Hopefully, the studio environment can morph into appropriate hybrids based on changing skills and methods in the design/planning fields, as the tipping point has been reached in my teaching experiences.

Key objectives of this memo-dialogue are: (1) to familiarize non-design students with the traditional studio process and culture; (2) to assess and evaluate the use of studio in the professional office environment; and (3) to explore studio hybrids that have direct application to the varied fields within design and planning, and encompasses the principles and elements of studio process while recognizing the differences between planning and design problem-solving objectives. In addition, the dialogue asks what process, means and methods can be taught as pre-studio preparation for all involved, to lessen frustration and unfamiliarity. I first started this exploration specifically targeted to urban planning students interested in urban design; I now expand that exploration to the established design fields after observations of beginning design students and their disconnect with a studio environment.

Studio Principles and Methodologies: Environment, Process, Culture

The Studio as Environment

Studio is a room, workplace or establishment where something is made (art, music, film, etc.); a problem is resolved. The key word is "made," a place and environment wherein a (creative) process results in a specific product. This varies from the terms "classroom," "auditorium," "meeting and seminar rooms," "recreation room" and "all-purpose room" that are associated with verbal discourse and (hopefully) visual presentations as opposed to the making of some physical/spatial composition.

This is a scene that is rapidly disappearing—work tables and play/design objects in use. Many design studios now are dominated by digital hardware. This was driven home recently as I flew home from Toronto, Canada, one of my favorite cities. I wanted some food and a glass of wine so I looked for the usual pub or pavilion in the gate area. I was confronted with a sea of monitors in front of every stool and chair. Everything was ordered via the monitors and a delivery person brought the results. Progress? Efficient, yes, effective, doubtful; visually it was distractive and the layout encouraged people to focus on the monitors and not on the environment or people.

A studio needs to be inviting as a start to alleviating initial fear and reticence in engaging a problem-solving process with semi-independent work—not simply efficient or streamlined.

The Studio as Process

Studio is a process of study that is progressive (proceeding in steps), evolutionary and conclusive. Its principles may be applied to many fields, altered by the specific needs of skill tools and methods. Studio contains the following essential elements and principles.

Elements

1. Individual work space suitable in size and arrangement for the skills and methodologies required to produce a product, not shared desk space
2. Instruction on the use of key basic materials and processes associated with that individual or personal space
3. A collective of individual work spaces that enable individual and semi-independent work as well as collaborative small and large group interactions (and the space to accommodate those interactions)
4. One instructor per fifteen student relationship
5. Student access beyond class hours with an understanding that the student–faculty interactions are dependent upon prepared work, usually done outside of class time, not talk
6. Meeting, display and presentation areas for large-format posters, photography, process models, etc., not limited to individual computer monitors or PowerPoint presentation—the key term is interactive area
7. Computer support space within the studio, not outside the space in order to eliminate studio-related absences from the studio environment (thus the inclusion of a computer station area within the confines of the studio space).

Principles/Components of Studio Process

1. CPS as opposed to normative or linear problem-solving
2. Non-goal oriented: a path of discovery using experimentation prior to exploration of an idea
3. Experimental rather than simulation-based
4. A combination of divergent and convergent thinking means and methods
5. Utilizes and depends upon manual dexterity methodologies in addition to computational design applications—a plurality of design and planning methodologies

6. Requires skills of element manipulation, object-learning: knowledge and practice with appropriate symbolic tools and techniques

7. Integrity in representation and simulation—avoidance of clip-art and "existing" images to represent design ideas and solutions

8. Repetition and practice with discovery seeking novelty and innovation

9. Interactive feedback

10. Spatially articulated and defensible product(s).

Studio Problem-solving

This is critical to studio operation and success, and can startle and frustrate some students based on the following differentiation between *traditional linear goal-driven problem-solving and CPS.*

Components of CPS (Cropley and Cropley, 2009)

1. The problem is not specified exactly

2. Students are expected to participate in problem identification and specification

3. The nature of the solution is largely open

4. The pathway to the solution is not specified

5. The criteria for recognizing a solution are open

6. Embrace complexity: context is more than a "setting" (CST Matrix)

7. Embrace ambiguity, avoiding over-focus

8. Discover and explore relationships not objects: meaning and functionality

9. Work through a system of scale-based relationships, defining their boundaries and redefining them as those boundaries dissolve and reassemble

10. Avoid compromise fallacies (unity, separation, fifty/fifty)—consensus by compromise is one more set of problems

11. Develop necessary skills and knowledge to participate in process through training, repetition and practice—avoid talking heads

12. Define a specific outcome/product

13. Assess its novelty and innovation potential.

Yes! Over-structure and over-focus are frowned upon in CPS. In an academic studio process, the faculty member frames the problem in a way that students are required to redefine the problem and approach for themselves. This does not mean loosey-goosey or helter-skelter, and requires significant effort in organization and meaningful structure. CPS requires openness not closed and restrictive thinking, divergent thinking, and an appreciation for ambiguity and complexity. Replace the traditional term "goal" with "aspiration" (a beginning notion) and "journey" (the act of traveling from one place to another, over and through).

In professional settings, a qualified project manager or project designer has the task of providing critiques and guidance within a contractual framework that specifies deliverables and costs. Within this contractual structure is also an unknown journey pursuing innovation and novelty. An experienced leader will rely on guided instruction and management that enables creativity and a continual learning process for participants, again within a time and budget constraint. This is not easy and is not simply performance based if creativity is to remain an integral part of the problem-solving process.

Studio Culture

A studio environment process has patterns of behavior that are different from traditional teaching and practice cultures as direct results of the process itself. There is structure and it is flexible, individual and interactive. In each studio population there is a diversity of personality traits that are represented, required to interact and potentially conflictive. Accept that as a given and an opportunity based on the following principles:

1. Each personality pattern has the potential for creative action
2. Each personality pattern has different means and methods of approaching the same problem
3. Each personality pattern has the ability to strengthen weaknesses and add traits that better enable creative action
4. Creative differences are essential to innovation
5. Creative differences are not encumbered by compromise fallacies.

Again, this challenges the instructor, facilitator and manager to understand these differences and be able to guide those differences in both individual work energy and group interactions.

A Culture of Innovation

Innovation is defined as the beginning or introduction of something new or novel (strikingly new, different). Solving a problem can be competent and devoid of creative outcome. Innovation and novelty can both solve a problem and advance the dialogue to distinctly new and different levels, referred to by Soja (1996) as "thirdspace."

Practical guides for students regarding innovation:

*   Be interested in your own unusual ideas. Do not discard them, as initially all are alternatives or possibilities—they will be sorted out by the process, not your fears or trepidations (this applies to the faculty person as well).
*   Do not be afraid of your own impulses. Regard them as a valuable source of ideas, a factor of creative difference—something that makes you stand apart from your colleagues.
*   Be aware of your preferred cognitive style and ascertain whether it facilitates or blocks the generation of innovation or novelty—do not compare yourself or your style/approach to that of your studio-mates.
*   Let your imagination go—confront the aspects of fear specific to your personality (fear of success, fear of failure, fear of comparison, etc.).
*   Seek wide experience (marginally related classes, practical assignments, case studies, etc.).
*   Look for links and relationships among pieces of information, especially unexpected links and emergent relationships, phenomena (unusual occurrences).
*   Look for relevant but remote associations (they assist in dissolving and/or expanding the boundaries of a problem dialogue).
*   Be willing to cross boundaries.
*   Try to build networks of related knowledge.
*   Transfer ideas from outside settings (including previous jobs and/or other fields) to new tasks.
*   Seek to go beyond the information provided by outside sources and clients/community.

- Avoid treating a new task as simply another example of the familiar, as this can lead to cliché design (dormer-ville, the act of adopting some other community's design codes, for example).
- Try to look at the new or unexpected elements of the task that made it different.
- Try to find multiple answers as there is never only one.
- Look for the unexpected but supportable answers.
- Ask yourself if you have generated effective surprise.
- Treat *failure with work energy* as a learning process—real failure is not doing anything, not applying your thinking and skills to a problem-solving effort.
- Be ready to defend your own ideas, even if they are unconventional.
- It is okay to be self-centered, as it means you have the confidence in yourself to accomplish the tasks you set out to do.

In CPS, look for the gaps and inconsistencies in the information and knowledge about a project, as therein may lie the gestalt.

Success as Failure

Yes, failure as success or success as failure. Both work. The word *failure*—the condition or fact of not achieving a desired end or ends—can have a negative connotation if defined as "nonperformance" versus "not achieving a desired end." There is a big difference: one can be a term of learning and the other one of defeat/fear. Frank Webb, American impressionist watercolor painter, puts it succinctly as "fear is a necessary ingredient in creativity"; and "failure" is a necessary ingredient in learning through experimentation.

Studio is an Integral Educational Process

Studio is the place where the theory, process, methods and skills are brought together to construct a story, argument, position, strategy, etc. in a spatial format that reflects the CST Matrix—space, culture and time aspects of community (more information not less). This involves whole mind–body thinking— the integration of cognitive thinking with the senses and intellectual mental processing of information and ideas. A key component of this in studio is manual dexterity—the physical/sensual manipulation of objects, materials and tools—something that is often lost in the use of digital technologies. This is not a battle between the two but a process of integration and appropriate use.

Studio Enables an Independent and Semi-independent Work Process

Studio leads to the production of a unique or novel design composition. Studio processes that produce a group product (common in urban planning and urban studies programs) require individual signature elements within that group product, necessitating and enabling both individual exploration and group interactions. Again, the instructor is a guide and enabler, to overcome the fear of individual responsibility in the making of a product.

Studio is a Learning Process

Studio process is not a demonstration of how much you already know! This is a departure from goal-driven processes that can state or imply predetermined outcomes that are weak or devoid of novelty and innovation. This principle can be troublesome for urban studies students and professionals not familiar with the studio process, as they expect or depend upon a rigid procedural structure—*tell me what to do and what you want to see as product.* CPS is neither linear nor predetermined by its very nature—openness, at times ambiguous and uncertain. Learning is a continuing process, changing behavior potential through experience. Of prime importance to the CPS dialogue is that learning takes place within a person and only occurs with experience or practice (i.e., *the act of doing)*, which makes studio such a rich experience.

Studio Discipline

Studio discipline is self-learning mixed with a dash of self-centeredness. The self-centeredness provides a confidence level of "yes I can!" and a focus for individual expression. The instructor is the guide and does not "teach" the student as the student teaches him or herself through action.

Studio is Both Non-linear and Multi-linear or Complex in Process

Studio is a process of entering the unknown, discovering new gestalts, and exploring new directions that have uncertain outcomes and discovery. Part of this process requires a definition and delineation of information and knowledge that sets known boundaries—a starting point for crossing or dissolving those boundaries through creative actions.

Studio and the Uncertainty Principle

Studio process is understanding the information and data; translating them into relationships (implying connections); discovering and observing emerging "stories" or realities; not predetermining outcome and working toward that (novel) outcome. Underlying this principle is one of creative action, i.e., *maintaining the integrity of the dynamic of the process* (Johnston, 1991).

Studio Also Requires Knowledge and Analysis

Studio requires the formulation of an analytical base, founded in knowledge (history), integrated with the identification of emergent realities that together can generate space-use programs (what, how much, where, when). These are based on the meaning and functionality aspects emanating from that knowledge/analytical base that define an *adequate context* within which the project is immersed—another beginning point.

Studio Desk Critiques

Studio desk critiques are a one-on-one dialogue between student and instructor related to the developing composition; this is a key educational element of studio that cannot be compromised and requires the following:

*   Direction of intent and expectation from the instructor with clear guidelines related to direction, process and general expectations of product type and format

- Advance preparation by the student of progress to be critiqued; requires out-of-class time commitment that increases the depth and quality of student–instructor or designer–team leader interactions
- A specification of progress and next steps
- Convention: preliminary analysis, concept development, testing, design/planning development, testing, final completion.

This principle also applies for the professional office between manager or project designer and team members.

Studio is an Individual Exploration

Studio is a process of individual exploration of design and planning processes with emergent products. I have found that students can work well as a team to collect and disseminate information and materials; then engage in individually defined problems related to the larger problem; and be required to be in constant interaction and communication with colleagues regarding directions and explorations related to the larger problem.

Studio Requires Interaction with Colleagues

Studio requires interaction with colleagues on data analysis, critiques, relationships to the larger dialogue, and coordinated presentations to community and client. Studio has a social aspect that can enable growth and maturity as well as creative pursuits.

Studio Requires Interaction with Administrative and Substantive Clients

Studio and the Community
This is about people and the complex relationships of people to people and people to environment, not objects, things, pie charts, data, etc.

Studio and Creative Traits
The studio process can identify and assist weaknesses in creative potentials of students based on the creative differences within any given studio team. Exercises in skill, process and attitude can increase a student's/professional's ability to engage in creative actions by recognizing traps, closed-mindedness, rigidity, skill deficiencies in spatial thinking and other barriers. Creativity is learned not bestowed.

Student Issues

Based on years of teaching instruction and discussions with design and planning students, many are new to the idea of "studio" and grapple with the following issues:

1. Independent work that may not be as structured as is comfortable in other courses; many students become reticent with a new structure and are unaccustomed to a new form of discipline: self-learning.

2.   Students are expected to gather information and engage in skills and methods with less instruction and guidance from the instructor.

3.   Inexperience with non-linear processes, i.e., "free fall" that requires multiple avenues of idea exploration and testing.

4.   One-on-one critiques with instructors—some students enjoy this process while others avoid the contact (fear manifestations).

5.   Resistance to the requirement for out-of-class work as necessary preparation for in-class critiques and interactions with faculty and colleagues.

6.   Lack of capability to prepare work suitable for critique and discussions (adequate portrayal of ideas and information in spatial formats)—skill development and practice.

7.   Uncertainty about instructor's expectations, deadlines, objectives.

8.   Disinterest in topic assigned.

9.   Lack of understanding of skills and methods needed for studio.

Example Methods Useful for Studio Process

1.   One- to three-day charrettes to establish directions, approaches, programs using parts/polarity analysis, delography (Verner) and other techniques.

2.   Brainstorming sessions: quantity of ideas over quality; criticism is not permitted because of its inhibitor effect; hitchhiking by attaching one's ideas to those of others is encouraged; wild or exaggerated ideas are welcome; visualize.

3.   Sketch problems: a one to three-day independent assignment without faculty assistance for concept development.

4.   Community workshops.

5.   Diagramming and visualization techniques to consolidate ideas and directions (all studio types benefit from these techniques to identify emergent ideas and patterns otherwise lost in a "data glut").

6.   Mid-term semi-formal/formal critiques.

Studio types can be varied and structured in response to the topic and client group. These basic principles apply to most if not all types.

Suggestions for Studio Quality

1.   Incorporation of studio methods and means discussions into fall and/or winter courses: communications, studio prep

2.   Introductory workshops in fall and/or winter quarter

3.   Earlier determination of studio topic, where possible

4.   Scheduled visits to active studios in planning, urban design, architecture, landscape

5.   Assessment of what is a studio topic and what is not suitable

6.   More contact with second-year students experienced in studio process.

Figure 5.1
Studio Environment

The studio team prepared contextual information for the project, including a chipboard model of the downtown Seattle urban center site and surrounding areas. The students used a combination of hand-crafted and laser methods to construct the model in a studio preparation course prior to the actual Fall Quarter Urban Design Studio in order to provide more time for creative problem-solving tasks.

Figure 5.2
Studio Duality

In this photo, student Tiernan Martin is working with a smaller discovery model and a BIM image of the same to explore and test urban design implications of the concept.

Figure 5.3
Studio Discovery Model 1

Student Katy Kay explores a new building type overlaid on an historic footprint and its relationship to the existing office tower.

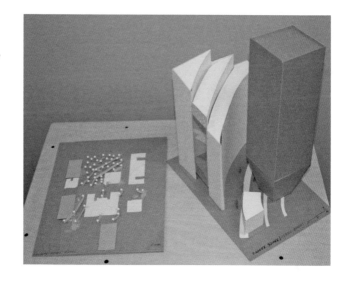

Figure 5.4
Studio Discovery Model 2

Students explore new building typologies for dense urban centers with one of the many paper discovery models for discussion in the studio.

*

A studio as an environment can take many shapes, from a classroom converted to a physical drop of water, to a warehouse where life-size models are constructed out of proposed physical environments, to playrooms filled with empty cardboard boxes. A studio is not a recreation room, a place to rest or take a break. It is a space of dynamic activity where things are made, created through the senses with tools, materials and objects. It is a place of direct experience and divergent thinking. The challenge for contemporary applications of studio environment focuses on the particular domain, the profile and composition of the team. In non-design domains, a studio environment can be a temporary space for experimentation for acting-out, physical mock-ups, movement experiments related to dancing or group movement patterns. The point being that the idea and construction of a studio is a creative act and experience in itself and has a direct influence on the "made" outcome.

Chapter 6

OBJECT-LEARNING WITH PLAY-TOOLS/SKILLS

Okay, here we go—we're re-entering Froebel's world of learning gifts, the symbolic objects of object-learning and play.

Before discussing object-learning, the role of skill development is important to introduce as a key part of the creative problem-solving (CPS) and object-learning process. Skill is a facility or dexterity that is acquired through training or experience . . . an art, trade or technique particularly requiring the use of the hands or body (*American Heritage Dictionary*, 5th Edition). Skill is both required in play and object-learning as well as learned through their engagement.

Skill Development

Skill is the ability to use one's knowledge effectively and readily in the execution of performance using motor skills, cognitive skills and motivation. Skills are learned and performed as a direct result of the integration of the body functions and senses and the processing abilities of the mind. Again, this is referred to as whole mind–body thinking.

Three key aspects of skill development include the following:

- *Biological network:* Processes of the body—effortful practice and training, movement and training using the nervous system (sorry, but a finger on a mouse does not qualify!)
- *Cognitive approach:* Processes of the mind—conscious and unconscious mental processes, neurological, using both sides of the brain hemispheres
- *Motivational approach:* Processes of attitude—overcoming physical and mental challenges; ability to develop, resolve and deal with fear; and the will to act, show passion, relaxed attentiveness; arriving at the state of "no mind" (Tomporowski, 2003).

Skill Necessity in Information Processing: Speed, Knowledge, Procedural Skills, Capacity

Skills are developed through an interaction of four components in information processing:

1. *Processing speed.* Information is organized, transformed and routed into perceptions and transformed into working memory. The working memory combined with knowledge and movement produces intricate actions related to emerging relationships and realities.
2. *Breadth of declarative knowledge.* This is the storage of declarative or factual knowledge that is extended through training and practice; and results in a more sophisticated organization of facts and rules to solve new problems (Tomporowski, 2003).

3. *Breadth of procedural skills.* Procedural skills reflect a type of implicit, nonverbal knowledge achieved through movement and action. Skilled performance requires action acquired through training, repetition and practice. I discuss the key elements of playful spatial diagrammatic (semiotic) activities in Chapter 7 that underscore the importance of visual skills in the creative thought process. *Procedural processes*, the manner in which something is performed, improve working memory by linking specific environmental conditions to specific mind/body responses. This is critical in design and planning as complex or complicated information is digested, assigned, organized and relationally composed.

4. *Processing capacity.* Working memory is the central unit of information processing. It is information that is compiled from the environmental conditions of the problem and the body/mind responses to them. This is the emerging CST Matrix, increasingly complex and limited in capacity. Design skills can modify the efficiency of the working memory limitations by compression and linkage.

In addition*, compositional processes* can collapse or compress the longer sequences of response production from information processing into shorter sequences and clarified relationships, thus reducing the demand on working memory. Again, visual diagramming skills and processes are one set of play-tools used in this compression and one that takes training, practice and repetition. A GIS map depicts information in a spatial context; whereas a visual diagram depicts relationships in a clarified and compressed expression. The other key aspect is the act of composing processed information, again into relationships, not layers of datasets.

Note: When perusing Chapter 7 on object-learning experiments, refer to this chapter for descriptions and demonstrations of symbolic objects as playthings, play-tools with their essential characteristics and principles. They are suggested exercises and are by no means a complete list, as play can enlist almost any object or media, including music, to engage the design process. And yes, this chapter takes us all back to kindergarten. As I mentioned in the Introduction, those of you in the *League of Ancient Youth*[1] will be very familiar with these "gifts." Younger readers may experience most of these playthings for the first time. In any event, they are meant to be integrated into the larger creative problem-solving process.

In order to reduce redundancies with the "gifts," I exemplify their use with a mix of abstract examples and domain-specific examples such as development typologies. The readers and instructors can fashion their own versions of play exercises using these as a base or starting point.

> [A]ll the tools and the techniques used to present and convey an idea have their technical possibilities, limitations and conditions. Consequently, is architecture [and landscape architecture and urban design] perhaps not just what is thought up in the mind or dreamt of, but also those things that can be visually conveyed with the tools available at the particular time?
>
> (Tomporowski, 2003, p. 123)

Learning with Symbolic Objects

This chapter highlights, describes and demonstrates the use of symbolic objects that lend themselves to the design and planning fields. They are useful education tools from high school art courses to undergraduate and postgraduate programs to professional offices.

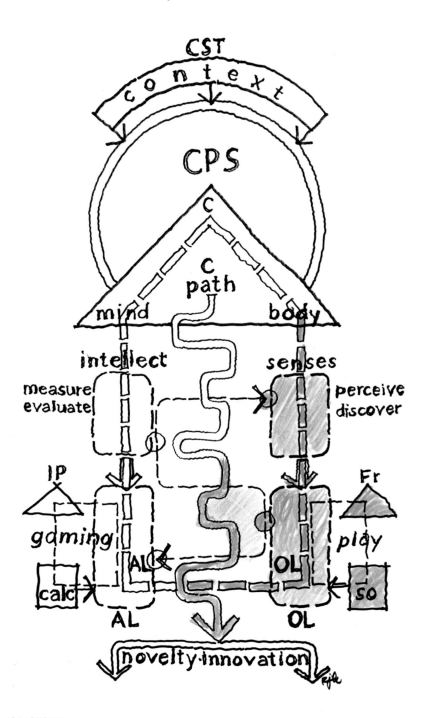

Figure 6.1 CPS Diagram

This aspect of creative problem-solving requires the use and skill development of real physical objects in a sensory learning process. The predominantly symbolic objects in this chapter are inspired by Froebel's gifts, and many have been traditionally used in the design and planning domains.

Cognitive pluralism in design and planning enlists the intellect, the senses (perception), tools, skills and materials in an integrated process. Add "play" and the creativity level can increase significantly. Change one aspect of that pluralism and the process is altered accordingly. Consequently, an appropriate use of relevant tools and materials is critical—not relying on one tool simply because it is convenient or popular. Again, I now teach students who have never used anything but a computer for problem-solving in design and planning, thereby limiting their discovery process.

Design as a creative problem-solving process is not conjured in the mind, as an intellectual notion. Design, as has been discussed earlier, is a whole mind–body process with intellectual and sensory cognition. How we go back and forth between the intellectual and mind-processing aspects of thought and the sensual manipulation of design tools and materials directly affects the design outcome. This is a component of design that we are quickly losing with a plethora of technological devices which exude the illusion that they are appropriate for every aspect of the design process. They have their role and they are not universal.

Consequently, understanding the tools and materials we as designers and planners play with is of prime importance for the design outcome.

Playthings as defined in this book are real objects, physical and symbolic, i.e., without an initial (or formal) identity, theme or signature. They are designed to be in contact with the senses; or comprised of and guided by other senses such as sound, touch, smell and movement. Play and object-learning can be with wood blocks, cardboard, yarn or paper; and it can be a dance movement performed as an individual or with another, or with a group. The objects, their compositional elements and principles such as movement, repetition with variety, etc. are symbols of a story being told or imagined; a spatial metaphor for meaning and functionality in (urban) design.

Play can enlist anything in its enactment to represent an aspect of the story or imagined scenario: a tree, part of the lawn, a cardboard box, wood blocks and a toy, to mention only a few. That is the power of play—the ability to infuse objects with meaning without fear of failure. The following discussion outlines the general categories of playthings and subsequently injects those that relate to the design professions. These are inspired by and an expansion of the gifts of Froebel.

Let's Play: Exercises in Meta-play

Meta-play is the transformational aspect of this free activity called play and includes an awareness of the self in the play.

The following materials, skills and related exercises are intended to stimulate and assist the player in engaging play in design and planning domains. They are not formulas or set programs and are simply places to start. They are later augmented by object-learning activators, again as places to start the composition process. Take advantage of spin-off ideas that can be generated as an exercise is engaged. This is where "discovery" emerges as the play activity progresses. Don't hesitate to change the rules as you progress. Don't evaluate prematurely, let the ideas flow, and embrace ambiguity and uncertainty.

I have organized the following sections according to the variety of symbolic objects that may be useful in design and planning domains. Please feel free to expand them to fit your unique or special teaching or practice situations.

As mentioned at the start of this chapter, play requires skill development in order to increase the quality and depth of engagement. The following exercises and experiments begin with simple elements, and increase in complexity and meaning as the chapter progresses. Feel free to change, alter and expand the exercises to suit your own personal preferences, progress and tools.

Symbolic Object-play

Symbolic objects can be translated into many types and signatures or identities through their manipulation and play. A cardboard box, designed to contain objects for storage, shipping, etc. is a symbolic object when used in play and translated into a spaceship, a building, a fort, an office mock-up, etc. Wood blocks are symbolic objects in the same manner, gaining identity through play and manipulation. Their advantage over contemporary tools and toys is their ability to be manually manipulated. Exploring play through symbolic objects for students ranging from high school to postgraduate studies is an excellent place to begin, due to the combination of the manual handling of real objects within the elements and principles of design composition.

Before we move to symbolic object-play, I want to address the differences between "toys" and "symbolic objects," and why "toys" are not highlighted in the work.

Toys

A toy as defined by the *American Heritage Dictionary* is an object that a child plays with for amusement. A negative connotation is also included: a trifle, something of little importance. Ouch! Toys in general are vehicles for imagination and creative expression, not trifles—with some exceptions. They can be a portal to fantasy and enjoyment, far beyond amusement, and they have limitations in their prescribed signature or identity, materials and form. This is a critical point in object-learning.

Theme toys

I define *toy* as a material object of play that has a specific identity for a defined purpose or use. Toys are usually designed and constructed by adults for use by children: the doll's house and space station, traditional and (historically) gender-oriented theme-specific toys. Lincoln Logs (1916) were notched miniature wooden logs invented by Frank Lloyd Wright's second son John Lloyd Wright; and the Erector Set (1913) was invented by Alfred Carlton Gilbert, and consists of metal construction toys. Both are related in that their material makeup and form dictate to a great extent the structure of a thematic outcome, i.e., log building and steel bridge structure. Lego has theme-based story packages for children. These are all toys with value for imagination and creativity. They are also defined or bounded by their predetermined themes, which initiate a contextual background for the player that does not necessarily emanate from the player. Not a negative issue, simply one with predetermined rules by inherent structure.

Computer Toys/Games

I include under theme toys the digital graphic programs that have a theme with predetermined rules, game board, competition goals and structure (regardless of the number of "options" programmed into the software program, including representations of building materials, forms, etc.). They lack contact with most senses, limited to visual and digital manipulation. They have value as a resource of images and are limited by that resource, with constraints within the methodologies of application.

Symbolic Objects

Symbolic objects (of play) are non-thematic or less defined material objects that can represent countless entities, limited only by the imagination of the player. Having said that, any shape or object brings with it a set of conditions based on its material, dimensions, color, proportions, etc. Is it rigid? Does it have "plasticity" of application? A cardboard box is generally a rectangular shape, and with that shape come beginnings and boundaries. The box provides a flexible object subject to many manipulations—one of its many advantages. In any event, the symbolic object is more abstract than real (thematic or representational), has flexibility that many other "toys" do not possess, is ambiguous in initial identity, and has minimal preconceived structure, enabling more experimentation. This is a critical factor in discovery through the manual manipulation of objects and materials—object-learning.

The traditional design fields have long practiced "play" with symbolic objects and materials, such as cardboard, clay, construction paper, balsam wood, foam, plaster and sand; and with two-dimensional media such as pencil, pen and ink, paint, etc. as functions of the larger art culture that influenced the early design schools. These objects are disappearing from design studios in many fields and are as relevant today as they have ever been, particularly when they can be integrated with digital technologies, as we will discuss. Again, for recent generations that have not had the exposure to these traditional symbolic objects, they are discussed and experimented with as valued and relevant playthings—they are classic, not "old-fashioned." Unfortunately, to gain access to some of the more useful traditional objects one must look into "antique toys"!

Figure 6.2 Symbolic Objects as Tools

Graduate student Katy is experimenting with a variety of play-tools or symbolic objects as she explores design concepts in the studio.
Model source: Katy Haima.

In my Urban Design Composition course, offered to graduate urban planning students as a prerequisite for advanced Urban Design Studios, participants learn to play with paper and cardboard in their early exercises—no computers. The reasons include a familiarization with flexible materials, manual dexterity skills and skill development, visualization of form through hands-on experimentation, and an introduction to playfulness without failure—a form of constructivism. Let's explore the objects of play.

Symbolic Object Reference Systems

- The Grid
- The Axis
- Compositional Structures.

Symbolic Object Materials and Types

- Paper

    o   Construction and art paper
    o   Cardboard (all types)
    o   Dense "chipboard"
    o   Poster and illustration board

- Wood

    o   Blocks
    o   Balsam (lightweight/density, easy to cut)
    o   Sticks
    o   Various flat shape objects

- Plastic

    o   Blocks
    o   Straws

- Clay

    o   Modeling
    o   Ceramic

- Pen and ink, Pencil (color, graphite)
- Paint and Pastels

    o   Watercolor
    o   Pastel pencils and sticks

- Yarn and String
- Wax
- Metal
- Glass
- Others.

Symbolic (Spatial) Reference Guides: The Grid

As in Froebel's gift lessons, the grid played a key role in providing a spatial/mathematical starting place or structure for play activity. The grid provided a guide and spatial framework or reference for experimentation with blocks, sticks, balls and all sorts of symbolic objects—all contained in a compositional relationship established by the grid (primary shapes: square and cube). In this section, various grid hybrids are illustrated with various forms of symbolic object-play. The type of hybrid grid affects the play-activity by establishing an underlying compositional structure, and is considered a variable as the grid adjusts and adapts to a specific spatial context. It also provides a starting point for play.

EXERCISE 6.1: GRID AS SPATIAL REFERENCE GUIDE

I used grid vellum sheets (architectural (eight per inch) or engineering (ten per inch)) to outline various grid hybrids as play-bases for the initial exercises, quickly using a Pentel Sign Pen freehand on bond copies of the grids. They can be laid flat on a table or glued to illustration board. The grid dimensions may vary according to the fractal object. For example, Halsam's Building Bricks are actually 7/8 inch by 1 3/4 inches.

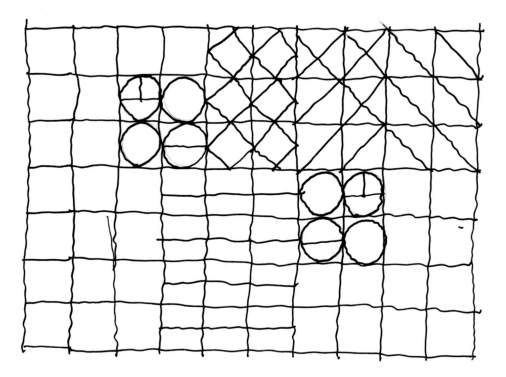

Figure 6.3 The Grid and Grid-derivatives

All grids are derivatives of the square and in this example they constitute squares, rectangles, circles and diamonds. Varying the type of grid hybrid can lead to different approaches to a design challenge.

The Grid in Context

Play is enriched by the complexity of the play-environment and the spatial context within which it occurs. Playing on a grid is a structured learning process, and is abstract until connected or overlain on a real terrain and/or urban setting. Then, the spatial/physical context strongly influences the application of the symbolic objects being fitted into the context—changing one and being changed by the other in an interdependent manner. Decisions regarding the types of symbolic object fractals that are compatible with the spatial context and how they relate to the grid are critical at the start.

A "playground" can be complex, with organic and meandering features and elements, not oriented toward a grid or other more formal composition. This playground can be formed by the elements: water, wind, ground-altering events, etc., and yet an underlying compositional structure can provide a design/planning reference system that initially guides the play process—as much a part of play as the symbolic objects arranged on it. More information is given in Chapter 7.

Paper

Construction and Art Papers

Numerous craft papers (Kraft, Craft, Art) are available for countless uses including three-dimensional process model constructs, two-dimensional design composition cut-outs and collages, and as additives to other play-objects. They include construction papers, tag board, art paper, poster and illustration boards, roll paper, to name a few. They are versatile and easily manipulated into form constructs due to their thinness, ease in cutting with scissors as well as crafting knives, whether representative of a single building, an urban block or a city district.

I use construction paper extensively when introducing students to design composition as a comfortable starting point with minimal skills needed. The examples below are from student exercises in "Urban Design Composition" (University of Washington) as students experiment with the principles and elements of design composition and simultaneously engage in a crafting process—composition and play-skill development. Urban Design Composition is a course in the Urban Design and Planning graduate program designed to prepare students without undergraduate design backgrounds to engage in urban design studios. The students are taught the elements and principles of design composition as they relate to and apply to urban design.

Additional examples may be found in *Urban Design: The Composition of Complexity* (Kasprisin, 2011). I use the construction paper for discovery models extensively in Chapter 7.

Figure 6.4
Student Construction Paper Experiment

Superimposition of grid and circle.
Source: Student Haima.

Figure 6.5 *(below)*
Construction Paper Volumetric Studies

Simple three-dimensional paper constructions advance the skill development with added vertical and horizontal planes. Illustrated are quick construction paper examples of various volumes useful as movable pieces in design experiments or interactive sessions—I use these in Chapter 7.

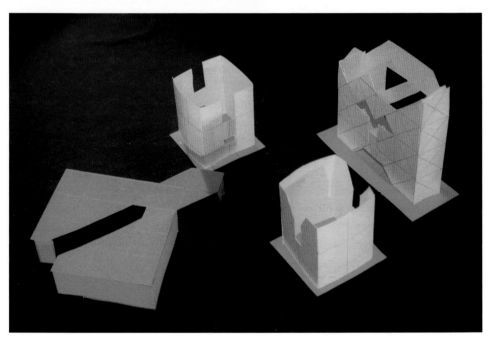

Figure 6.6 Craft Paper Process Model

Craft and art papers are fast and flexible materials to envision emerging ideas, and as a means of playing with design notions in short time spurts. This quick study of a houseboat design for Seattle's Portage Bay was one of a half-dozen or more playful renditions used to explore various massing options. Each process model, as it was crafted, contributed ideas to the development of the next—thus my reference of "discovery models." They are fragile and not meant for a prolonged existence; they are fast, expressive and for the client a clear and touchable process model for review and discussion.

The Paper Collage

A collage is an assembly of diverse elements ranging from paper, to paper and yarn, stones, sticks, etc. In this context, it can be an assemblage of various materials pasted over a surface, often *with unifying symbols and colors.* This last part is critical to their use in (urban) design, in that a collage can filter out detail and focus on critical aspects of composition. Examples include unifying or organizing symbols (axes, centers, boundaries, etc.) and color and value (light to dark). There are often pitfalls in the design process with premature detail captivating and capturing the process. The collage offers an abstract or semi-abstract compositional play-tool for experimentation with broad general patterns in the experiment. Many of the previous two-dimensional experiments are collages.

EXERCISE 6.2A: ABSTRACT COLLAGE PLAY—FREE PLAY

- *Intent.* Begin with any form using the grid and build off it in any direction or with any impulse that comes to mind. There is no goal here and there is no failure, just play. The initial form can be any derivative of the circle, square or line.
- *Rule.* As a guide, use derivatives of the primary shape as a starting point. Maintain their essence or essential characteristics. For example, a square can be defined as simply four corners; a circle by a center and a radius, a line by its linearity—longer shaft than its width. Then introduce other materials (in this case yarn and wood slats for variety).
- *Tools.* Colored construction paper, scissors, glue or frosted tape on a grid, yarn and wood slats.
- *Skills.* Basic manipulation of scissors and glue.

Figure 6.7 Abstract Collage

This is a warm-up exercise to begin design composition studies. To get started I chose the square and line or axis as the two shapes to manipulate into an abstract composition. I drew a grid on the paper to be cut and began manipulating the various pieces into a diagonal dominant composition.

EXERCISE 6.2B: SEMI-ABSTRACT COLLAGE PLAY—INITIAL NOTION

- *Intent.* Begin the same exercise as above with a basic or raw idea or notion. For example, the following exercise is initiated with "spaceship." It has the same rules as above and uses varied materials in the concoction of the imaginary spaceship.

Figure 6.8 "Let's Play Spaceship"

On a grid, I began arranging construction paper cut-outs of circle and square derivatives in the form of an imaginary spaceship, building off the initial emerging composition. The intent is to begin with a notion not a plan. Have the student (from high school to graduate school) find a place to begin (in this case I began with the purple mass as the aft portion of the ship) and simply built on where various pieces suggested rather than trying to conceptualize a final product.

The following exercises advance the student into the three-dimensional realm with construction paper, again easy and flexible to use. Basic compositional structures, principles and activators are used as starting points. There are numerous examples in Chapter 7, as the construction paper is easy and fast to use in assembling semi-abstract compositions.

EXERCISE 6.3: REPETITION WITH VARIETY

- *Intent.* Use vertical planes on a grid to create repetitive shapes with variety (horizontal and vertical).
- *Rule.* Use the grid as a spatial reference as curves are constructed.
- *Tools.* Construction paper, glue or tape, yarn.

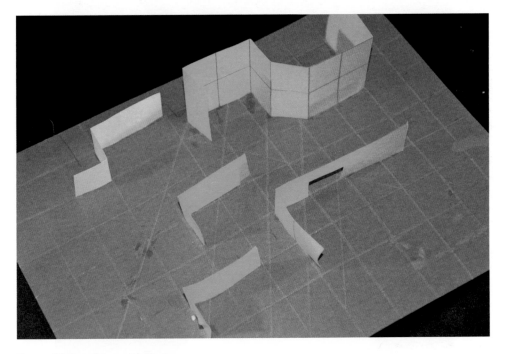

Figure 6.9 Repetition with Variety

In this quick example, vertical grid planes are repeated with variety in length and height.

EXERCISE 6.4: LINEAR VERTICAL PLANES IN MOTION—DIRECTIONAL MOVEMENT

* *Intent.* Same as previous exercise.
* *Rule.* Generate additional movement in the space with additional vertical planes and yarn.

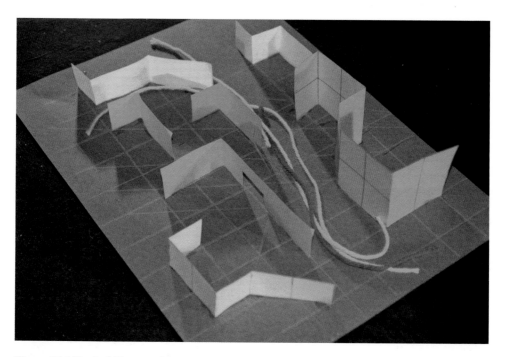

Figure 6.10 Vertical Planes in Motion

I used the same base as in the above and added additional yellow vertical planes and colored yarn to increase the directional or movement pattern.

Cardboard

Corrugated Cardboard

Cardboard comes in numerous formats, from dense, flat sheets, usually 1/16 inch to 1/8 inch in thickness, to corrugated and non-corrugated boxing formats. It is a versatile material, and is easily manipulated into multiple shapes and configurations with knives and scissors. In design play, the cardboard "object" takes shape as building/site typology or use-program forms.

A classic symbolic material long used in architecture and urban design explorations to construct symbolic objects, *corrugated cardboard* is a versatile material that provides domain-specific play-objects at varying scales. Again, the nature of preparation (i.e., cut into orthographic or right-angle pieces) becomes a fractal that is represented in the larger formations.

The corrugated cardboard can represent the translation and interpretation of need into meaning and functionality; or it can represent a space program that consists of a specific dimensional development type or manifestation of identified needs, activities or typologies emanating from the analysis of a CST Matrix. These symbolic objects are easily incorporated into a play and gaming process to explore the organization and structure of urban design compositions. They are flexible, and easily manipulated in various physical contexts. The following examples portray semi-abstract patterns as warm-up exercises.

EXERCISE 6.5: CARDBOARD GRID PLAY

- *Intent.* Cut out primary shapes in various amounts and arrange in abstract patterns on a grid.
- *Rule.* Use a compositional structure to begin play: repetition with variety, diagonality, radial burst, etc. Mix vertical and horizontal planes to form a composition.
- *Tools.* Corrugated cardboard, X-acto knife.
- *Skills.* Basic manipulation of cut-outs on a grid; becoming familiar with the material.

Figure 6.11a Cardboard Play

I used simple grid-based cut-outs to create repeated patterns with variety. The corrugated cardboard is versatile, easily cut and the cut-outs serve as game pieces in team or community interactions, workshops and charrettes or intensives. They are a classic material for design and planning, and remain a useful contemporary tool. Keep the initial constructions simple and build to more complexity.

Figure 6.11b Group Cardboard Interaction

Students work together at concept development using the cardboard cut-outs as building types and development configurations.

Cardboard is also a flexible material for three-dimensional constructions, again representing anything from rock walls to building masses. Cardboard cut-outs are used extensively in "programming and typologies" later in this chapter due to the material's flexibility and ease of manipulation and shaping. The set-up time consists of cut-outs that mirror building typologies. Once these are done, the construction of alternatives is fast and effective. Imply volumes with planes as a starting point.

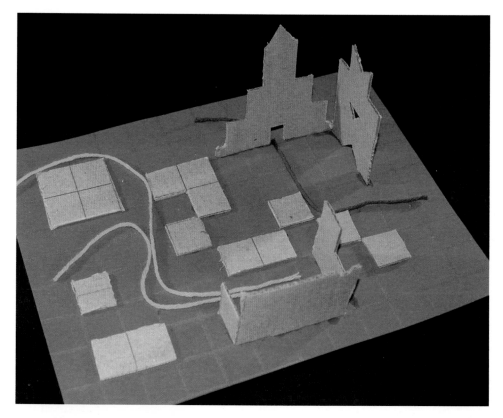

Figure 6.12 Cardboard Compositions

Cardboard is suitable for horizontal and vertical plane construction to represent any type of space or building component. These simple cut-outs were constructed in minutes not hours, ready for use in various settings.

Chipboard or Fiberboard

Chipboard is a dense cardboard material composed of pressed recycled paper and glue. Thicknesses range from .015625 inches (1/64 inch) to .125 inches (1/8 inch). Most commonly used thicknesses range from .022 inches to .125 inches. Sometimes the word "point" is used to denote the thickness and essentially describes the decimal value, i.e., 22 point equals .022. Chipboard is available in many sizes and has been a mainstay in architecture and landscape architecture for decades as a means of crafting buildings and topography base constructions. The material can be hand or laser cut depending upon the application. Laser cuts can be limited by the size of the laser width: 24 inches is common; hand cutting is effective for larger models—using the appropriate tools.

Chipboard is applicable for both two- and three-dimensional constructs, ranging from surface or site features such as parking lots to building forms and configurations. It has been a standard convention for architects in process/discovery models.

EXERCISE 6.6: CHIPBOARD SPACE-PROGRAMMING CUT-OUTS

- *Intent.* Construct a series of existing built form masses including space-program cut-outs for design and planning development typologies for use in design-gaming situations. This is expanded in Chapter 7.

- *Rule.* Familiarize yourself with the principles of development typologies for various contexts and replicate in chipboard with horizontal and vertical dimensions; color code.

- *Skills.* X-acto and box cutter or matt knife use, straight edge and chipboard. When using straight edge for cutting, avoid plastic (T-squares, scales, rulers, etc.) as they will nick and present problems later. See Figure 6.11b.

Figure 6.13 Chipboard as Context and Process Models

This is a portion of the UW Rainier Square Urban Design Studio wherein the existing buildings and topography are constructed of chipboard with hand-crafted and laser-cut methods. To set the context for a complex urban design studio, the students learn the types of buildings and their uses as they construct the chipboard base model.
Model construct: UW Urban Design Studio (2014).

This stage of the process model encompasses preliminary design ideas in white tagboard inserted into the base context model. Students can easily manipulate and evaluate their design ideas in a three dimensional frame of reference.

Paper (Poster Board, Tag Board, Railroad Board)

These flat panels or boards have more density than the construction and art papers, making them suitable for quick-study three-dimensional constructions. Poster board is less dense than illustration board and is suitable for fast concept or study models. The denser the board, the sharper and more durable is the required cutting tool (X-acto blade, matt knife, laser cutter). Poster board comes in numerous colors.

EXERCISE 6.7: POSTER BOARD CONCEPT MODELS

This stage demonstrates a more finished approach to the design concepts again using poster board in white for the recommended massing solutions. The materials are easy to cut and construct.

Figure 6.14 Poster Board Constructions

It has long been standard procedure to differ new development scenarios in a process model from the existing context. In this case, poster board, tag board and railroad board are used to represent the design recommendations as insets to the contextual model. Model construct: Scott Bonjukian.

Wood Blocks

Wooden objects are classic play-tools that have captivated children for centuries. In Europe, wooden toys emerged as thematic objects: miniature castles, bridges, wagons, etc. Froebel used the wood block as the foundation of his play-gifts, with the pyramid, sphere and cylinder among other shapes. They are versatile, flexible and durable.

In a studio discussion with graduate students on the importance of play, the topic of Legos (1973) emerged, including when they were available on the US market. Based on a quick computer search by students, it seems they were introduced into the US market in 1973 with no other references to wooden play blocks. "Aha," I laughed. Why then did I play with my wooden Lego-type blocks under the dining room table as a boy in the 1950s? I can still remember the scent of the green carpet, kept so meticulously clean by my Croatian mother—a temporary and safe playroom. Another search: this time it is suggested they search under "antique toys." We identified my beloved toys as American Wood Building Bricks, Halsam Products Co., Inc., 4114–4124 Ravenswood Avenue, Chicago, USA. There lie my beginnings as an architect.

After two dogs in the historic family household, they eventually went the way of the happy chew. I am now pleased to possess Set No. 60/2, complete with an original instruction manual along with other partial sets. And at the bottom of page 4, it states after a discussion about the use of the manual and examples: "It's more fun to create a new model than it is to copy." How profound! We will play with these later in the book, in Chapter 7.

Wood building blocks come in numerous forms, and range from the antique brick-like Halsam's and non-interlocking Playskool Blocs, to many contemporary blocks made from sustainable woods. Sets vary widely and those I recommend include less specific architectural shapes (arches, columns) and contain more basic shapes (squares, rectangles, triangles, pyramids, cylinders, etc.). These allow more flexibility in symbolic play. Melissa & Doug's Standard Unit Blocks are based on 1 1/2 × 2 × 5-inch standard size. There are many to choose from and include but are not limited to Haba Basic Building Blocks, KidKraft, Guidecraft, Jonti-Craft, School Outfitters, Barclay Blocks and more.

I highlight a few in this section because I use them in Chapter 7 due to their flexibility in making complex compositions.

Halsam's American Wood Building Bricks

The American Wood Building Bricks come in two sizes: 7/8 inch by 1 3/4 inches, augmented by 7/8 inch squares and 45-degree shaped blocks. Red and yellow were available in the 1950s. The blocks are oriented to a grid pattern in their right-angle configurations, rectangle and square. Given this condition, the two sizes provide ample flexibility and variety in forming compositions. Scale is a variable and can be assigned depending upon the scale of the game board. One inch can be 30 feet (townhouse depth), 80 feet (stacked flats double-loaded corridor depth), etc. Again, the play factor involves the handling of the material object and the experimental assemblies that are almost endless.

I appreciated the interlocking nature of the building bricks when constructing models, enabling them to hold together longer.

This series of exercises uses an underlying grid with Halsam's American Wood Building Bricks (1943) as the basic symbolic object set, augmented by colored yarn (movement, fluidity). There are two sequences of play, from a warm-up exercise to more complex compositions. Halsam's "bricks" constitute

Figure 6.15 Halsam's American Wood Building Bricks

Halsam's blocks measure 1 7/8 inches in length by 7/8 inch in width by 1/4 inch in height and are dowelled and pegged for interlocking assemblies. They come in two colors: red and yellow.

a specific fractal geometry, with unit sizes of 1 7/8 inches in length by 7/8 inch in width by 1/4 inch in height; a half brick at 7/8 inch square; as well as a triangular brick with 7/8-inch square base and a 1/2-inch altitude. Their fractal shape is based on the square.

EXERCISE 6.8: TWO-DIMENSIONAL PATTERNS WITH WOOD BUILDING BRICKS

- *Intent.* On the appropriate grid, assemble a two-dimensional pattern with the wood building bricks. Play and experiment with the multiple variations that will become apparent as you manipulate the objects on the grid.
- *Rule.* Use basic compositional structures as a starting point and incorporate colored yarn as an element of connective directional movement.
- *Skills and Materials.* Grid, wood bricks, colored yarn, scissors. This is a simple start up exercise for beginning students who lack basic crafting skills and helps them build confidence and capability for more complex compositions.

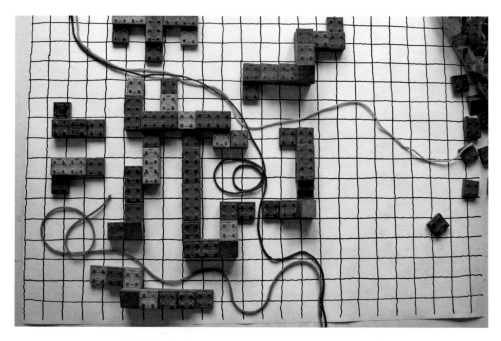

Figure 6.16 Two-dimensional Combinations of Line and Square (Repetition with Variety)

On a grid, I arranged yarn in an abstract movement pattern as a starting point and followed up with Halsam's Wood Building Bricks to respond to the yarn movement. The power of the axis (yarn) is experimented with in Chapter 7.

EXERCISE 6.9: COMBINING AND MANIPULATING THE PRIMARY SHAPES IN THREE DIMENSIONS

- *Intent.* This series of exercises provides yet another element of complexity by adding the vertical dimension. I had no notion or objective to the pattern-making—I simply began arranging blocks and soon realized how the symbolic object as a fractal influenced the pattern—linear and consisting of right angles.
- *Tools.* Blocks, yarn, grid.
- *Skills.* Basic manipulation of blocks into compositions.

As described in the caption, begin to experiment with various compositional structures and transformational actions to evoke playful compositions. Adding another symbolic object can also open new directions. Use caution as to not create distractions through varying objects. I limited this exercise to wood blocks and yarn on the grid. And do not try to visualize a final product or composition before starting--jump in and begin to move objects around, making frequent changes. Play . . .

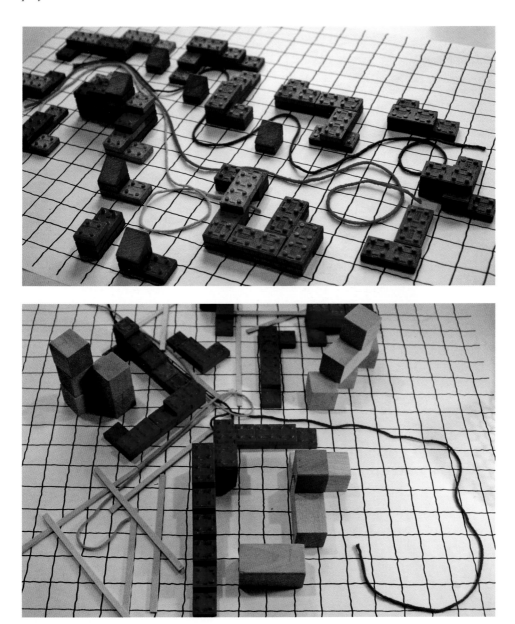

Figure 6.17a and b Setting the Directional Movement

Each play-tool has special characteristics based on their shape, size, orientation, etc. These characteristics affect the compositional response of the player as he or she manipulates one tool in response to another. In this case, I reversed the process by playing with the yarn strands in various spontaneous ways. I made several efforts to find a pattern that had some compositional strength as an axial form. I found that at least three strands contributed to a complex axis as a starting point. After playing with the evolving pattern, looking for ways to add variation and repetition, I decided to begin adding patterns that responded to and compositionally complemented the original pattern directed mostly by responses such as solid/void, portal axis, diagonality and directional movements. Lastly, using yarn strands, I emphasized axial movements within the semi-enclosed spaces formed by the bricks. The addition of the yarn axis dramatized movement and direction in the overall composition.

Once I had an axial composition, without a significant amount of analysis or evaluation (simple movement and direction with some minor repetition), I began arranging blocks in response or reaction to the established axial form. Obviously multiple variations are possible and are abstract with the absence of a contextual framework. I can also add other elements such as green patches within the axial forms as a softer two-dimensional pattern that again emphasized the coiled axis.

Figure 6.18 Compaction

As a change from the linear influence of the bricks, I delved into more compact compositions, beginning with a single form and ending with multiple forms responding to one another. This exercise brought home the fun or enjoyment of not knowing the end result, instead following the lead of emerging forms. The compositions, some with more harmony and coherence than others, all evolved as a result of the fractal objects and the manner of connecting them with fascinating discoveries regarding cantilevers, solid/void or positive/negative effects.

Figure 6.19 Compaction Cluster

Letting the forms drive new forms, I made four massing compositions and manipulated them into various cluster configurations. The example consists of a smaller mass oriented at a 45-degree angle to the central and largest of the masses. I then placed the yarn strands to reinforce visual connections along the key angles as a final unifying action.

I had planned on moving to another sequence using another symbolic object, but instead decided to continue this sequence to a more complex composition that resulted from the play actions above. I began assembling a composition of bricks as an initial random placement, interlocking them as sometimes dictated by the emerging arrangement, with only a vague notion of a larger mass construction. Based on their physical characteristics, principles emerged regarding ways to guide the compositions.

Figure 6.20 Brick Mass A

The first brick mass emerged as a solid-void, stepped composition with an implied orientation via an opening on one side and a solid higher form on another.

Figure 6.21 Brick Mass B

A second brick mass was constructed as a response to the first (A) characterized by a void corner oriented toward mass A. I then constructed a concave lower form to "receive" and complete the implied axis from mass A; and to engage mass B with the shorter end of the concave edge.

Figure 6.22 Brick Mass C

I utilized a previously constructed mass to complete the larger composition.

Figure 6.23 Brick Mass D

Once the various parts are produced they can easily be manipulated into other compositions and in this case with added yarn movement patterns.

Figure 6.24 Brick Mass Additives

Additives, in this case a paper pyramid, are many and varied, and bring additional dimensions to the dominant material and forms.

Playskool and other Wood Blocks

Playskool Blocs, founded in 1901, was formerly a Milton Bradley company (Canada) and is a subsidiary of Hasbro Inc. of Pawtucket, Rhode Island. There are wood blocks available in multiple shapes, ranging from vintage basic colored blocks to multiple-shaped blocks offering more variety in composition. They are easy to manipulate and move around the grid.

I am using classic "toy" wood blocks in various shapes as initial symbolic objects. They are available in various basic sizes, colors and dimensions suitable for many design-play activities. I avoided using arches and other more specific architectural forms for these exercises to maintain an abstract character to the composition. The exercises use cubes, triangles, cylinders and rectangular volumes as the basic fractals or pieces. I prefer the natural blocks when combining with other objects.

These objects do not interlock as do Halsam's bricks. This changes their application characteristics, adding a little additional flexibility in composing arrangements.

EXERCISE 6.10 (NOT ILLUSTRATED): MANIPULATING THE PRIMARY SHAPES WITH WOOD BLOCKS

I found these exercises to be useful in guiding the student in three-dimensional massing studies through quick manipulations of the blocks, replacing construction paper with simple block shapes.

- *Intent.* Manipulate the primary shapes with wood blocks in as many ways as you can, as complex as possible and do not lose their essential identities.
- *Rule.* Maintain the essence of each primary shape. By now, the critical characteristics of the primary shapes are becoming apparent, adding to the freedom of the play-activity.
- *Tools.* Playskool and other wood blocks.
- *Skills.* Basic manipulation of blocks and a developing understanding of the elements and principles of composition and compositional structure.

Figure 6.25 Wood Blocks

Some wood block sets come with uniform sizes and other with multiple shape blocks. I find the multiple shapes to be flexible in design-play, as is exemplified in the experiments in Chapter 7.

Cylinders

The cylinder is one of three shapes (gifts) utilized by Froebel in advanced play-activities. Again, in these warm-up activities, I began with an underlying grid and without much analysis selected a starting point and basic compositional structures to guide the play. In Sequence One, the structure is *diagonality,* a *cross* and *repetition with variety* (Kasprisin, 2011*)* by essentially enabling the pieces to organize themselves within the two larger compositional structures further activated by repetition with variety. I mixed color into the composition to reinforce that variety.

It was certainly an option to "arrange" the pieces helter-skelter but I chose an initial rule—to be broken later on—to insert compositional structures as an initial guide, a starting point.

Figure 6.26 Cylinders

The composition of cylinders is a curvilinear form with a center highlight. The cylinders work well with other shapes and represent more point sources in their circular shapes.

Pyramids and Triangles

Continuing the explorations with one type of shape element, I played with the pyramidal shapes, reflecting their triangular characteristics in the compositions. Using a diagonal axis provided a strong starting point with the triangles' apex emphasizing direction and movement.

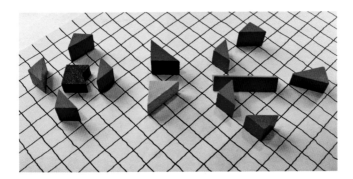

Figure 6.27 Pyramids and Triangles

A combination of compositional structures guides this assemblage, including a cross and square around a positive/negative axis.

Balsa Wood

Balsa wood is a lightweight wood easily manipulated into variable shapes. The Balsa tree is grown in Brazil, Bolivia and Mexico, and can grow to 90 feet in six to ten years (Midwest Products). It is used in architectural modeling, model airplane construction and other constructs, and is an excellent and flexible wood for experimental play-activities due to its light density. It is a flat, thin material and I find it less useful in experimental compositions, more suited to advanced process or final models.

Wood Slats

Wood slats were used by Froebel as one of his gifts for creative play. They are linear and flat, suitable for both two- and three-dimensional constructions. In Figure 6.28 Wood Slat Pattern, they are arranged on a white background with black grid.

EXERCISE 6.11: WOOD SLAT PATTERNS

- *Intent.* Construct a "free-form" two-dimensional pattern with movement and direction.
- *Rule.* Construct the pattern on a grid base using key characteristic components of the grid (e.g., centers, corners, diagonals of squares).
- *Tools.* Slats or other flat wood pieces linear in nature, grid on color background for additional contrast.
- *Skills.* Hand manipulation.

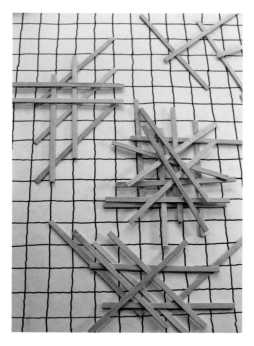

Figure 6.28 Wood Slat Pattern

The flat and linear characteristics of the wood slats make them more effective when combined with other play-objects. They are akin to lines in that their complexity depends on the density of slats in a given location.

Pick-up Sticks

Slender skewer-like sticks bring another linear component to the play table. With a porous base, the sticks can be versatile regarding vertical, horizontal and angular placement for various play-activities. They are symbolic objects that can assume many identities. Like the wood slats, they provide a vertical additive to other play objects.

String and Yarn Materials

Again, linear elements in the form of string and yarn materials are easily manipulated in a playful and experimental manner. They provide flexibility and color to a composition, and can act as linkages among major elements. Their fluidity works well for crafting movement and direction in compositions, as well as calligraphy, transparent frames, etc.

Plastic Blocks

Plastic blocks come in solid and molded forms, ranging from pattern blocks with variable flat shapes to plastic interlocking bricks and multiple thematic toys. The pattern and brick types are of interest here, again due to their more symbolic nature.

Plastic Brick Blocks

Lego is the most common name in plastic brick toys. The word "lego" is Danish, meaning "ley godt" ("play well"). Begun as a wooden toy manufacturer, the company under founder Ole Kirk Kristiansen began manufacturing plastic bricks and distributing

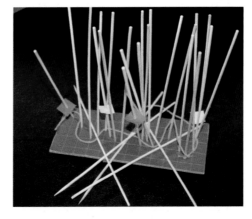

Figure 6.29 Pick-up Sticks

Pick-up sticks or skewer sticks are linear shapes that are useful for vertical demarcation elements, creating movement and direction, and as horizontal directional elements.

Figure 6.30 String and Yarn

The yarn can serve as vertical constructs when combined with pins, sticks, and even starched, as well as horizontal movement pattern elements. Kids' stuff? Use it in compositions as movement and directional elements; as aerial elements; as spirals and coils, etc.

them worldwide, establishing a US outlet in 1973. Similar to the Halsam's American Wood Building Brick, the interconnecting plastic brick was introduced in 1958. The variation of blocks is represented by Lego Building Plates, Lego Duplo Brick Set and more recently the robotic Mindstorms sets. Along with Halsam's Bricks, the Lego bricks can be applied at multiple scales, representing multiple design typologies. The first Christmas gift I gave my nine-month-old granddaughter was the larger block set of Legos, a gift she still enjoys. I enjoyed watching her quickly evolve from taking the bricks apart to connecting them with great focus and enjoyment. As she grows they take on ever more complex identities.

EXERCISE 6.12 (PARTIALLY ILLUSTRATED): LEGOS AND PRIMARY SHAPES

- *Intent.* As with the Playskool Wood Blocks, use the Legos as a means of manipulating the primary shapes in both two and three dimensions. The difference in this version is that they interlock.
- *Rules.* Maintain the characteristics of the primary shapes.
- *Tools.* Various Lego types and colors.

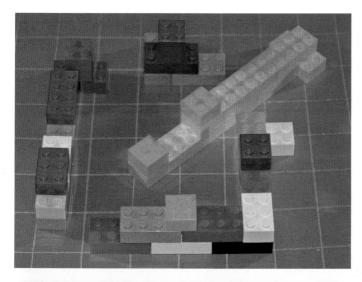

Figure 6.31 Manipulating Primary Shapes with Legos

Similar to Halsam's Wood Building Bricks, Legos are interlocking pieces that are flexible and easily manipulated. The main difference between the two is their use at appropriate scales, although Legos come in numerous sizes as well. This example uses a square compositional structure.

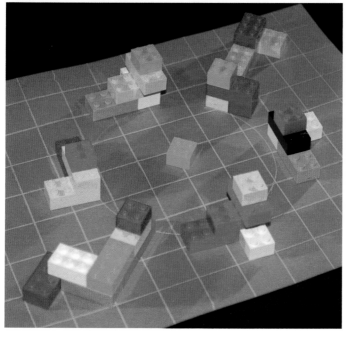

Figure 6.32 Legos as Circular Compositional Structure

The circle is used as a void and the Legos define arcs and diameter, essentially a radial burst with uniform radii.

Clay (Modeling) and Wax

Clay is a misnomer when referring to modeling clay in that many types of modeling clay have no clay in their ingredients, as they vary significantly. Types of modeling clay include ceramics (fired for hardness), oil-based clay (retains pliability without drying), polymer clay and paperclay. Generic names of modeling clay range from Plastilin (1880), Plastatine (1892) and Plasticine (1897), and the clay has been a mainstay tool for artists for centuries.

The oil-based modeling clay is the more common and other variations can be made at home. Recipes include: cornstarch, salt, water and food coloring; flour, salt, water; cornstarch, baking soda, water or oil. The recipes are many and may be found on the Web together with detailed instructions.

Modeling clay is pliable and not hardened with heat, suitable for design mock-ups and conceptual studies of three-dimensional form. The manipulation of the clay may be done with the hands, a palette knife and other cutting and shaping tools—a direct connection of mind–body visualization.

The modeling clay block is an easy place to have students begin additive and subtractive transformational exercises. The block may be used as two cubes or as one large rectangular volume, or cut into smaller grid cubes, etc. The material is flexible and easily manipulated.

Figure 6.33 Clay Blocks or Bricks

I must admit to impatience when working with the clay blocks—it takes care and focus to cut them into desired shapes. They are pliable and flexible, and that is their value in model-making. They are not as flexible as wood interlocking blocks such as Halsam's Bricks and plastic Legos for hard-edge effects. After experimenting with them I used them for organic, free forms rather than chiseled or orthographic geometries.

Wax

Artist wax work, including encaustic painting, is a versatile two-dimensional medium. The waxes are generally beeswax applied with a pen-like device or as molten wax heated to the desired temperatures. The wax may be applied on many varying surfaces, making its use similar to painting and collage. The various kinds of wax used include the following:

- Beeswax (block-form strip or "spaghetti" form)
- Paraffin wax (cloudy-transparent made with oil)
- Carnuba wax (natural plant wax, golden in color)
- Micro Crystalline wax (oil based).

The pigments are referred to as "dirt" and are mixed into the various wax mixtures, usually resulting in blocks that are $1\ 5/8 \times 7/16 \times 15/16$ inches.

Metal

I include metal art in this section due to both its use in (urban) design and its integration with glass and the printing (Giclee) medium. It is less the conceptual material and more the final product. Its applications range from three-dimensional sculpture to surface and wall art forms. Metal art uses the following materials for small and larger installations:

- Steel
- Stainless steel
- Copper
- Aluminum
- Bronze
- Zinc
- Titanium
- Iron.

Sculpture

Sculpture is a broad category of art and design medium with many applications, ranging from study model to artwork to art installation as in environmental art—the landscape itself. It is the shaping of figures or designs into the round or in relief on many scales. It is akin to architecture in that it can be an artwork within a space and an artwork as the space. Sculpture may be used for concept study models using lightweight materials and tools that permit loose and fast applications, i.e., with modeling clay, sand and paper among other materials. As discussed in Chapter 4 with the work of metal sculptor John Luebtow (Langley, Los Angeles), part of John's play and preparation activities includes scouring junk yards for strange and intriguing shapes.

I mention it here as a separate play-tool, and it is discussed in various other sections such as process models and paper tools.

Drawing

Drawing: To inscribe a likeness or image with a marking implement. Characteristics of drawing include manual dexterity, applying a mark with a force or pressure using an implement such as a pen or pencil, connected directly to the cognitive plurality of the mind–body thought process.

Drawing is one of the most direct contact media, and unnecessarily frightens beginning designers. Drawing is a learned skill that increases the user's confidence as skill development improves through practice and repetition. Given the advent of digital tools, many aspects of drawing are no longer familiar to emerging generations of designers and are worth a new look. Types of drawing tools include the following:

- Pen and ink
- Graphite pencils
- Color pencils
- Pastel pencils
- Charcoal
- Crayons
- Color markers
- Watercolor pencils.

Traditional two-dimensional playthings include drawing, painting, collage and photography. The play is affected by the type of tool (pen, brush, etc.), the material being drawn upon (vellum, mylar, etc.) and the type of pigment or residue transferred to the drawing surface.

Drawing has many varying skills and techniques: too many to address in this book. The reader is referred to resource books available from many authors, including Ching (1990), Doyle (1999), Kasprisin (1999), Wu (1990), Kasprisin and Pettinari (1995) and others. Important in this context is the play aspect of drawing, the joy of experimentation and visualization, and the telling of stories. In the following examples, I focus on fast, loose, freehand drawing techniques that are as much an art form—a part of the visual *thinking* process—as opposed to visual representations.

There is a major shift in design fields from drawing as the main form of visual thinking to computational design and building information modeling (BIM). See David Ross Scheer (2014) for a discussion:

> [T]he elimination of the human body as the common foundation of design and experience; the transformation of the meaning of geometry when it is performed by computers; the changing nature of design when it requires computation or is done by a digitally enabled collaboration.
>
> (Scheer, 2014, Introduction, n.p.)

Let us review the role of drawing as a tool for the language and alphabet of the design process.

The Doodle Sketch

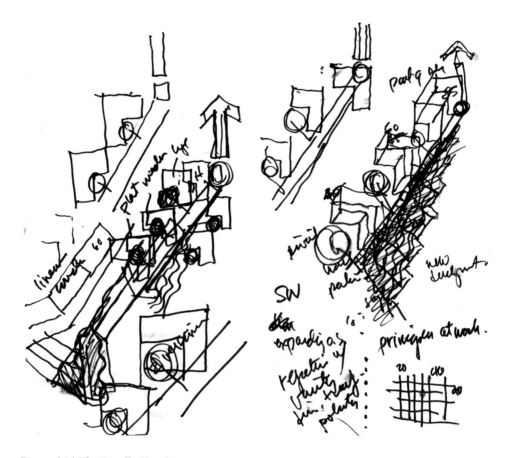

Figure 6.34 The Doodle Sketch

There are thousands of examples for the doodle sketch. Check out restaurant tables, napkins, etc. where designers have had lunch or dinner. The key is that it is a conceptual drawing or diagram that compresses and relates an idea in sketch form.

The Perspective Sketch

The perspective sketch is a classic visual communication tool used by designers and artists for centuries. It is as valuable today, perhaps even more so with computational design, as a means of quickly expressing ideas and connecting the designer's intellect to the physical visual image through crafting tools. Learning how to draw also imprints the elements and principles of design and composition within the designer's psyche.

Figure 6.35 The Playful Perspective Sketch

This quick sketch is for a public interactive event regarding improved access to the Sechelt BC waterfront. It is designed to be informal, "sketchy," and to represent ideas not hardened proposals. People enjoy looking for little references to local personages or places as they review the concepts portrayed within the sketch—playful.

EXERCISE 6.13: DRAWING COMPLEXITY (UNCERTAIN OUTCOME)

- *Intent.* Create a drawing "story" with no initial script or goal.
- *Rule.* Draw any shape as the first move and build off that shape until a notion or concept emerges from the drawing, not the intellect.
- *Tools.* Pen and ink (various tools), vellum or mylar.
- *Skills.* Basic drawing skills, including an understanding of perspective, preferred but not required.

The Axonometric Drawing

Remember that the axonometric drawing is a paraline drawing wherein all lines that are parallel in plan, elevation or any other orthographic (to scale) drawing remain parallel in the axonometric drawing. That is the beauty of the axonometric for design studies in that the distortion of a perspective is eliminated and the "plan" remains embedded in the drawing (see Kasprisin (2011) for many examples). In Chapter 7, I display examples of axonometric drawings used extensively in the Tsunami Vertical Evacuation Community Design Charrettes (University of Washington, 2013) for coastal communities in the State of Washington. The axonometric drawings were fast and easy to construct during public meetings with people gathered around a table.

Figure 6.36 The Axonometric Drawing

This is a simple axonometric drawing that was used in a design guideline study relating to existing architecturally distinct houses in commercial districts. Remember: all parallel lines in plan and elevation remain parallel in the axonometric drawing. Pentel Sign Pen on vellum.

EXERCISE 6.14: EMERGING COMPLEXITY

Using a pen-and-ink grid of one-inch squares and occasional smaller grids within the larger one, play with an axonometric drawing with no initial notion.

- *Intent.* Construct an emerging building complex that responds to each incremental drawing effort and incorporates a curvilinear shape within the grid.
- *Rules.* On the grid, draw a curvilinear form without a lot of preparation or forethought—start with a diagonal directional movement. Begin an axonometric shape anywhere on the grid; add new axonometric shapes, large and small, onto the previous incremental effort; continue as a

pattern emerges. Respond to the diagonal curvilinear form as the pattern progresses. When you have completed the drawing pattern and decide to make changes, add a trace overlay and draw new hybrid(s) and see what they merge into.

- *Tools.* Pentel Sign Pen or similar felt-tip pen, grid vellum—no pencil or eraser—there are no mistakes in this exercise.
- *Skills.* Basic drawing skill with minimal pen-and-ink experience. Knowledge of axonometric drawing (freehand—without any straight-edge tools).

Color Markers

Color markers have been around for decades as a useful tool in design/planning work for many fields. They are disappearing from the desks of many designers, replaced by computer graphic programs.

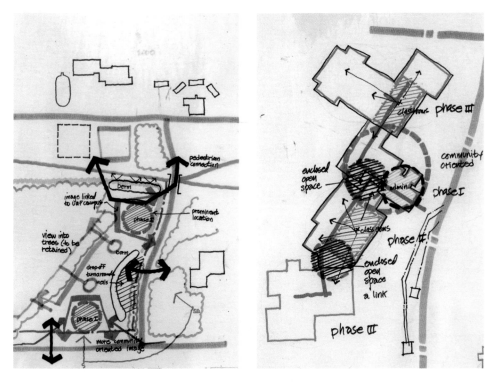

Figure 6.37 Color Marker Diagrams

Since the diagram with marker is discussed in more detail in Chapter 7, this example serves as an illustration of the use of markers for semiotic diagrams. Consistency in line weight, size and other factors, as in all languages, is critical to the quality and readability of the diagram. As in speech, any variance or inconsistency can lead to confusion of the message. As in this diagram, maintain consistency in line quality and characteristics. I have used these before from a campus master plan in Fairbanks, AK with Bettisworth North Architects. After the programming and design phase, I assembled over 125 marker diagrams as a part of the process for both design evolution and client interaction. These diagrams were taped to the corridor wall at the University of Alaska Facilities Office so that ongoing progress could be assessed at every meeting. The diagrams provided a record of progress and decisions that were accessible at any time during the meetings.

They still have a place alongside that computer for appropriate play-activity as they have the capability to execute quick and effective images, particularly in the diagram stage of design, free from dependency on a monitor view and suitable for public interaction events with poster and story boards. Refer to the section on "Semiotic Play" (Chapter 7) and examples of diagram construction.

Color markers are generally high-key or intense pigments carried by means of a chemical to keep the pigments suspended and fluid. Historically, they were toxic and have been sanitized significantly, though not completely. There are many brands on the market for use, and range from markers to watercolor markers. Markers are less flexible than some other media in their applications, as they do not mix well and rely on pre-made colors (see Doyle (1999) for applications of color markers and mixed-media applications with color pencils). I use markers extensively in diagrammatic drawings and as templates for symbols, especially for design and planning intensives, charrettes and other public involvement formats. Doyle's quality drawings are more for representational depictions of design outcomes or design progress.

Color Pencils

Color pencils are classic (not obsolete) tools of the design and planning fields. They are wax- and clay-based pigments that are guided by hand pressure for value and intensity. I use them extensively to highlight and dramatize pen-and-ink drawings. Unlike color markers, they are sensitive to the touch and

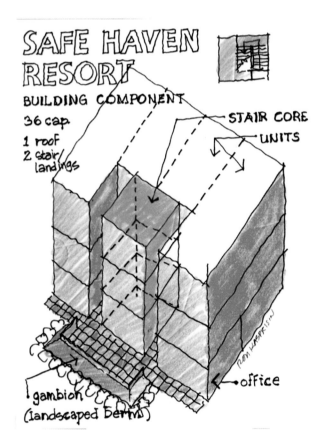

Figure 6.38a
Color Pencil Example

I use color pencils extensively as a mixed medium with pen-and-ink drawings for public meetings. When on-site in a community, many technological assists are not available or are time-consuming (e.g., finding plotters and printers on weekends). The simple bond print or original drawing if no printer is available works well with color pencil highlights and emphasis. The softer the wax the better, in my experience, is the application. This is an axonometric diagram drawn during an on-site design charrette along the Washington Coast in a small community away from standard services.

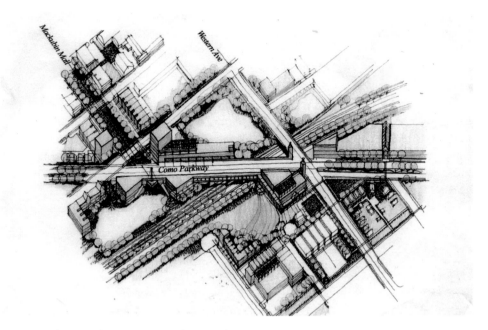

Figure 6.38b St. Paul Connection (Color Pencil)

This axonometric pen-and-ink drawing has the value and texture added in ink, and the color pencil is added on bond prints as an overlay for presentation and publication. The drawing depicts the Como Parkway as a connecting element between Minneapolis and St. Paul, MN.
Source: Professor James Pettinari.

can produce varied results, again through pressure. I used them extensively in *Urban Design* (2011). The key to color pencils is pressure of the hand for variations in density of line, etc.

Additional examples are given in Chapter 7.

Painting and Pastels

Painting is the application of pigments to paper, canvas and other materials through various media or carrying vehicles (including oil, water, alkyds, acrylics, clay, egg tempera, wax, etc.), applied with specialized brushes and tools that are directly related to the carrying vehicle. The physical nature of the medium determines the effect: oil is viscous and not obviously or immediately affected by gravity and evaporation; consequently oil paints are applied with thicker or stiffer brushes and palette knives. Water is fluid, affected by gravity, evaporation and paper type, and is applied with brushes that can absorb water (and pigment mixture) in their hairs. Acrylics can do both to a degree—they can be fluid with more water and viscous with less, thus making them a popular medium. Paint effects can be generated digitally and, again, the argument is that without manual dexterity, the play, experimentation and discovery aspects are reduced or non-existent.

Oil painting is used less in playful loose exercises due to its viscous nature and consequently is not discussed in detail. The oil medium is opaque and requires more set-up or drying time than other types. In oil painting, the artist can generally work dark to light, as opaque light pigments can cover darker pigments.

Architects, landscape architects and graphic designers still use painting as a play and experimentation vehicle in design (e.g., Steven Holl). References for playing with watercolor may be found in *Design Media* (Kasprisin,1999), *Architecture in Watercolor* (Schaller, 1990), *Painting by Design* (Reid, 1991), and *The Pastel Book* (Creevy, 1991) for pastels. Of the many quality watercolor painters, I chose two in particular—Reid and Schaller—and encourage the reader to spend time with their books. Reid is an impressionist who mixes most pigment washes on the paper for an energetic and loose style (even though his methods are deliberate and concise). Thomas Schaller's work as both an architect and a fine artist is inspirational on one professional's ability to bridge the professional use of watercolor and use it so expressively in his fine art.

Watercolor

Watercolor painting has long been used as a study medium for oil painters due to its loose, fluid and fast application. It is now a valued fine art medium in its own category. Watercolors are both transparent and more opaque (guache). Transparent watercolors allow the light to pass through and reflect back off the paper, producing luminosity. Opaque or guache watercolors, used largely in representational drawings because they are easier to paint over and suitable for detail, are chalkier and cover other pigments, restricting the light reflectivity. Transparent watercolors are also used in representational or rendered drawings, and are valued for their transparency (Schaller, 1990; Hook[2]).

This section provides some basic guidelines in the use of watercolor as a playful tool in that it has less precision in its outcome than other media. Since water is the vehicle or carrier, remember that it is wet, flows with gravity, absorbs into the paper and evaporates over time depending upon environmental temperature—in other words, it is less predictable. Its qualities for CPS play are fast-and-loose methods of application, color and value characteristics that all contribute to a conceptual signature.

Some basic principles of watercolor application include the following.

Pigments

There are three basic palettes or families of color: Delicate Palette (Azo or Aurelian Yellow, Cobalt Blue, Rose Madder with Veridian Green as a mixing color); this palette produces bright, clear colors which are also fragile in that they can be lifted from the paper to varying degrees once dry.

The Transparent Staining Palette (staining colors such as Permanent, Intense, Pthalo—Winsor Newton (WN) Yellow, WN Blue, WN Red, WN Green, Alizarin Crimson); this palette produces bright, intense colors and is often used to mix dark and rich colors with mixtures with other palettes.

The Opaque Palette (Yellow Ochre, Cerulean Blue, Cadmium Red); this palette produces muted, somewhat chalky colors.

There are many other pigments available, with more introduced regularly, as all pigments are now synthetic. It is beneficial to use a basic palette depending on the lighting mood desired and then export other colors into the mixture. This can help establish a color harmony in the work.

Brushes

Student and professional grades are available at varying costs. The key principles include: water retention *plus* spring-back (bend wet brush over and see if it comes back to vertical position—if not, don't buy it). Medium to larger size brushes are best as small brushes do not hold a sufficient charge of water: suggested range is no. 12 to no. 18 rounds.

Paper

Student and professional grade papers are available and in either case use at least a 140lb watercolor paper, spiral pad, block and loose sheets. For concept sketching and play, spiral pads, sketch-books and blocks are sufficient. Lighter weight paper will not adequately absorb water and will curl, forming ravines for the washes to settle in—not pretty.

Palettes

Palettes for pigments and mixing purposes are available in plastic (round and rectangular), enameled metal and metal. Always use a palette that has at least eight pigment wells and at least three or more larger mixing areas. Small palettes are inefficient for studio work and may be suitable for fieldwork at best.

Application Techniques

For fast-and-loose watercolor applications, there are a number of methods:

* Wet on wet (paper area to be painted is wet with clear water and pigment wash is added while area is still wet or damp)
* Wet on dry—the direct method (pigment wash is applied to dry paper)
* Merging and mingling (pigments are mixed on paper rather than in palette for the most part)
* Glazing (applies to all of the above) is the application of two or more layers of wash on top of a previously *dry* wash application
* Others include stippling, spattering, dry on dry (go to oils), etc.

Color and Value

Color and value are key to painting success with value having more importance, as it defines and strengthens the composition through the light-to-dark relationship. Use a five-scale value: light, mid-light, middle, mid-dark, dark. Keep color choices simple to avoid overworked, muddy or dirty and busy outcomes. Sometimes keeping to the simple color opposites works the best: blue and orange, yellow and purple, red and green. *Hint:* pick one and what is left is the opposite or complement. Pick blue and what is left? Yellow and red—orange; pick purple (red and blue) and what is left? Yellow; and green (yellow and blue) leaves red.

Watercolor painting is considered complex due to the fluid nature of water and principles of color and value painting. Read, attend workshops and play-practice; and by all means avoid comparison and competition. As a way to reduce the anxious avoidance factor, I suggest that the painter set up a small area dedicated to painting so that when the urge arises it is a simple matter to sit down and begin play immediately. This medium represents the real connection between player and product through the senses. Obviously it is a medium that I truly love and relish.

General Guidelines for Watercolor Painting

1. The medium is water: wet, affected by gravity (pulled downwards), affected by temperature (evaporation), capillary action (the drier part of the wash will pull and soak up a newer, wetter wash application).

2. Always prop your paper up at an angle of 30 degrees or more (the steeper the angle the more downward movement of your wet wash edge).

3. Wash edge: the "bead" is a good effect, as gravity is pulling the wash to the dry edge of your wash application; this is what you work with as you go back and forth to your palette and paper; the wash will not dry and set up for you as fast with the bead—the smaller the bead the faster the drying process.

4. *Never, never* (yes, there are exceptions) go back into a wet wash, capillary action, since you will get a blossom or blemish in wash as the less damp wash will pull water from the damper, newer wash; do not paint in vertical stripes, as drying times for each stripe are different at top and bottom; the exception is to drop pure pigment into a wet wash for brightness and, because it has very little water in the wash, it will not spread or blossom.

5. Lighten up on pressure on the brush by holding the brush further up the handle or you will get banding.

6. Wash directions: most washes are top-down either straight horizontal strokes of the bead or at an angle, but always down in order to allow gravity to participate; washes can be aggressive or slow (faster drying); banding will occur initially (too much pressure); too wet (flooding); too dry (white spots and friction)—all a part of the learning process.

7. Do not take a fully charged brush to your pigment wells as you will dilute the bank ($); regulate the water in the brush by slatting (shaking your brush charge onto the floor or at the dog), dabbing on a synthetic damp sponge or towel or TP; this controls the amount of water in the brush. More water/pigment may be added from the mixing wells.

8. Avoid a "swimming pool in your mixing well—too diluted; seek a "clinging wash"; remember that your wash will dry about 30 percent lighter than it looks on the palette.

9. *Safety*: even though lead has been removed, the synthetics in pigments are not good for your organs so do not suck on brushes or get pigments in your mouth, etc.; and always know where your coffee cup is located!

10. Have fun, enjoy, relax, don't be precious about your work (think it is hot!).

11. Palette arrangement: arrange your colors from warm to cool (i.e., yellows to blues in pigment wells); I like to separate my staining colors as they are strong and I know where they are.

Lots more . . .

The following are some sample exercises to get you going.

EXERCISE 6.15: WET ON WET/WET ON DRY/GLAZING/MERGING

Do not use yellow, as it does not show brush characteristics as well as darker colors; use blues, sepias, reds, etc.

- *Intent.* Practice the mechanics of painting and learn the characteristics of the various colors.
- *Rule.* Draw four sets of six 3 × 5 triangles (you can draw any shape you want: tree mass, circle, etc.), six per wet on wet, six per wet on dry, etc.
- *Wet on wet.* Clear water is applied to paper first, then pigment charge is added as water starts to evaporate and disappear into paper (shininess disappears—paper is still wet as water is in paper, not on it).
- *Wet on dry.* Pigment charge is applied to dry paper, essentially carrying the water to paper in brush.
- *Glazing.* Light wash is applied, allowed to dry, then painted over with another layer of a different color—begin with yellow, add red, add blue (lighter to darker).
- *Merging.* Combine two or more colors at and into their edges to get them to merge and also retain parts of parent or original colors (you need to push the second color into the first wash).
- *Tools.* Pigments, round watercolor brush no. 16 preferred, wash water container and other supporting supplies.

EXERCISE 6.16: GETTING TO KNOW YOUR TOOLS AND BASIC COLORS/VALUES

- *Intent.* For each of the pigments in your palette (a minimum of 8), learn the ability of each color to go from light to medium to dark values.
- *Rule:* Draw 3 × 5 triangles, three per color, in your spiral pads; for each color, paint a light, medium and dark value application using either wet on wet or wet on dry.

Do not be cautious and it is okay to goof up, so for the dark, try to make it as dark as you can, even if it is too much (goes flat and even shiny, as it is almost solid pigment). If your supposed dark value is cautious and weak you will not be able to bring the needed strength and closing values to a painting as your darks are really mid-value.

Why do these?

1. Play and practice with brush, pigment and water combinations
2. Play and practice with brush strokes and applications
3. Understand the value range capable for each pigment: they are not equal.

EXERCISE 6.17: COLOR WHEEL

- *Intent.* Learn how to mix colors, concocting primary and secondary colors by family or palette.
- *Rule.* Using at least two-inch diameter circles for each family of palettes (transparent delicate, staining, transparent opaque), do a circle of color mixtures beginning with yellow at the top, then yellow orange, orange, red orange, red, red purple, purple, blue purple, blue, blue green, green, yellow green, yellow. There are many variations of the secondary colors (orange, green, purple) depending upon the amount of each pigment used in mixing.

This will keep you busy.

Figure 6.39 The Roman Forest God

The mountain goat provided an excellent opportunity to play with various wash techniques, including wet-on-dry applications (my dominant approach) with merging (mixing washes on the paper not in the palette). The merging is evident in the shadow on the body to the right and direct applications of pure pigment into a wet wash are evident on the horns.
Source: Part of the collection of Tim Williams (ZGF), Seattle, WA.

Figure 6.40 Bruno

Bruno stands in the Piazza Campo di Fiori, Roma, brooding and silent. I painted the entire statue in one initial wash, changing colors as I moved down the figure, and kept right on going into the left background. Observe the base as the blues and oranges have a smooth transition at the same value from one color to another. Only then did I go back and add detail.
Accepted for Exhibition: St. Louis Artists Guild.
Source: Part of the collection of Mat Tonkin, Seattle, WA.

Figure 6.41 Red Rider

Red Rider exemplifies two key principles: (1) merging techniques of mixing colors on the paper instead of on the palette; and (2) the use of simple color opposite or complementary applications—in this case red and green on the first rider and blue and orange on the second rider. This was fast and loose—and fun.
Source: Part of the collection of John Schevenell, London, UK.

Figurer 6.42 Blue Boy

Blue Boy is one of my favorites and was again a large juicy wash approach with simple color complements (blue with orange highlights); a wet application of pigments and abstract background of greens and some reds. Accepted for Exhibition, Salmagundi Club, NY.
Source: Part of the collection of Levon, Seattle, WA.

*

Obviously, painting can occupy an entire book due to the complexity of the subject and techniques. I chose four works that illustrate the major techniques and approaches discussed above: wet on wet, wet on dry, and merging. These works represent a fast and playful style as opposed to a realistic representational style, accurate and detailed. Enjoy.

Pastels, Pastel Pencils, and Crayons

Pastels, pastel pencils and crayons are pigments carried via clay and wax, respectively. Pastels are sticks, blocks and pencils containing clay chalk mixed with pigment. Application differs from painting in that

Figure 6.43 Pastels: Haines, Alaska

I have used this sketch before (Design Media, 1999) as an example of a fast-and-loose pastel sketch—Barracks Building in Haines, AK. The pastel is a fast-applying clay-based tool that builds up a density of clay pigment to a point of saturation. Again they are quite versatile in generating ideas with color and texture. I used both pastel pencils and sticks, with simple color complements.

you are applying and spreading an opaque dust of fine particles over the paper. It is really about density of application (lighter density allows light to come through while darker density does not). As the clay particles build up and become too dense to absorb more particles, the work can be fixed with a spray material (fixative) so that additional clay applications may be applied. Pastel pencils are versatile tools in design and planning studies. They are applied to paper, wood, canvas and other surfaces. They are affected by pressure applied by the player similar to other pencil applications. Texture and variability in line weight are key characteristics of clay and wax carriers. Pastels are flexible and may be manipulated in that they can be spread into a smooth application with the finger or blending stump. See Kasprisin's *Design Media* (1999) and Creevy's *The Pastel Book* (1991).

Basic tools for pastel work include palette knives, razor blades, chamois (for blending and spreading), erasers, tortillons and blending stumps (rolled paper tools for blending and spreading), sponge brushes, foam rollers and holders.

Wax crayons may also be blended using various pressures on the stick. They are useful in public involvement interactions as a familiar and easy tool to use on large paper displays for public input.

Models

Crafted Models

As the reader will discover while reading this book, I used process or discovery models extensively in many experiments, since they were easily constructed and manipulated as a prelude to more definitive models and materials.

Crafted models in the design and planning fields come under a number of categories.

Semi-abstract Models

Semi-abstract models are less specific in spatial context or representation and focus on principles of composition rather than details. They may be used to represent negative as well as positive space (solid/void). They are useful for visualizing and playing with overall composition augmented by compositional relationships (movement, repetition with variety, etc.). By maintaining an abstract level of expression, they enable the player to be free from the pressures of finality and specific detail when experimenting with spatial compositions. I give numerous examples in Chapter 7.

Process and Discovery Models

The key difference between a process model and a representational model is completeness and finality. Process or discovery models are hand-crafted, conceptual, three-dimensional crafted models that are less finished and evolutionary. They are constructed for the purpose of exploring, experimenting and testing design concepts; thus the term "process." I use the term "discovery" to emphasize a difference between process and discovery in that a process model may be a pause in the design process for testing and evaluation. A discovery model is done as a means of uncovering new paths through the crafting and manipulation process. Their value in the design process is as a means of finding new and different directions through playful manipulations. Many designers who work with computers also rely on process models to visualize the three-dimensional aspects of a design forged on the two-dimensional computer monitor, regardless of the three-dimensional (3D) digital software. In many professional offices, the process model has replaced drawing as a visualization tool. A design is crafted into a model which can be scanned for digital manipulation.

A process model is in movement, experimental, exploratory, and less finished in physical form, and is used to study emerging design concepts.

Representational Models

A representational model depicts a final outcome and is used more for presentation and visualization of a final state for a client, financier, community, etc.

Representational models are not discussed in this context.

Gaming Models

Gaming models are process models that are used to explore, evaluate and strategize design concepts, usually as a group activity. They are a game board with gaming pieces (buildings, etc.). I use them in public participation events to illicit in-depth participation by community members. As an example, on an aerial photograph at a standard scale, participants " play" with cardboard cut-outs that represent design elements (buildings, landscape features, parking lots, etc.). With ongoing facilitated discussions, concept compositions are assembled, new cardboard parts are constructed as needed, and a concept is photographically documented for later review and discussion. Basic rules are established at the onset of the game, always subject to change as the group discussions and *model-manipulation* advance. This form

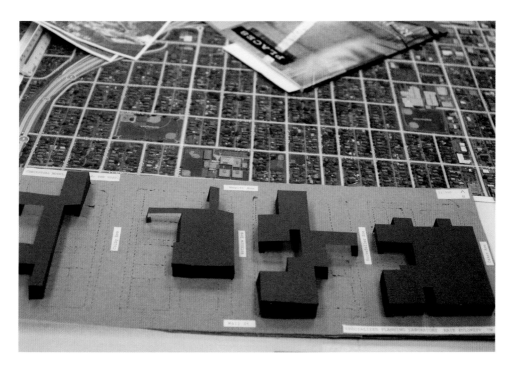

Figure 6.44 Semi-abstract Models: Everett Voids A

Student Kaie Kuldkepp devised a paper model to represent the void space within a downtown Everett, WA urban block as a part of her investigation into the nature of remnant space and its potentials.

Figure 6.45 Everett Voids B

The same student looked for movement direction opportunities within the void, again using construction paper inserted into a chipboard context model.

Figure 6.46 Everett Civic Center

To break out of a standard process, student Tim Lehman played with colors that represented use types within the contextual model, adding another visual dimension to the discovery process.

Figure 6.47 Gaming Model

A corrugated cardboard model is prepared for play with various pieces representing uses and building types for both individual and class interaction.
Source: UW Studio, photo by author.

of visualization in community forums can increase the understanding and participation of laypersons interested in urban design impacts.

In studio, planning students with a few exceptions slowly gravitated toward the use of models, from cardboard and paper constructs to Legos, after overcoming reticence regarding the possible triviality of playing with "toys" and after luring them away from their BIM programs. Once they allowed themselves to open up and experiment, they became players.

An astonishing thing happened during the process: they found a relationship between doing models by hand and concept processing with their BIM programs—a pluralistic use of methods in design. More later . . .

Since Chapter 7 is extensively about model building, I illustrate just a couple process models from student studio work.

Spatial Movement as Play

Design and planning fields can also utilize many forms of spatial play-activities that are less conventional than drawings and models, particularly in association with public involvement exercises and other group-related functions. I refer to these as *movement constructs* in that they enable participants to experiment with spatial compositions using movement sequences. In my teaching and professional experience, conventional play-tools often intimidate laypeople, whereas movement exercises and story-telling may be more familiar and perceived as fun activities.

Dance

Dance is a spatial activity, defined by the extents of movement sequences, and the space containing the dance whether with one person or many. Many forms of spatial dance interpretation are possible for both community involvement and design experimentation. Given a preliminary script with ambiguity and uncertain outcome, the player-dancer can interpret script over a grid surface while being videotaped and otherwise recorded. Dance may be used to express emotions, aesthetic arousal and spatial preferences. This does not necessarily require specific skills, merely a reduction in the fear of performing in front of or with others; and practice and/or guided instruction.

Other Movement Constructs

There are many movement constructs that can be imagined given the context and initial script or storyline (issues, opportunities, problem to be resolved). An example of a movement construct useful in some public involvement processes is "flocking." Usually performed with nine people in three rows of three (more are certainly possible including larger groups), the construct is set up with each person facing the same direction. Participants are instructed to be aware of the person in front and on each side and repeat whatever movement they do (it may be any one of the three). All are asked to close their eyes and the instructor taps one person in the front row. That person begins the movement construct after the others have opened their eyes. He or she can perform any movement: bend, walk, wave one arm, etc. As they turn and the entire formation turns in kind, someone else in the new front row begins another movement . . . and on and on. It can be a lesson in horizontal leadership, or an exercise in group cooperation that does not focus on one person.

Drama/Acting Out

Similar to dance movements, play-drama or acting out certain roles and situations can lead to novel or innovative ideas and outcomes in a design process. Again, given a skeletal script with key information and no determined outcome, the drama may be used to discover design ideas, share ideas with community clients with interactive feedback, and stimulate ideas as people engage the drama either as participants or observers. Similar to story-telling, the drama is constructed by participants based on the actions of an initial and guided sequence. Participants and/or observers can then suggest changes or additions to the first sequence to create a new and connected dramatization. These are recorded for later discussion and evaluation. One form of recording consists of assembling key factors or principles exhibited in each dramatization on large note cards placed on a wall in an emerging matrix (gestalt). This enables participants and observers to view any emerging patterns or ideas that result from the sequences.

This is also an excellent opportunity to introduce other play activities as inserts to further experiment and to explore emerging ideas and challenges.

Story-telling

I have always been a fan of story-telling in the planning and design fields because it is a pathway to and from the cultural characteristics of a community as told through the voices of that community. Stories can be spatially descriptive, defining space through the story metaphor. They can be used to describe how things were constructed in past generations by cultural characteristics. Story-telling can be used to record actual historical memories related to spatial contexts; or they can be used to construct future preferences using the uncertainty principle, inviting participants to contribute to an evolving scenario, "piggy-backing" onto previously introduced ideas and comments.

Drama and story-telling "tools" require advanced preparation, including a beginning script, an initial context description or setting, a time period and beginning characters (usually three key characters), etc. An experienced facilitator can act as director and assist the group in identifying emerging patterns and ideas, always advancing the activity until a conclusion, vision or ending (albeit temporary) is achieved.

An Example

Select a minimum of three volunteers, each representing a fictional character in a given context, set in a triangle. Other participants will replace each of the characters at prescribed periods during the evolving story-telling event (relieving anxiety or reticence). Each participant builds upon what the others have suggested. In a pause or stall in the process, a participant is replaced by another assuming the same character who contributes to the story. This can be repeated numerous times until the process has been saturated or an emerging pattern solidifies. A visual wall matrix of ideas begins to track, record and categorize the emerging storyline. There are many variations of this basic concept.

Games and Gaming

Again taken from the *American Heritage Dictionary*, *game* is an activity engaged in for amusement and/or recreation and is often associated with winning or losing, rewards and, above all, competition. I do not include "game" as play. "Playing" a game means to participate in the game and its structure; it does not mean a free-activity with little or no failure. "Playing" a game on my computer by moving my fingers on the keyboard or screen is not playing—it is an oxymoron; it is "gaming" with a structured and programmed toy.

Gaming plays a significant role in creative problem-solving and is introduced here as a methodology that can incorporate play. Game theory is a mathematical decision-making process in which a competitive situation is analyzed to determine the best course of action: enter computational design. In addition, gaming is effective in evaluating emerging concepts and discoveries within the larger CPS process. This approach has application in creative problem-solving processes later in the development of novel and innovative emergent concepts. For example, I can establish a site/product context (i.e., an older shopping center available for redevelopment), and set up a gaming situation with students to both play (with cardboard and block representations of building square feet, parking, etc.) and strategize on ways to achieve a resolution that meets the program requirements. This is a blend of gaming (strategizing and analyzing) and playing (free manipulation of materials and objects with a set of initial rules in order to

Figure 6.48 Gaming

In the key diagram, gaming is represented as an interactive evaluation activity integrating the intellectual and sensory domains of the CPS process. Interaction points as indicated are opportunities for the testing and evaluation of concepts and ideas. Here, students evaluate and test various design notions generated with the discovery models.
Source: UW Studio, photo by author.

experiment and discuss new ideas that can be assessed through gaming) to explore ideas and experiment with new ideas in a free activity.

In this definition of game, "reward" is replaced with "novel" and "innovative" as it relates to compositional quality, space-program satisfaction, aesthetic quality with meaning and functionality and place-making. The idea of "reward," in my experience in practice and teaching, has tainted the design and creative problem-solving processes. In practice, it can be driven by "bottom-line" evaluations and over-dependent upon cost factors; ignoring the larger integral process of smart design, similar to the inclusion within the CST Matrix of multiple factors and forces. In academia, "reward" can range from grades to adulation or failure, both negative results of a supposed creative process. Is *"gaming"* not a part of the creative problem-solving process? Quite the contrary: it is an important tool in the processing and evaluation of creative solutions or discoveries once they begin to mature and attain specificity.

Gaming (not *playing* games) involves a criterion of achievement for evaluation, and provides a mechanism to explore the multi-layers of that criterion for a given project. Play can still be incorporated into this gaming process as the need for further innovation remains. In the analysis and evaluation of accepted alternatives, gaming can test the strengths and identify the weaknesses of the performance of each alternative against client/community needs and aspirations—the criterion.

Most board games do not lead to "novelty" and "innovation" as they are highly structured around a reward system—capturing opponents, amassing wealth and collecting the most points—of fun and stimulating activities, unless the aim of the game is to change the game. Board games have set pieces and set contexts with highly structured rules that cannot change in order to maintain fairness for all participants. It is basic algebra with two equal sides around an equal sign—play does not have an equal sign.

The principles of the board game can be transferred to planning and design. The following is a hypothetical example of a planning/design board game:

1. A given context adequately displayed at a standard scale (not a GIS scale!) with key reference elements (streets, land forms, buildings, etc.).
2. Participant figurines represented in cardboard, wood, paper cut-outs, etc. for the various actors and constituents in the client/community-user-group (and it is important here to include the polarity of participants); public jurisdictions can be indicated within the board context while other pieces capable of movement are represented by figurines.
3. Outcomes: redevelopment of a neighborhood block or site with certain set achievement parameters of square feet, use, zoning envelope, etc.
4. Barriers and incentives: within the rules, barriers and incentives can be identified, not unlike the cards in "Monopoly" wherein unknown aspects are revealed based on the movement and location of a given participant; a barrier can be an ordinance, a soil condition or a community group factor; an incentive can be an environmental credit, a community-oriented design feature credit, etc.
5. A participant "movement" can be represented by making planning and design actions or attempted actions; or movements of people through a given project area in search of design features, compositions and place-making, etc.

A "playful" gaming situation can occur with an uncertain outcome, more ambiguity and a more complex context. Once the structured predetermined controls are removed or altered and an uncertain outcome is permitted, a playfulness can enter the game, seeking novelty and innovation.

I have used gaming extensively in public involvement formats and with students with hand-crafted three-dimensional cardboard models using pre-constructed board pieces that represent building types and square footage, parking lots and structures, etc. that can be moved around and discussed. There is an element of play given again more uncertainty and ambiguity. The tighter the controls on outcome, the less play occurs and more controlled or goal-dominant the gaming becomes.

The Game Board

Play involves the senses not merely the intellect. In preparation for a creative problem-solving process and the associated play-process, the player(s) prepare a "game board" that includes an identified project site and surrounding area and a larger adequate context—an area that has a high level of influence on the project site area. Overstating this game board(s) is recommended. The game board can be represented in multiple scales and forms as long as they are referenced and oriented properly.

Caution: I have observed students "gather" base maps, aerial photos and other game board resources and . . . limit their access to the computer. When I enter the studio I expect to see physical maps and displays on the walls for easy visual and physical access so that there is a sharing of information and idea-formulation through group interaction and manual dexterity, not through individual laptop screens.

Photographs, plans and other visual resources are made available in a physical format so that play can occur individually and in groups. When presenting ideas and information to a community group, one does not direct the audience to laptop computers; one directs their attention to displays and story boards that can be continually revisited during a dialogue—touched, pointed at and scribbled upon.

Lastly, as the game board is identified and prepared, its scale must be conventional, usually at an engineering scale (1 to 10 through 1 to 60) or similar metric. Many students are baffled when they instruct the "computer" through GIS to print out a document at a standard scale (e.g., 1 inch equals 400 feet), and the actual printed scale is different. In workshops, brainstorming sessions and design intensives, handheld scales are still the backbone of accurate dialogue and testing mechanisms—and they are standard scales that become useless when confronted with maps at 1 inch equals 433 feet, for example, when actually printed out.

Chapter 7

OBJECT-LEARNING APPLICATIONS IN DESIGN AND PLANNING

Creative problem-solving Object-learning and Play Applications

This chapter experiments with creative problem-solving (CPS) object-learning through play in the following design and planning applications:

1.   The Semiotic Diagram
2.   Brainstorming (Public and Private Environments)
3.   Design/Planning Intensives and Charrettes
4.   Design/Planning Applications

     •   Development Typologies
     •   Concept Development
     •   Design and Planning Explorations.

Object-learning applies to all aspects of the CPS process, both in the intellectual/processing and sensory thinking components. The list above includes applications common to all (urban) design and planning domains. They are used in this chapter as example applications for object-learning and play exercises and have transferability to other facets of design and planning. Play is possible in most facets and is particularly successful in concept development through various formats.

The M.J. Approach

And play is the glue . . . the experimental free activity that can also be utilized in data-gathering and analysis, exploration and evaluation of ideas, as well as the discovery of novelty and innovation. The following example illustrates the importance of play in conventional data-gathering/analysis processes. Years ago in high school, while taking an advanced Latin course, I and a friend, M.J. (now a retired brain surgeon), enjoyed competing for the top grades in Latin tests, tests augmented by extra credit questions. I studied diligently, translating every word of the assigned lengthy text. M.J. devised an alternate way of studying the text: he inscribed the translations on a continuous role of restroom hand towel paper, unrolling it on the floor as he progressed through the text. He then hung sections of the toweling around his room and studied it further. What did he do? He found a way of playing with a potentially tedious task and stimulated his thought process through a manual and visual play-skill, absorbing more information

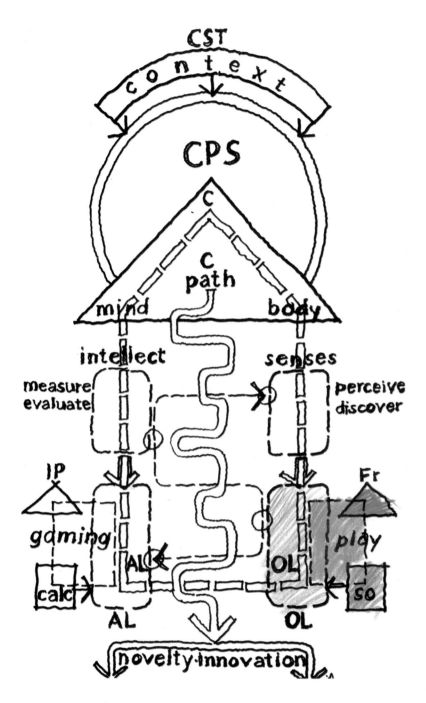

Figure 7.1 CPS Diagram: Play Diagrams

This chapter is about object-learning through play. The exercises and experiments are examples of various approaches toward conceptualization, imaginal and sensory thinking. They are meant to be fragile, fast and not precious—definitely fun and a learning process integrated with a "failure as learning" element in the discovery models.

by lessening the study stress through play. He replaced the memorization task with a playful activity to accomplish that task. M.J. got all of the extra credit questions correct as well and demonstrated the power of play.

In all aspects of creative problem-solving, these formats contribute to the creativity of the process and the innovation of the product because they rely on visual thinking play-skills to relate and transfer information, relationships and ideas in stimulating ways. Edward Tufte in *Envisioning Information* (1990) discusses the importance of visualization methods in understanding and interpreting data for oneself, one's colleagues and the community. For example, he assessed both Space Shuttle tragedies and described the lack of visual creativity in data analysis and interpretation—an inability to see critical relationships with appropriate visualizations—that led to those disasters due in part to an overreliance on standard and conventional methodologies (charts and tables) and on "apps" such as PowerPoint.

The Semiotic Diagram

Object-learning play-activities are integral and inherent in all aspects of design as a creative problem-solving process. As stated previously, object-learning is a direct sensory or cognitive perception process, performed primarily through manual dexterity—hence the use of play. Play is a free activity with an uncertain outcome, occurring in a creative environment with its own set of rules that emerge and change as the activity progresses; and is without significant fear, failure or reticence. The initial rules of play set the stage for action, skills and context. Play can be the tipping point between linear data-gathering—between data-gathering and analysis and an in-depth understanding of the relationships embedded within that data. Creative problem-solving is a novelty (innovation) generating process that employs whole mind–body thinking tactics that generate variability and complexity with self-direction (meta-cognition) which all results in a creative product.

Here is a first-hand educational example of the importance of the semiotic diagramming process; and the need to understand and visualize relationships within the data. I gave an assignment to urban planning graduate students that involved the diagramming of land-use relationships. Note the key word "relationships." The majority of students found this difficult and challenging as they kept looking at the data graphics, the Graphic Information System (GIS) maps, repeating the data patterns in diagrams. Noooooooooooo . . . The assignment was to diagram the relationships within the data patterns. Initially they simply iterated what the GIS map presented, not extracting the relationships and meaning. The semiotic diagram required them to ask what the patterns meant beyond conflict or land-use quantifications, density, etc. The related task of visualizing the relationships—issues, conflicts, "stories" within those data—added to the challenge and the entire thought process.

Diagram

A plan, sketch, drawing or other graphic designed to demonstrate or explain how something works or to clarify the relationship between the parts of the whole (*American Heritage Dictionary*). A diagram explains through visualizations the complex relationships embedded in information in compact form.

Semiotics

Semiotics is the theory and study of signs and symbols as elements or aspects of language and other forms of communication. Their construction as symbols add a major communication dimension to urban studies and design in that they can summarize, dramatize and distill the essences or stories embedded in urban data. They can assist the designer and planner in crystallizing complex information and actions in the analysis and pursuit of community meaning and functionality.

If you cannot diagram the issues and relationships, you cannot adequately design for them.

In the design fields and in particular in urban design and planning, diagrams are used to explore the organizational (functional) and structural (assemblage) relationships of the CST Matrix. Planning and design decisions cannot precede this process for the following reasons:

- Diagrams are semi-real descriptions of relationships that in general are *in-process explorations* of information, analysis, ideas and concepts.
- The relationships begin to describe a story or stories inherent in the information that eventually form the basis of spatial metaphors defined through architecture, landscape architecture, urban design and planning.
- Without these relationships and their organizing principles, there is no story—simply recycled data, convention and cliché.
- Diagrams are semi-real in that they are in most cases context specific and scale-referenced and -oriented, yet filter out unnecessary data or detail, and are thus semi-real. Exceptions to the context-specific application include certain aspects of space organizational programming.

I consider the construction of the semiotic diagram to be a critical skill in object-learning/play-design for the design and planning domains.

Every composition from a room to a house to an office building to a city block to a city has two major sets of relationships: organizational and structural. The organizational relationships describe the connections between and among uses and functions, needs and wants, opportunities and barriers in a composition. The structural relationships describe how those organizational components are assembled and composed as a spatial entity. The manner of assembly can distinguish two similar organizational relationships from one another. For example, two chairs can have the identical organizational relationships (four legs, flat seat, backrest) and have very different appearances based on materials and their assemblage or structure. These elements of relationships are not new to design and planning, and bear repeating when we explore the role of play-diagramming as both skill and process.

Organizational Relationships

These are the connections and interactions of meaning and functionality of a system (e.g., a city), including the needs, wants and requirements of the population. These relationships are defined and described prior to assembly or spatial placement of those relationships in a spatial context.

The main categories of information that form the basis for organizational relationships include and are not limited to the following:

Cultural Elements

- Social (individual to group interactions)
- Political (public and private decision-making processes)
- Economic
- Jurisdictional (including administrative and managerial)
- Workability
- Use and functionality
- History periodicities
- Meaning.

Spatial Elements

- Bio-physical:

  o   Geology
  o   Soils (subsurface, surface)
  o   Hazards (earthquake, flooding, tsunami, landslides, etc.)
  o   Surface features (topography, water (recharge, discharge, wetlands, rivers, ponds and lakes), vegetation, etc.)
  o   flora and fauna habitats
  o   bio-functions (air, water, land processes)
  o   bio-functions and their spatial characteristics (enclosures such as watersheds, edges such as shorelines).

Structural Relationships

These are the assembly of organizational relationships into structural constructs which are also relationships—spatial: plans, neighborhood design, master plans, site plans, the built environment including buildings, open space, etc. In structural relationships, materials, their physical characteristics and methods of assembly are combined with context, environment and organizational relationships to form reality—something made. The urban form diagram is an example of this type of semiotic diagram where spatial features and components are related via symbols and signs into a visual representation of the dynamics of the form.

Structural components are the assemblage of organizational components, composing them with specific mechanisms and materials into a relational pattern.

They are both intentionally composed structures and natural structures. Examples include and are not limited to the following:

Compositional Structures

- Circle/sphere and derivatives (radial burst, arc, etc.)
- Square/cube and derivatives (grid, diagonal, triangle, rectangle, etc.)
- Line/axis
- Scale ladder

- Built form structures:

  o   Existing (reality) context by scale patterns (block, neighborhood, district, city, suburban, metro, rurban, rural, etc.)

  o   Emergent (reality) context(s)

  o   Transportation infrastructure

  o   Other infrastructure (sewer, power, communication)

  o   Large-scale typologies (grid, curvilinear)

  o   Districts and nodes

  o   Development configurations (subdivisions, crossroads, etc.)

  o   Building typologies.

Natural Structures

- Watersheds
- Land forms and features
- Recharge and discharge areas
- Natural edges and transitional zones
- Etc.

Time/Historic

This relates to the periods of time within which significant events occur (periodicities) as well as time/historic and phasing.

  They include the following:

- Current periodicities (time frames within which key events and actions occur)
- Historic periodicities
- Historic/time patterning
- Visual time indicators
- Sequencing/phasing.

Techniques for the Semiotic Diagramming Process

Remember that motivation and intellect are not sufficient to engage the creative problem-solving process components and methods. Effective skill is required to adequately think visually through this process. The following are selections to exemplify the art of diagramming relationships with base information— finding and making connections. The following techniques provide a basis for semiotic interpretation and representation of CST relationships. They are followed by selected examples.

Diagramming Principles and Tools

As in writing, the visual thinking/communication process has a separate language and accompanying "alphabet." This alphabet is composed of graphic symbols that are organized and structured to express ideas, analyses, concepts, etc. Significant research supports the advantages of communicating to people (lay and professional) in visual form (Tufte, 1990). Information is retained by connecting visualized ideas, analysis and concepts to specific contexts as far as possible. As in writing, the accuracy of that language is critical to quality communication. There are conventions and there are personal choices on how spatial manifestations of culture, space and time are represented (and their interrelationships). This is a critical place for play in constructing diagrams. There is a lot of leeway in visually interpreting information in relationships. Key aspects of visual–spatial communication, similar to writing with letter symbols, are as follows:

1.   Accuracy of convention as used by an area of study or field of design
2.   Consistency in symbols, size, value, etc.
3.   Clarity of representation
4.   Value or tone for emphasis and weight
5.   Size and weight
6.   Objects = nouns
7.   Actions or principles = verbs
8.   Reference and orientation to a specific domain or context.

The following are some guidelines and principles based on cognitive perception (thinking with the senses).

Accuracy of Convention
Conventions of application exist within the various fields of design and planning, and need to be honored when constructing diagrams. In planning and design, they range from color conventions for land use to symbols and line weights for other spatial constructs from watersheds to urban blocks.

COLOR
In GIS and crafted applications where many categories or degrees of categories exist, each primary or secondary color can be further broken down almost to a point of confusion where differences between hues are weak; a combination of patterns and color can correct this situation.

*   *Yellow.* Single-family or low-density residential (sometimes accompanied by letter symbols).
*   *Orange.* Multiple family residential uses with variations depending upon the specific densities.
*   *Brown.* Often used for higher density residential uses.
*   *Red.* Commercial (retail, general, wholesale, etc.) indicated in variations of red and/or with hatching or letter symbols accompanying color.
*   *Purple.* Usually industrial (black is sometimes used but is discouraged).
*   *Blue.* Public, semi-public uses.
*   *Green.* Open space, again all with variations.

There are reference books that identify these conventions for all applications, including GIS.

COLOR INTENSITY
Color intensity is the key or brightness of a color. Primary colors (red, blue and yellow) and secondary colors (purple, green and orange) can be represented in high keys. Adding the missing primary (i.e., yellow to red and blue (purple)) produces a muted effect—a colored gray. In diagrams, a high key color is used for emphasis and a muted color for less emphasis, background or lower priority importance.

COLOR TEMPERATURE

Color temperature is expressed as hot and cold, warm and cool. Warmer colors have more yellow in their mixture and cooler colors have more blue. Temperature is relative, as a purple (red and blue) may be the "warmest" color in use next to cooler purples and blues. In many color applications, there is a color temperature dominance for consistency and harmony.

COLOR AND VALUE

Value is the relationship of light to dark, often expressed in five stages: light, mid-light, mid-, mid-dark and dark. Color can add mood through temperature and local identity (stop signs are red); and value adds emphasis, a scale of importance. Used together they form an effective visual communication.

LINE WEIGHT AND SPACING

As in writing, line weight determines a scale of *emphasis*. Bold, italics and underline are all used on your computer programs for visual emphasis through value (bold letters in relation to fine letters); difference (italics or slanted letters in relation to straight letters); and attention (underlining). So too is line weight *convention* critical to the visual-spatial alphabet: the smaller or thinner the line, the less important or priority the information; or, the minimum position in a spatial hierarchy. The heavier the line weight, the more attention is drawn to the shape or symbol—the higher priority the information or communication. For example, on a site plan, a curb line is the thinnest line (closest to ground plane) whereas a building outline may be thicker (more noticeable) and the farthest from the ground plane. This is important in conveying accurate information without words.

LINE TYPE

A solid line represents an actual edge to a physical shape (curb, building outline, etc.); a dotted line (broken with thin dashes) indicates a physical element that is rudimentary or almost non-existent, i.e., a trail. Dashed lines can also indicate a proposed element (future road, outline for a building that is no longer there, outline of an existing element that is either above or below the referenced horizontal plane (a second-level deck outline or overhang that is indicated on a ground or first floor plan)) or a future element. The width of the lines indicates their hierarchy of importance and/or size. A line with a combination of lines and dots is a convention usually used for administrative/ownership elements. For example, a property map can indicate parcel lines as a line-dot-line or line-dot-dot-line. Why? They are administrative not physical boundaries. A wetland or water edge is often indicated as a squiggly (natural not manufactured) edge with a line-dot combination. Why? The water edge is adjustable and can vary.

LINE TYPE AS MATERIALS INDICATOR

Contours or the edges of shapes can indicate the material or type of element in a plan, section, etc. The curb and building lines are straight (even if freehand, they are consistently "straight"—look at my drawings, as they are mostly if not all freehand); a forest or group of trees can be curly, squiggly lines representing organic materials or elements—smaller squiggles indicating smaller organic elements and the converse. Size and line type are relevant, and communicate meaning and priority or dimensional differences.

VALUE OR TONE FOR EMPHASIS

Perhaps the most important aspect or principle in visual communication of any kind, from planning diagrams to a watercolor painting, is value or tone: this is the light to dark relationship, in line density,

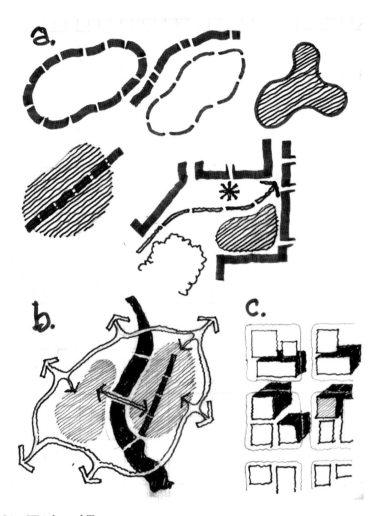

Figure 7.2 Line Weight and Type

I put emphasis on line weight in every course and book because of its importance as a part of the semiotic language. It is no different than the distinction between a lower and upper case letter—their relative sizes mean something (sound or hierarchy). The lighter the line in most cases means the smaller the emphasis, scale or importance in information.

color, etc.; the lighter the value the less the emphasis; the heavier or darker the value the greater the emphasis; speaking quietly versus shouting. Planning and design generally use five values: (1) light (white), (2) mid-light (light gray), (3) mid- or medium (gray), (4) mid-dark (darker gray), (5) dark (black). In line work, GIS and crafted methods, we often use line density and patterns to emphasize value: fine lines close together in a 45-degree angle (1); same angle and separation going in opposite direction overlapped with (1) making (2); a vertical pattern (same consistency) overlain (1 and 2), making (3); a horizontal pattern, etc., making (4); solid black, making (5). In many GIS applications the spacing of the line weights is not consistent, too separated, etc. and inaccurate.

SIZE AND WEIGHT

Again, size indicates a hierarchy of importance or stature as does weight (line, etc.).

OBJECTS = NOUNS

Objects or elements are the nouns (subject/object) of visual communication: shapes, lines, dots, symbols, etc. These objects are derivatives from the circle (sphere), square (cube) and line (axis).

ACTIONS OR PRINCIPLES = VERBS

Actions and principles are the verbs of visual communication: movement, direction, diagonal, repetition, repetition with variety. See Kasprisin (2011).

Reference and Orientation to a Specific Domain or Context

This is the Monopoly Board (Parker Brothers) where *Park Place* is a reference with location. Directional orientation (n, s, e, w, up, down, inclined, etc.) indicates a conventional orientation that is universally accepted, usually and preferably on a scaled map or diagram.

SPACING

Symbols clustered together such as a dashed or dotted line are located close to one another and not separated by excess space: Why? Spreading the symbols out makes it difficult for the eye to discern the pattern, and implies a series of independent shapes (rectangles) in a line—confusing. In GIS map work, excessive spacing of symbols is common, problematic and confusing:

W   a   e   r   water   l   a   n   d   u   s   e   land use

Be careful not to lose the principle of the dashed line; keep it compact with close spacing for clarity of meaning.

CONSISTENCY OF SYMBOLS

Do not change or alter symbols that represent a spatial element unless there is a change in that element, as that change indicates a variation in information being communicated. For example, in writing, capitalizing a word in one sentence that is not in other sentences changes its meaning or emphasis and is not consistent. That is why templates are critical to preserve this consistency. In GIS, if I am using a cross-hatch pattern, say, 45 degrees lower left to upper right with one-eighth-inch spacing, I must maintain that pattern and spacing for all similar applications. If I change the spacing to one-quarter-inch for the same information I have changed the information. Be consistent.

Consistency is adhering to the same principles established for the entire visual communication. If I am using an asterisk to indicate shopping centers, I do not mix a circle and an asterisk when referring to the same meaning. I use larger asterisks for larger shopping centers and smaller ones for shopping plazas, etc., consistent in meaning and variable in importance or degree. This is critical for the understanding of information, avoiding unnecessary distraction or inconsistent messages. This applies to all symbols and is often violated in GIS applications due to a lack of understanding of these principles.

CLARITY

Be clear, able to see well, and avoid too much visual information on one diagram; is there a hierarchy of information apparent and clear to the observer? Is the message muddled, crowded, lacking in emphasis and a hierarchy of symbols according to what is important in the message?

Directional Movement with Symbols

Arrows are linear lines, axis, with a "head" or tip indicating emphasis and direction, as in a north arrow; I prefer to use 45-degree arrow heads; 30 and 60 degrees are also common. If you get sloppy with arrow

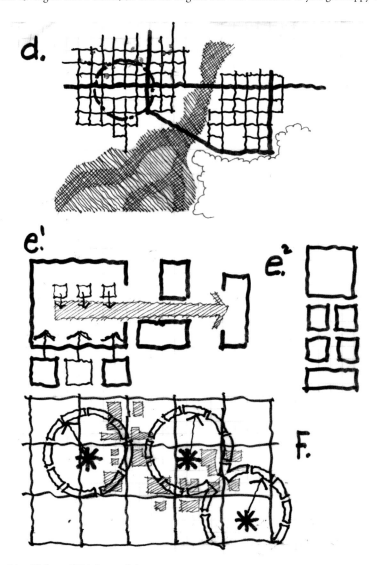

Figure 7.3a Line Values, Weights and Arrangements

These are a continuation of examples I provide to students in the visual communication course as guides to various symbols in diagramming. They represent various line values, weights and various ways to arrange the symbols to indicate relationships.

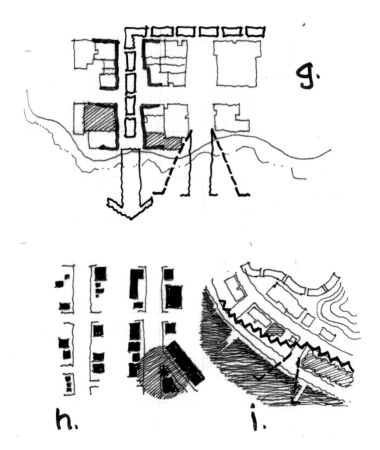

Figure 7.3b Symbol Types

The player can construct varying symbols to represent land forms, buildings, view corridors, slopes, etc. in semi-abstract ways. In (g), building forms are represented with a lighter pen as they are for reference, whereas the continuous building fronts are given more value with the darker and larger continuous line.

heads in a diagram and they start varying in size and consistency you are implying a change in information; keep them the same or change them for a reason. An arrow may be straight, curvilinear (indicating a variation in path, direction, etc.), broken, etc. Avoid decorative and visually "busy" arrow symbols as they overstate their importance and can confuse the message with distractions.

The application of these graphic symbols involves relationships of information analyses and planning concepts. Data do not exist as separate items and relationships are to be presented in context. For example, stating the number of single-parent households in a community does little for the planning process. Identifying and locating those households, adding age and gender groupings, speaks of relationships that have implications for housing stock and type, cost, rental vs. ownership, etc.

Historic/Time Patterning

The project area/district is placed in perspective regarding the evolution of the natural/built form patterns over a given time span composed of periodicities (time-sheds similar to watersheds). For example, the

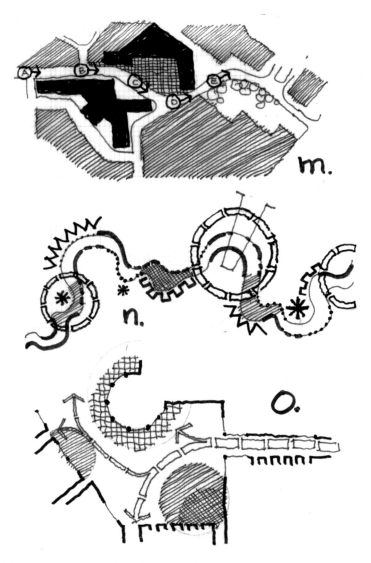

Figure 7.4 Movement, Direction, Spatial Characteristics

Again, varying line weights and types help compose a series of built form and spatial activity diagrams. The player is only limited by his or her imagination.

waterfront in Portland, OR along the Willamette River can be graphically portrayed from 1900 to 1930 to 1986 and beyond in plan diagrams that simply have built form information. In many cases, this form of diagram can identify remnant patterns within the landscape—clues for future planning. Doing them in a crafting mode helps the designer and team to visualize historic changes and relationships without relying on outside and disconnected methods.

All of the above represent elements within the physical world. The interactions between and among them are relationships, the connections and by-products of those interactions. These are the key elements

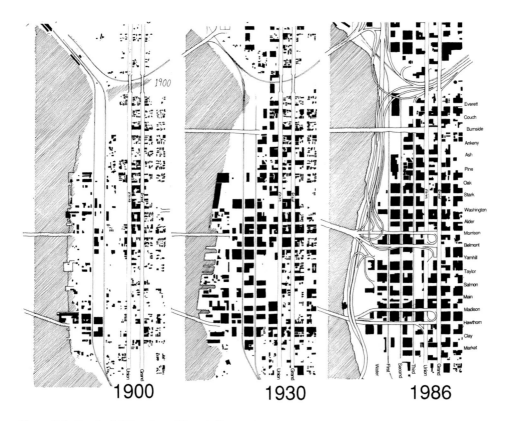

1900 **1930** **1986**

Figure 7.5a Portland Waterfront Historic Patterning

These three diagrams were done as part of a study of the river district by the Department of Architecture, University of Oregon in 1989, led by Professor James Pettinari. The diagrams are pen and ink on mylar. Obsolete? Hardly. An example of direct connection between the student and the built form through crafting.

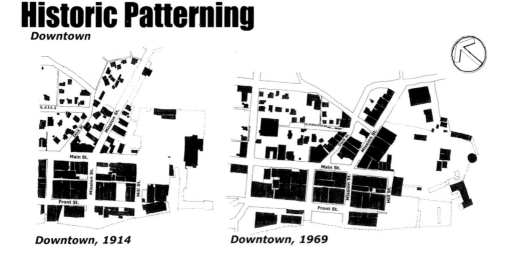

Historic Patterning
Downtown

Downtown, 1914 *Downtown, 1969*

Figure 7.5b Ketchikan Historic Patterning

Similar to the Portland Waterfront, this diagram tracks urban form over time for the downtown of Ketchikan, AK, an isolated waterfront community at the base of the mountains in southeast Alaska.

140

to be diagrammed. It is not sufficient to simply locate elements within the environment; or define or compare sets of information through GIS. What matters is how they relate and are changing—regressing or emergent—that is the story to be communicated. Not until all three components of the CST Matrix are brought into play through best efforts can the designer advance in the design process. This makes the planner/designer's task complex and challenging.

Existing (Reality) Context

The existing context is complex in that the present form relationships are in various states of reality: descending (aging), transitional, emergent (new hybrids, phenomena, unusual occurrences, etc.), static or stable. This is critical to understanding the underlying dynamics of the CST Matrix and requires critical analysis.

The existing context includes compositional structures that contain and sustain key organizational relationships. They assemble and relate elements and principles in the built form. This can have significant importance in design guideline development and review in cities: assessing a project in relation to the compositional structure present or desired rather than detail to detail.

Figure 7.6 Existing Context Diagram Series

Since this is about play, this illustration is one I did years ago in Ketchikan, AK during a comprehensive planning process with the Gateway Borough Planning Department. Sometimes it is refreshing to step back and look at the big picture. This is actually one-half of the original pen-and-ink drawing on mylar. I did the drawing by stitching together a series of photos. It is a contextual visualization that was also fun and rewarding to draw.

Scale Ladder

For any given project from a site to a neighborhood or urban district, define the larger context that the project area is within—and a part of—Seattle to King County to Western Washington to the Pacific Northwest to the Cascadia Watershed (bio-region (preferable)). This requires multiple map diagrams with just enough information for reference and orientation.

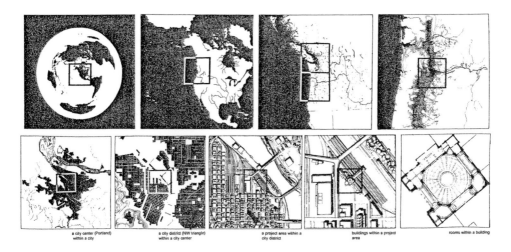

Figure 7.7 Scale Ladder (Planet to Room)

This series of nine images represents a ladder of increasing scale or focus from a planetary view to a room. The scale ladder provides a progression of information and context, with each view offering differing sets of information and relationships.
Source: Professor James Pettinari, University of Oregon.

Natural Structures

- Floodways (linear/curvilinear axis)
- Flowages (linear fan-like structures, ribbons)
- Watersheds (regional to local, nested, various shapes)
- Aquifers, recharge/discharge areas.

See Figure 7.8.

Emergent (Reality) Context(s)

The changes in context or reality are clued in the environment, with systems and structures changing—regressing, maintaining stability or coherent and emerging. The value of visual communications to highlight an emerging development pattern is vital to public discussions. (See Figures 7.9 and 7.10.)

2-6 Regional Forces. The aerial perspective places the study site in its regional setting and identifies the moraine as an organization principal that is further diagrammed at the study site scale.

The glacial landscape of tall grass prarie, forest, river and lake is Milwaukee's origin and structures its urban form and culture. Natural and human systems converge at this site and can find integration in a lake edge moraine land form which will help shape the evolving culture and physical growth of the city.

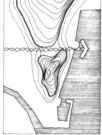

The new moraine form reflects the origin of the regional landscape.

The **moraine** mediates highway scale from regional to local, and . creates a portal to the city.

The moraine molds cultural subdistricts within the city.

The moraine extends the forested green belt into the city.

The moraine directs and organizes transportation while buffering recreation.

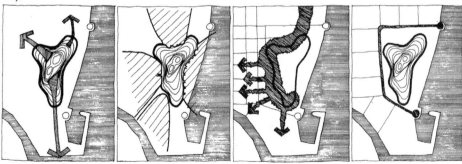

Figure 7.8 Natural Environmental Structures

This diagram demonstrates the identification of an historic glacial moraine in downtown Milwaukee, WI along the waterfront that was then compared to the built form encompassing it. The moraine, as interpreted in the smaller diagrams, became the basis of a major design recommendation connecting the downtown to the waterfront.
Source: Professor James Pettinari, Visual Thinking for Architects and Planners (1995) with Ron Kasprisin.

143

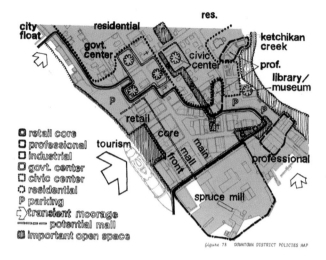

res.

city float

residential

govt. center

ketchikan creek

civic center

prof.

library/museum

retail

core

main

mall

front

tourism

☐ retail core
☐ professional
☐ industrial
☐ govt. center
☐ civic center
☐ residential
P parking
↗ transient moorage
----- potential mall
important open space

professional

spruce mill

figure 73 DOWNTOWN DISTRICT POLICIES MAP

Figure 7.9
Downtown Ketchikan
District Diagram

This is a basic policy diagram indicating development trends within the downtown Ketchikan, AK district and sub-districts as a basis for further detailed urban design recommendations. An existing base map with building footprints provides reference and orientation, and the overlain symbols are kept simple for clarity.

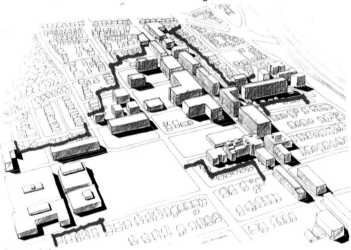

ROOSEVELT COMMERCIAL DISTRICT
Zoning Visualization Project

Prepared for:
ROOSEVELT NEIGHBORHOOD ASSOCIATION
University of Washington Urban Design Program

Figure 7.10 Roosevelt Commercial District: Emerging Reality

I use this as an example of an emerging context in that students were asked to use axonometric drawings to portray the existing zoning allocation for a north side Seattle neighborhood commercial center. Controversy swirled around the 65-feet allowable building heights adjacent to single family residential areas. Needless to say, residents became upset by these visualizations, as they perceived them as proposals and not established zones. The visualizations accomplished their mission: zoning was changed within the district to reflect the community concerns and land-use transition edges. I consider the axonometric drawing to be a powerful diagrammatic tool.
Source: UW Visualization Course.

Compositional Organization/
Structure Diagrams

ORGANIZATION

These are the functional relationships of need, desire and requirement as described previously. Too often, these components and their relationships are lost in the collection of data. Summarizing and compressing them into spatial diagrams retains the important relationships and advances the design/planning process.

STRUCTURE

These are the structural compositions or assemblages, the built form that manifests and is manifested by the organizational relationships in the bio-physical/historic context. Planners deal with these as larger scale use/environment spatial patterns; designers deal with them as spatial/environmental constructs.

There are many applications of playful diagramming exercises that apply to all levels of design and planning. These examples highlight techniques that use crafting skills to assemble. They can be constructed on a computer but I have found through experience that the initial conceptualization of the diagrams is effective when done by hand, then scanned and made a part of a larger presentation or copied using a digital graphics program for consistency in the presentation. There are numerous other diagrammatic examples illustrated in the remaining portions of the book.

Please refer to *Urban Design* (Kasprisin, 2011) for more information on diagrammatic symbols.

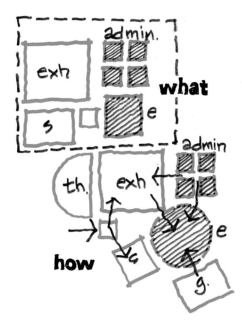

Figure 7.11 Space Programming Organization

This is a fast organizational diagram in two parts: the upper is a spatial list of needs (what) for an Eagle Rescue Facility in southeast Alaska; the bottom portion is the organizational relationships (how) for the various activities. They range from exhibit space (exh), gallery space (g), injured eagle area (e), theater (th), administration and classrooms (admin), and service (s) area.

**Figure 7.12
Spatial Programming Structure**

The organizational relationships are now assembled or composed into the emerging forms of a building structure with the various parts placed around key circulation patterns.

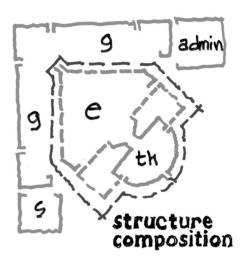

145

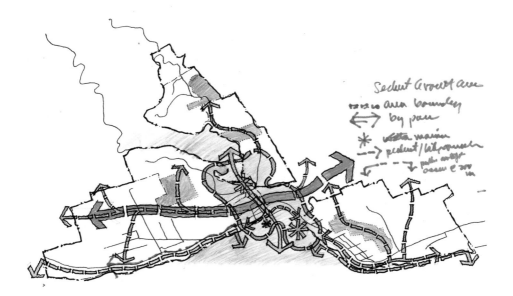

Figure 7.13 Sechelt Growth Area Diagram

Compressing information into semiotic diagrams enables the larger patterns of growth and other issues to be illustrated during and in preparation for public meetings; in many cases using the diagram as a talking point. As each scale is explored, data changes, and increases in detail and focus.
Source: From "Visions for Sechelt, British Columbia," with John Talbot & Associates, Burnaby, BC.

Play Applications for Brainstorming

Before engaging the aspects of play in an (urban) design process, the process of "brainstorming" is discussed as an essential component of design/planning thought that exists in all levels of creative problem-solving. It has many manifestations, and is supported and improved with the addition of play-activities, especially in group interactions. The basic principles are outlined and discussed below.

Play is both an individual and group free activity. Brainstorming is utilized as a means of identifying problem parameters, emergent boundaries, directions, approaches and ideas of a given problem. Key principles for brainstorming include the following:

1. A comfortable and creativity-oriented environment (open, adequate work space for individuals and team members, flexible, wall space for poster and story boards)
2. A facilitator with graphic visualization skills
3. An introduction of the traits and characteristics of play
4. An information base that has relevance and accuracy
5. An emergent statement of the problem, subject to alteration
6. Emphasis on the initial quantity of ideas, not quality
7. Suspension of criticism (facilitator can act as referee)
8. "Hitch-hiking" permitted and encouraged wherein one player can build upon the ideas of another
9. No idea is a bad idea: wild ideas, exaggerations are encouraged as the process itself will eventually sort and evaluate

10.   Visual and graphic thought and synthesis processes (this requires skill development for most players and facilitator).

Two applications of brainstorming are discussed below: internal team sessions and public interactive "delography" sessions (Verger, 1994).

Internal Team Brainstorming

The use of visualizations, crafted and/or digital, are critical tools in any brainstorming session in that they provide a contextual base and starting point with supportive information, and a visual pattern that emerges as the process evolves through layers of discussion and exploration.

Digital visualizations can provide jurisdictional and bio-physical supporting data for an initial contextual base such as parcel configurations, use and zoning, built form, and other base data. The sharing of information is critical to the success of the session. Consider the following guidelines for the use of visual information:

1.   Use large-format poster or story boards in order for all participants to be able to refer to and reflect on the contextual data during discussions.
2.   Crafted preparation of the poster boards enables participants to review and interpret in diagram form the data and information rather than relying predominantly on graphic information systems that can reduce quality contact with the information. When teaching graduate students in the use and construction of diagrams, too many repeated the information provided in digital form and did not perceive the relationships between and among the data—they were not playing.
3.   Working from projectors and individual monitors or cell phones reduces or prevents the shared experience and draws the participants' attention away from the group process.
4.   A common wall or large view plane allows the building of relationships during the evolving discussion with summary diagrams and other visualizations.

Public Interactive Brainstorming

In public involvement brainstorming sessions, the key word is "interactive," with the public as active participants rather than as passive listeners.

A process developed by Verger (1994) for school planning, programming and design, called "delography," advances the dialogue through a series of evolving scale-based small group discussions that are shared with the larger group and repeated in small groups with a change of scale, from broad-based issues to finer detail.

There are a number of ways to implement this method and they all include visual summarizations of information and ideas.

Emerging Visual Story Boards

Using large sheets of paper, butcher paper, grid flip chart paper, etc., a visual recording person, equipped with color markers in most cases, listens to the discussion and characterizes or cartoons the essence of what is being said onto the wall paper. As discussion continues and evolves, the story board expands and through the visualizer begins to distill even further various ideas and challenges put forth by participants.

I have used this extensively in brainstorming sessions and design charrettes. It works effectively for both internal and public interaction events.

A Community of Learners: Opportunities for the Redmond Elementary School Site (University of Washington, 1996, Center for Architecture and Education) conducted two creative events that sought ideas and concepts related to the future use of the former elementary school building in Redmond, WA. The workshop included educators, parents and city officials, and a university design team consisting of

Community of Learners

powerful opportunity exists in the City of Redmond on their historic school site. Four generations of learners have graduated from what was originally Redmond High School and is currently the local elementary school. Many former students now live and work throughout the community. Some graduates are not directly involved with the current school activities, but many warmly identify with the old building as the place where they were introduced to new ideas and experienced social interaction while growing up. It continues to be a symbol of learning for the community with programs and after school activities.

In his book The Different Drum-Community Making and Peace, M. Scott Peck defines community as "... a group of individuals who have learned how to communicate honestly with each other, whose relationships go deeper than their masks of composure, and who have developed some significant commitment to "rejoice together, mourn together" and to " delight in each other, make other's conditions our own." Elsewhere he says that community is and must be inclusive. In other words no one can be left out of the true definition of "community." What better place to create a "community of learners" than a school site centered in the heart of the City of Redmond.

Lake Washington School District (Redmond Elementary joined the district in 1949) encourages community interaction within the school through a variety of outreach programs which involve local businesses, children's and service clubs, city organizations as well

as parent volunteers. The task for the University team was to maintain the existing outreach programs ties, conceptualize other ways to reach out and physically connect the school to the surrounding neighborhoods and then propose practical solutions for their implementation.

A community of learners means that the school is reaching out and the community is reaching in. There are many different communities (neighborhood districts, business organizations, church and senior groups, athletic clubs, parent associations, etc.) that currently exist within Redmond, all with their own unique desires, goals and learning requirements. If Peck's definition of "community" is correct, that of being inclusive and able to communicate openly and honestly, then the Redmond Elementary School site provides a good foundation for activity much like a "mother-board" within a computer to link all the various components together. The conduits or connections are visual, physical and spiritual. The green pathways connecting the hills through the parks and finally to the river, are physical and visual connections. Providing places for unique learning opportunities allow for that "spark" of an idea that inspires one to learn more. Teachers may draw on outside expertise to come within or move their students out to view active examples of what they are teaching. People may tap existing resources within the new school, the site, the future uses in the historic school building or interconnect to a variety of sources via a "shared" network supported by the school but located throughout the community.

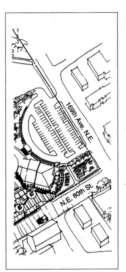 

*The prototype school **parking lot** design provides for an automobile drop off zone from 169th Avenue.*

*The slope along 169th allows for the potential of an entry to a **parking lid** **structure** over ground parking at 80th.*

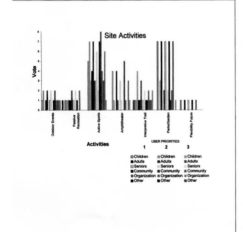 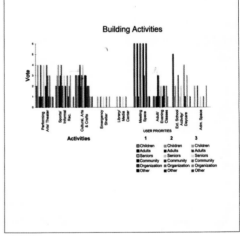

Figure 7.14 Redmond Elementary School

The chart summaries were augmented by axonometric and perspective design examples of the information represented in the charts for ease of public communication.
Source: UW Studio led by author.

faculty from architecture, urban design, landscape architecture and education, and augmented by a team of urban planning graduate students. I label this a brainstorming session versus a charrette, as it was a shorter term event, fewer than three days of on-site work.

The first event identified the community's needs and hopes for the site, surrounding areas and continuing lifelong learning aspirations. The second event enabled the assembled diverse team to interpret and compose future space-needs programs and design concepts for the building, site and surrounding area for community evaluation.

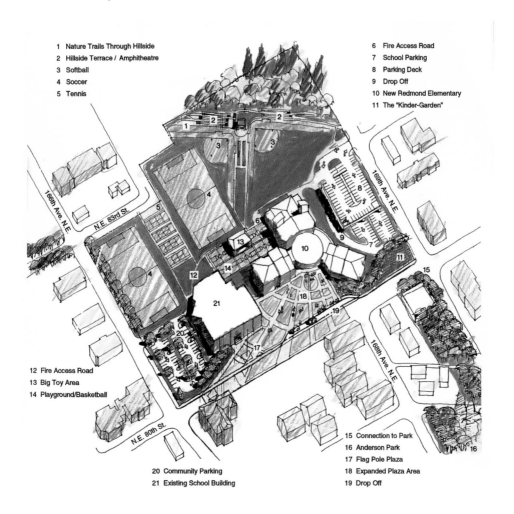

1 Nature Trails Through Hillside
2 Hillside Terrace / Amphitheatre
3 Softball
4 Soccer
5 Tennis

6 Fire Access Road
7 School Parking
8 Parking Deck
9 Drop Off
10 New Redmond Elementary
11 The "Kinder-Garden"

12 Fire Access Road
13 Big Toy Area
14 Playground/Basketball

20 Community Parking
21 Existing School Building

15 Connection to Park
16 Anderson Park
17 Flag Pole Plaza
18 Expanded Plaza Area
19 Drop Off

Figure 7.15 Redmond Elementary School Design

Three axonometric drawings (one axonometric is illustrated) summarized the final design concepts for further public involvement and input. All drawings were completed in fast-and-loose styles. This is not an easy task and requires skill development, as many images are constructed within an hour or less as a part of the brainstorming time frame.
Source: UW Studio led by author.

As a part of the brainstorming sessions, the discussions per Verger (1994) were progressive—moving from broad neighborhood issues down in scale to site and building programs and uses. After each smaller table discussion, participants were asked to summarize their ideas and perceptions on large note cards that were then amassed by the students and placed on large wall papers in an evolutionary matrix of ideas and challenges. It is important to note that the facilitator at each table also acted as a referee in order to identify and terminate any effort at argument or compromise.

The preferences of all participants were summarized into potential off-site activities, site activities and building activities. These were summarized in both chart form and urban design visualizations for final discussion.[3]

Design Intensives or Charrettes

Design intensives differ from workshop and brainstorming formats in that they are accomplished on-site, over an extended period of usually three to five days, and with a final product at the end of the intensive. Workshops and brainstorming formats can be similar and are carried forward, but usually do not have a final product attached to them at the end of the on-site session and are shorter in duration (one to three hours or one to two days versus three to five days for an intensive).

A design intensive requires a hands-on crafted approach to design solutions as opposed to digital graphics. This observation is based on years of design intensive and charrette participation for local and national American Institute of Architects events, University of Washington Design Charrettes, National Main Street Programs and many other events in the USA and Canada. Crafted methods are preferred for the following reasons:

- Crafted methods and skills enable direct interaction with the client (community members) where a designer can draw as participants are providing ideas and critiques; perspectives and axonometric drawings are particularly useful in this situation.
- Crafted methods enable presentations and discussions beyond the monitor, with wall posters and graphics that are fast and easy to produce in a short time frame.
- Digital graphics require equipment such as scanners and plotters not always available on-site; they are useful for final presentations where the equipment is available and enough time exists for preparation of PowerPoint and similar display formats.
- The designer can imagine and produce ideas and outcomes without relying on technical support staff; if scanners are available, crafted drawings can be incorporated into digital technologies for presentation purposes requiring a longer time span to complete.
- Local design professionals often participate in design intensives, requiring team coordination and interaction not readily available, with participants working on individual monitors (this may be remedied with new technologies).

Digital technologies can be integrated into the production phase of a design intensive as crafted work is scanned, manipulated and incorporated into a final report. Intensives rely on speed of information processing and speed and clarity of design interpretation in an interactive format with the community clients.

Key Attributes Necessary for Charrette Involvement

Playfulness

Playfulness is essential in design intensives when working with the community, providing a stimulating and personal approach to community involvement through the use of visual skills. The ability to construct fast study models and to draw concepts and ideas working on-site with community members present is exciting, and contributes to the community's sense of involvement and ownership of the process. There is a big difference between five people hovering around a computer monitor with one person in control, and a larger group focused on crafted displays hung on walls used as talking points. Interactive cardboard study models can be used in gaming and brainstorming sessions with community members, with each idea recorded photographically and available for later discussion, evolution and integration into final digital products. This process can be an anxious event for newcomers. I have found it useful to remind myself that I am not the star of the show—the participants and work process/product are—thus taking a lot of pressure for performance from the shoulders of the team members. This is where a sense of playfulness pays dividends.

Skill-competence

Design intensives require accomplished play-skills. "Talking heads" are not sufficient to conduct the interactive dialogue in intensives due to the informative power of fast and effective visualizations.

Play-tools for design intensives are varied and subject to the project context. Commonly used tools include the following, based on experiences and case studies.

Drawing with opaque inks provides a sharp line quality for reproductions during a design intensive. Pencil lines can be non-uniform in line density and do not reproduce as well as pen-and-ink drawings. Color pencil and pastel work is effective and requires a scanner or printer capable of color reproductions, which is potentially more expensive to incorporate into a final product. An alternative is to apply color pencil or pastel to bond copies of line drawings for display and discussion. These are fast, and the coloring can be done by support staff.

The most effective drawing types for design-intensive play are plans, plan diagrams, axonometric drawings and perspective sketches. Axonometric drawings enable the presentation of ideas in three dimensions that are essentially all of equal value—no vanishing point(s) and no foreground versus background, larger versus smaller images. Drawing can be both sketch quality and more finished line work. Since the time frame is shorter regarding the production of a final product, freehand drawing is preferred over precise straight-line work. I often work on grid vellum sheets that provide a reference and orientation for axonometric drawings and plan diagrams. They are easy to transport, set up and use during charrette events that are away from conventional supply sources. The personal quality of hand-drawn graphics is stimulating for community participants. Drawing tools include Sharpie Pens (durable and permanent inks), Pentel Sign Pens and equivalent, color markers and pencils.

CASE STUDY ONE: SECHELT VISION PLAN, SECHELT, BC, CANADA

Sechelt, British Columbia is a forty-minute ferry trip north from Vancouver, BC on the "Sunshine Coast" along the western edge of the mainland, facing Georgia Strait and Vancouver Island. As a part of a larger vision project (Talbot & Associates, 2009), two design intensives were conducted at key points in the year-long project to develop ideas and test concepts and implementation strategies. The project involved both hand-crafted graphics and digital assistance (plan production, word processing, final report presentation).

- *Project Overview.* Design intensives as part of a longer one-year visioning process focused on two issues: downtown redevelopment and housing subdivision reform.
- *Time Period.* Five days.
- *Team Composition.* Community Development Specialist/Coordinator, Urban Designer, Architect, Urban Planner, Meeting Facilitator with visualization/caricature skills, two digital technicians.
- *Intensive Environment.* Community center (large meeting space with loft).
- *Overall Process:*

  – Community and Stakeholder Committee introductory and brainstorming sessions
  – Personal interviews by key team members and community individuals and small groups at half-hour intervals (eighty people interviewed) for confidentiality
  – Team assessment of information: analytical diagrams, issues and opportunities summary, preparation of "game boards": maps, plans and other resources
  – Meetings with local officials, staff, etc.
  – Field trips as necessary

Figure 7.16 Sechelt Intensive Conservation Diagrams

This page is from the "Vision Plan for Sechelt (BC)," John Talbot & Associates, prepared as a part of two intensives or charrettes in Sechelt. This series of drawings by the author represent examples of conservation zoning for residential areas; part of a review of existing subdivision ordinances in the district.

Conservation Design:

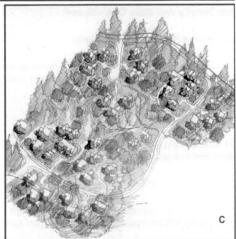

Rurban Hamlet:

A rurban hamlet is density neutral and arranges the units in a mixed building type cluster (referred to as "mixed density") on only a small portion of the overall site. For example, on a 10 acre site with an allowable density of six units per acre, or 60 units overall, it can locate all 60 units on four to six acres, saving or conserving six to four acres, respectively, in contiguous open space. All with conventional building types using detached, attached and multiplex homes.

The following sketches illustrate rurban hamlet development in the urban/rural interface. The right hand sketch shows multiplex housing (single-entry with three to five units, a shared front porch and shared garage); single-family detached bungalows, including one with an attached in-law suite; attached cottages; a shared garage; and a studio/potting building. Each unit has a private yard that connects to shared open space.

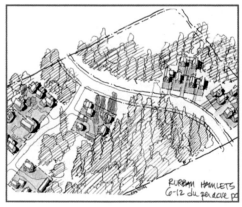
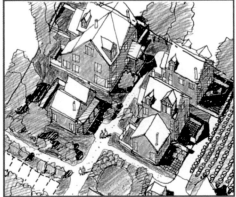

Figure 7.17 Sechelt Rurban Hamlet Diagrams

As a continuing discussion on subdivision ordinances, the design intensive explored and exemplified housing options, including the concept of Rurban Hamlets, development configurations intended to maintain current density (density neutral) and to increase the amount of contiguous conserved or protected open space. The axonometric drawings were fast and effective working from sketch plans, most completed on-site as a part of the design intensive.
Source: "Vision Plan for Sechelt (BC)," John Talbot & Associates, 2007; drawings by author.

– Team design interpretations of community input open to the public for specified periods
– Team preparation of community meeting presentations (PowerPoint and wall posters)

(Note: PowerPoint presentations and slide presentations are limited in their ability to "linger" on an image and have that image available for community dialogue while others are being viewed—thus the importance of the wall posters of material being digitally presented)

• Team and stakeholder committee review of community meeting results
• Team reinterpretation of community input with open periods for additional public input
• Team presentation of results to community at large for final feedback
• Preparation of final report.

Play-tool Factor

Key aspects of play during the intensive included the following:

1. Plan diagrams of information and relationships in a visual format with hand-drawn color graphics using digitally produced base maps at standard scales
2. Impromptu visual diagrams on butcher paper during brainstorming sessions by a graphic facilitation specialist, using caricatures, symbols and cartoons to capture ideas and concerns, engages participants' attention in a fun and often humorous manner

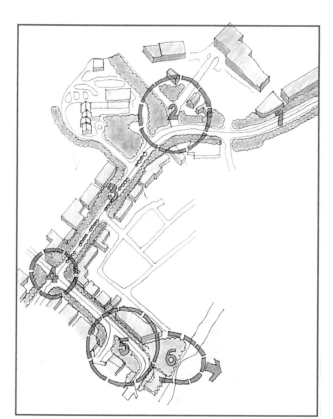

**Figure 7.18
Sechelt Gateway Diagram**

As a part of the intensives, the entries to Sechelt were explored as gateways to the "land between two waters," as the major coastal highway traverses through downtown Sechelt. The simple and fast plan diagram, pen and ink with color pencil on bond copies, provided a reference document for detailed axonometric and perspective drawings of key parts of the gateway corridor.

3. Impromptu visual diagrams and notes placed on digital wall maps during the interview process by team designers, strengthening the capture of ideas and issues with involvement of interviewees

4. Team design interpretive sessions: axonometric drawings, plan diagrams, some perspectives; fast, effective drawing process

5. Team design concept presentation drawings: same as above with full team cooperation.

CASE STUDY TWO: PROJECT SAFE HAVEN—TSUNAMI VERTICAL EVACUATION ON THE WASHINGTON COAST

The Cascadia subduction zone fault lies off the coast of North America and extends from British Columbia, CA to Northern California. This fault can generate a 9.0 magnitude earthquake. If this occurs close to shore, as is suggested to have happened by geological evidence in 1700, many coastal communities may not have time to evacuate based on the time available and damaged infrastructure, necessitating local evacuation alternative: Safe Havens.

- *Project Overview.* The University of Washington (Seattle) initiated a community-driven Planning and Design Studio process to plan for vertical tsunami evacuation facilities within coastal communities, "Project Safe Haven: Tsunami Vertical Evacuation on the Washington Coast" (UW, 2011–2013). Participants included the University of Washington, Washington State agencies, local communities, and tribal and county officials. The format for the studios for each community was a two-tiered design and planning intensive or charrette process. Tier 1 included a planning and science team working with communities to understand the tsunami hazard and to discuss possible location options for vertical evacuation structures. Tier 2 included the insertion of an urban design team to solidify those locations and prepare design options for vertical evacuation structures that served multiple public purposes as parks, festival areas and building components. The science team provided the planning and design teams with data indicating the size, capacity (ten square feet per person) and heights of vertical evacuation structures based on community locations along the coast.

- *Team Composition.* Lead urban planner and team for Tier 1 (graduate students, scientists); lead urban designer and team for Tier 2 (Architect-Planner, two or three graduate student assistants, representatives from state and local emergency manager agencies).

- *Time Period.* One- to three-day design charrettes on-site.[4]

- *Intensive Environment.* Community centers, tribal halls, conference centers in each community.

- *Overall Process.* Each design charrette or intensive was preceded by a "café" format public involvement activity for two days to inform and collect input from community members regarding the nature of issues and project objectives: wave dangers and specific information regarding wave heights by community location; and the café process identified potential sites within communities for Safe Haven structures (tower or berm). The café format is a series of interactive exercises for participants to share information and ideas in small groups.

- *Field Trips.* Field trips preceded each intensive to meet with local officials and survey the area and community built form and infrastructure.

- *Issue Identification Sessions:* Due to the hazardous and catastrophic nature of the subject (tsunami waves), geologists, wave specialists and other engineering experts provided information via digital graphics regarding the extent and severity of wave action for each community and neighborhood as a prelude to the café and intensives. This information provided the space program for structure heights and capacities of people (ten square feet allocated per person).

- *Community Revisitation of Selected Sites.* Based on field studies, updated engineering data and community facility needs and wants, the design team tested and modified sites selected at the cafés. Key issues focused on the multiple uses of structures and their integration into the built form (habitat viewing towers, festival facilities, school play berms, building components, etc.).

- *Design Team Interpretation.* The design team interpreted community needs with site context and tsunami engineering data to produce design concepts for each community, with sessions open to the public.

- *Community Meetings.* Final products were completed at the university from the design-intensive products rather than on-site due to budget and technical limitations. The presentation meetings allowed one final community input session for the design team prior to preparation of the final product.

Play-tool Factor

Key aspects of play during the intensive included the following.

A café process led by the lead faculty urban planner occurred over a two-day period. The participants circulated among a group of small tables facilitated by graduate students, emergency manager personnel and scientists set up to display and discuss specialized information regarding the tsunami and to select possible sites for community facilities. Each table then shared information with participants as they moved among the displays.

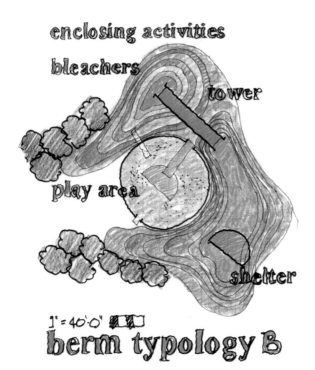

Figure 7.19
Long Beach Safe Haven Play Berm

The Long Beach Elementary School playground became a key site for a Safe Haven berm structure embedded into a play mound. Much of the mound will wash away due to tsunami wave action with the hardened Safe Haven berm remaining in place. The plan drawing was prepared during an on-site design intensive with direct community involvement.

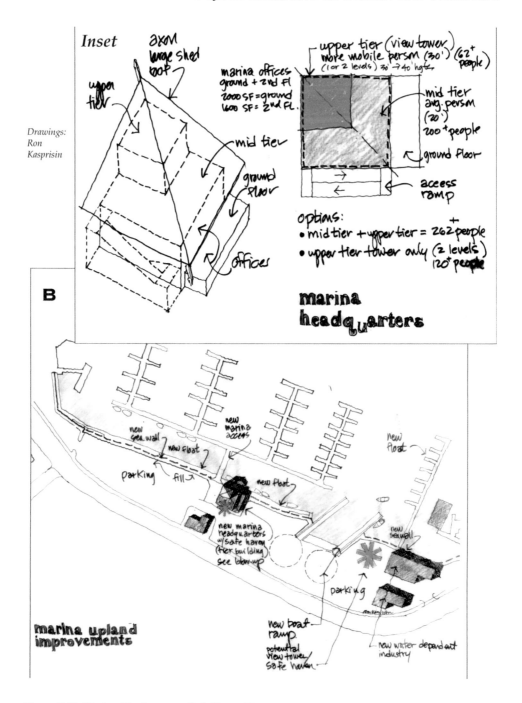

Figure 7.20 Marina Headquarters Safe Haven Diagram

As sites were identified based on possible infrastructure proposals or needs, Safe Haven opportunities were developed for community input. This illustration combines a reference plan diagram locating possible Safe Haven structures with an axonometric drawing of a Safe Haven structure embedded into a new building at the marina.

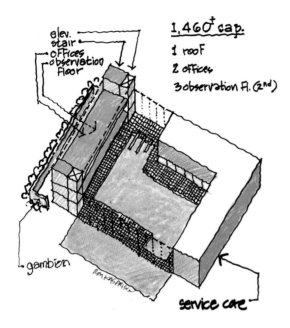

1,460⁺ cap.

1 roof

2 offices

3 observation fl. (2nd)

elev.
stair
offices
observation
floor

gambion

service core

SAFE HAVEN POOL
BUILDING COMPONENT

**Figure 7.21a
Building Component:
Community Pool**

This diagram and associated design ideas stimulated local officials and designers to incorporate Safe Haven structures into new building components. This idea developed during a design intensive and is now being applied to new school structures, fire stations and other public facilities. A portion of the building is hardened and the remaining parts are sacrificial in a major tsunami event. The axonometric drawing aided participants in understanding the concept and applying it to other situations.

**Figure 7.21b
Building Component:
Commercial**

During the charrette process, business owners asked about incorporating Safe Haven structures into new commercial developments. This axonometric drawing was done quickly in the meeting, illustrating various building components that can be "hardened" against earthquakes and tsunami wave action.

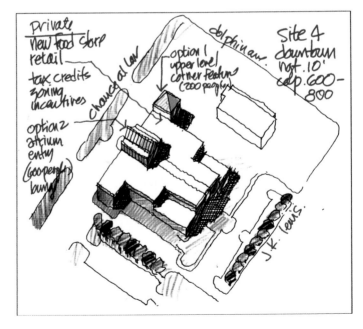

For the design intensives, the time frame varied from one to three days depending upon the attendance due to local population numbers. The design team worked on-site, visiting optional sites, and prepared plan diagrams and axonometric drawings of information and relationships in a visual format with hand-drawn color graphics using digitally produced base maps at standard scales, including the following:

1. Drawings with intensive participants at round tables using axonometric drawings, aerial photography and plan diagrams; limited use of perspective drawing
2. Construction paper cut-outs of berms and towers for community participants to arrange and "play with" on aerial photographs to standard scale; recorded with camera, constructed by graduate students
3. Cardboard and construction paper examples of berm structures at standard scale for community visualization purposes, constructed by graduate students
4. Color pencil additive for presentation purposes; drawings later scanned and included in final reports.

From these on-site intensive design concepts, a number of sites were selected for detailed architecture, landscape architecture and engineering design work. This project has resulted in the implementation of a number of Safe Haven projects in communities in Pacific and Grays Harbor Counties.

The role of play in community involvement projects has the following positive aspects:

1. Participants can be stimulated by the skills used in the development of ideas and concepts through visual methodologies. Even rough or rudimentary sketches and/or diagrams are foreign to many laypeople and there is appreciation for both the ability to use the drawing skill and for the representation of information and ideas contained in the visualizations.
2. Play can be an interactive and group activity as well as individual. This allows participants to be drawn into the authorship of ideas as they participate in play-activities such as moving cardboard parts around on an aerial photograph.
3. The *arousal motivation factor* applies to the participant-observer as well as the designer-player in that the excitement gained from observing or participating in a visualization or play process can lead to further stimulation and participation. Sitting in a meeting watching a PowerPoint presentation of pie charts and bar charts after a long day of work may not do a lot to stimulate further involvement and public interaction.

Other play-tools useful in design charrettes can range from simple to complex assignments for stakeholders and general participants. Examples include the following:

*   Playing with cardboard/paper model cut-outs in small groups with associative dialogue and recording. Criticisms are not allowed and all ideas have merit (facilitator/referee).
*   Locating issues and opportunities on a wall map with dots or stickies, while an old and overused method, still fascinates people and informs them of spatial references regarding key information; it is not sufficient in and of itself as an interactive method.
*   Facilitating progressive round-table stories of community culture and events, current and historical, can inform and lead to discoveries of cultural resources.

- Facilitating progressive round-table stories of possible futures for a community enable people to work with other community members on the construction of a probable scenario that is a gestalt, a thirdspace never before realized, initially without anticipated outcomes, emerging as the story-play continues; accompanying visual characterizations strengthen this method.

- The use of traditional games applied to charrette play activities. An example is the treasure hunt. During a charrette process, usually while design team members are working in semi-seclusion, participants are given a list of objects, issues, problems and opportunities to uncover in the community. They find, photograph and record context settings for review and discussion in a later portion of the charrette, and the results are shared in a summarization session prior to returning to interaction with the design team.

- Acting out a given situation in the community that highlights an issue, opportunity or emergent phenomena, found through on-site discoveries. Examples that I have had planning students participate in include the following:

  o Putting on a skit in a local pub for locals, students and other interested participants (a lot of fun was had by all and the skits were revealing for the identification of historic cultural aspects)

  o Constructing a "book" using photo-collages of a given or selected topic related to the larger project to communicate issues and opportunities for placement in the local library

  o The same may be done with videos, music, etc.

  o The wall collage where participants paste or tack ideas onto a wall map with note cards or symbol cut-outs to specific sites or districts within the larger project area, sharing and piggy-backing ideas as the collage grows and changes; this is repeated in cycles as emerging associations and relationships are observed, shared and recorded, and repeated again

  o These all require planning and structure for the play-activity to be as free and meaningful as possible.

Development and Building Typologies

Play has rules and boundaries. These can always change and evolve during the play-activity. Beginning a play session with them provides structure and a point of origin—a beginning. In the design fields, and in specific domains such as architecture and urban design, the play requires accuracy and thoughtfulness based on the analysis of cultural, spatial and historic information. In the (urban) design fields, there are conventions and typologies (principles for organizational relationships) for various uses that provide guidelines for design and planning experimentation. These real objects can change with discoveries of novel solutions; they are important places to begin the path of discovery.

Built form conventions and typologies include the following:

- Grid circulation system
- Curvilinear circulation system
- Site development configurations
- Residential building typologies
- Commercial and office typologies
- Open space typologies

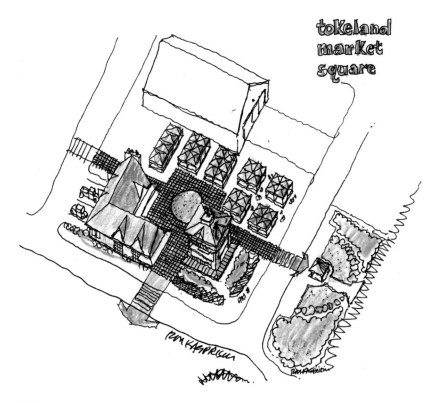

Figure 7.22
Tokeland Festival Market Safe Haven

This axonometric illustrates a Safe Haven tower as part of a proposed market area on the waterfront in Tokeland, WA. The team worked with a local economic development group during the intensive to develop and incorporate the tower into the market area. It also serves as a wildlife observation tower and information booth—a fast, effective axonometric drawing, with color added to a bond copy during the intensive.

Figure 7.23 Golf Course Safe Haven

This is a fun example of a quick sectional sketch drawn for a group of intensive participants who were golf enthusiasts. The coastal communities have numerous courses due to the high visitor volumes during the summer. The Safe Haven berm is embedded into a tee-off mound with sloping ramp as access.

- Support services such as parking lots, structures, etc.
- And many more.

As play begins, symbolic objects can be denoted as various typologies that apply to a specific domain. For example, when experimenting with a residential development design, the objects that are being manipulated can reflect the needs or wants of a client, community or market demand. A cardboard cut-out for townhouses may be twenty feet wide and thirty-two feet wide per unit, stacked two high. Another cut-out for a double-loaded corridor stacked flat residential building can range from sixty to over eighty feet wide by various width increments based on the number of units per floor along the corridor. This specificity adds value and accuracy to the playful manipulation of objects on a made-up game board.

In (urban) design, typology objects can represent buildings, open spaces, parking lots and other associated use-objects. For the play to be accurate, the play-elements require real descriptions regarding typology forms, as these typologies represent principles of organization of specific uses. As the play progresses, these typologies can dissolve as new ideas emerge—hybrids and even novel solutions. As I discuss in *Urban Design* (Kasprisin, 2011), typologies are a valid place to begin, and are not absolute or sacrosanct.

When working with faculty on design competitions in architecture school, play was dominant in the design process, especially for short-time event competitions. The preferred play-tools were dominated by pen-and-ink drawing and model-making with symbolic objects. Drawing was done freehand with Graphos and Rapidograph technical pens—attributing an artful (aroused and aesthetic) representation to presentation drawings. The cardboard and construction papers are and still remain versatile materials. As symbolic objects, they have the capacity to represent many urban objects, their characteristics and shapes; and the specificity of those objects was (is) critical to the creative potential of the play. This is more than historic methodology—it remains classic object-learning.

Understanding the Grid as Flexible Typology

I use the grid extensively in the book as a spatial reference starting point for students. It is an effective means to establish an underlying spatial mathematics to a design and planning context. A key point for students to understand is the flexibility of the grid to adjust to varying contextual influences—it is less rigid than assumed.

Building and Development Typologies

Based on the analysis of given space program requirements of a design or plan, derived from client/community needs, the uses of space can be identified along with a range of building types that accommodate those uses. For example, if a medium residential density is indicated as a part of the program, the design team can identify a range of building types from townhomes to stacked flats in double-loaded corridor or stacked flats common lobby configurations. Each has a range of preferred or experienced dimensions. These can be reflected in the shapes of the symbolic objects—cardboard in these examples—as play-pieces.

The symbolic objects and materials such as corrugated cardboard can be fashioned into many different typology templates. The last building-type example uses Lego plastic bricks to construct a live/work composition in cluster form.

Figure 7.24
The Flexible Grid Typology

In this illustration, the grid consists of (a) a rectangular grid, (b) a square grid, (c) a broken or partial grid, and (d) a meandering grid.

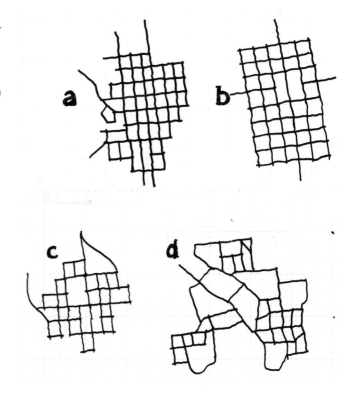

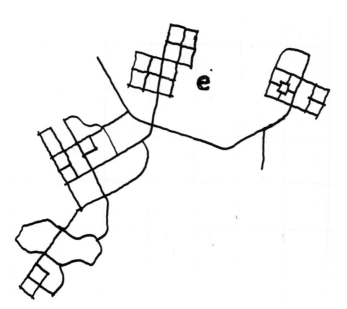

Figure 7.25 The Composite Grid Typology

Grids can be assembled in various compositions for different parts, yet retain the key characteristics of the grid mathematics.

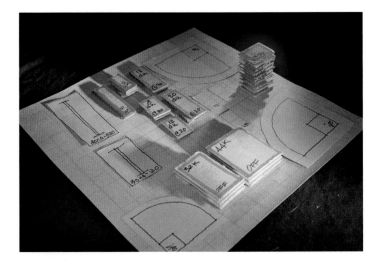

Figure 7.26 Basic Typology Shapes

The cardboard cut-outs represent various types of buildings that can be made into templates and manipulated into various compositions during design intensives or internal design and planning explorations. The examples range from townhouses (attached two- and three-storey structures each with a separate entrance); double-loaded corridor stacked flats (vertical layers of one-storey dwelling units organized around a central corridor with units along both sides); high-rise residential buildings (typically with a central core for vertical circulation, many with a mixed-use pedestal at ground level). In the high-rise template, without spacers it is a twelve-storey building and with spacers it becomes twenty-four storeys in height—fast and flexible. The designer or planner can develop multiple typology templates for play from flexible materials such as cardboard, blocks, etc. Other templates displayed include office typologies, retail facilities, parking lots and structures, and recreational fields, including volleyball and tennis courts and baseball fields.

Figure 7.27 Office Typologies

Office configurations vary considerably based on the projected types of uses (basic open office space, laboratory and institutional space, etc.). This is where the flexibility of the symbolic object is a distinct advantage when playing with design experiments. Establishing a basic grid framework can help set a beginning point for office space, increasing or decreasing the total number of grid cells based on square-feet program requirements.

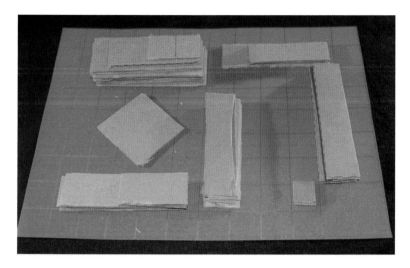

Figure 7.28 Shape Variability and Flexibility in Composition

Once the templates are constructed, their play may be varied and flexible—moving pieces around a game board to form various compositions that meet program requirements respond to context and other factors. In this example, the symbolic object templates from the previous illustrations are combined to form a mixed-use building complex.

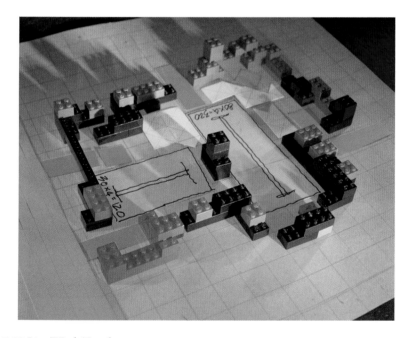

Figure 7.29 Live/Work Typology

I find the Lego bricks and Halsam's Wood Building Bricks to be among the most flexible objects for urban design studies due to their pre-made sizes and interlocking characteristics. This example explores a live/work cluster complex using the Lego bricks, accompanied by paper cut-out templates for parking areas. Again, this is valuable in particular for group interactions: community meetings and team design sessions.

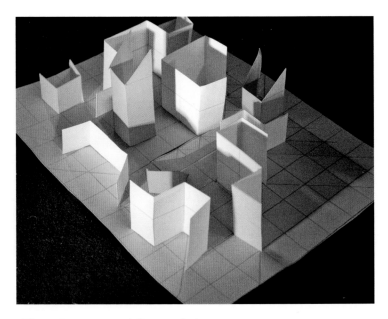

Figure 7.30a Plazas, Concourses and Courtyards A

Quick experiments in open space compositions can begin with semi-abstract paper cut-outs with construction paper and tag or railroad board easily cut with scissors or knife for scoring the folded corners. The plaza may be used to connect existing buildings and other vertical features or used to structure new buildings and features.

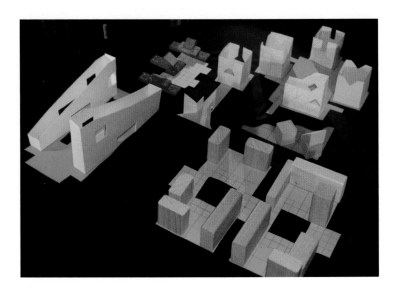

Figure 7.30b Plazas, Concourse and Courtyards B

I simply used construction paper to assemble various templates for plazas, concourses and courtyards that may be used over and over again in discovery model processes. They also combine well with varying materials and objects.

Figure 7.31 Promenades and Axes

The promenade is often a linear structure that can form an edge (waterfront) or be the axial compositional structure for an urban development, as in this illustration. In this example I highlight the structuring capabilities of the various axes, from the main axis to the crossing yellow axis to the smaller green (landscape) cross axis.

Open Space

Open space typologies are as varied as buildings, from plazas to courtyards to concourses to promenades to natural areas. They all have specific physical characteristics depending upon their uses. These play-pieces may also be constructed in increments for flexibility and manipulation. I illustrate only a few using basic grid shapes and vertical planes to define their edges.

The elements that can be represented with cardboard and construction paper are limited only by the imagination. They are easily manipulated in a play-activity, with outcomes easily recorded and saved for later advancement.

Object-learning Activators for Play-activities

The design/planning process begins with *need (problem), program (what and how much) and context* (see Figure 7.1). They represent the initial organizational relationships at the onset of the CPS process. *Context* begins the process of relating the organizational relationships to the spatial framework or spatial reality within which the *need* occurs. It is multi-dimensional and far more complex than "setting." As context begins to influence initial spatial compositions, the designer/planner begins the form composition process, bringing everything together into a cohesive whole: not easy. Form and composition clues emanate from context, need, program and design/planning criteria (typology, assembly, phasing, etc.).

There are aids that can provide starting points for conceptual explorations of creative outcomes. I call these object-learning activators—actions and principles to begin the exploration of spatial aspects of the design/planning process. Activators may be considered initial rules or starting points and spatial verbs to begin the play process, and may be changed and altered as the play progresses. These activators are used in the following section as guides for exercises and hopefully will stimulate additional activators for the reader.

It bears repeating that design/planning have spatial outcomes and are not merely intellectual analytical processes. The composition process relates and integrates organizational and structural relationships into a cohesive and coherent whole. The following list suggests ways to engage and guide object-learning in association with context, need and program.

Object-learning activators include and are not limited to the following:

1.   Do anything (the Phu Process)
2.   Manipulation of primary shapes
3.   Compositional structures
4.   Transformational actions
5.   Metaphors
6.   Remote association linkages
7.   Bridging as thirdspace

The main categories that I suggest as activators are summarized and discussed in the following sections.

1.   *Do Anything (Maltese Class)*
There is almost always a notion or aspiration or kernel of an idea that initiates play activities. As a loosening-up exercise, the process described in Chapter 5, removes the pressure of focus and frees the mind/body to be open to any emergent composition, starting and building on an initial "unnamed" form(s) toward a composition. In addition to the Phu Surrender series, I executed a hybrid in watercolor: I did study the image and composition of a grizzly bear head in pen and ink. Because I was in a funk, unable to let go and be loose with my painting, I reviewed the studies, then went to a blank sheet of watercolor paper and, without any references to view, I began painting, starting with the eye of the bear. I proceeded to continue the painting exercise without any pencil lines or frame of reference. The first half of the process was more analytical/strategizing and the second half was letting go and a suspension of analytical thinking. This was almost a "do anything" exercise and it helped me let go of some over-concentration that was interfering with my painting efforts.

2.   *Manipulation of Primary Shapes*

The primary shapes (circle/sphere, square/cube, line/axis) and their derivatives are excellent starting points for design exploration, especially for less experienced students. The basic initial rule is to maintain the essential characteristics of the primary shape during the compositional play activity, pushing those characteristics almost to "breaking point." This helps students understand the level of complexity that can be accomplished with those shape elements and their essential physical characteristics. For example, the circle may be identified simply by a center and an arc or radius; the square by three corners, etc. The following two- and three-dimensional examples demonstrate the compositional sequence from the start to a more complex composition with a circle, square and line or axis.

3.   *Compositional Structures*

Compositional structures are specific geometric frameworks that assemble or provide the specific structural composition for organizational relationships. Rudolph Arnheim (1969) defined the structures as two: the circle and the square, primary shapes. Goldstein (1989) expanded this to fifteen categories that all emanate from the circle, square and line (author's addition). These include the following and are valuable in establishing a starting point for any composition, and can be manipulated to suit most spatial contexts. They, like the primary shapes, can be manipulated almost to breaking point without losing their structural and geometric characteristics—part of the fun. They include the following:

- The Grid
- The Circle
- The Triangle
- The Diamond
- Central Location
- Two Centers
- The Bridge
- The Cantilever
- The Even Spread
- The Radial Burst
- Diagonality (dominance)
- Horizontality (dominance)
- Verticality (dominance)
- Curvilinear Dominant
- The L-shape.

(Goldstein, 1989, pp. 202–233)

4. *Transformational Actions*

Transformational actions change a basic composition through various actions and are summarized in Kasprisin (2011). Cropley and Cropley (2009) expand those actions from a different perspective in creative problem-solving processes. They all have spatial applications and manifestations. The examples that follow illustrate their power in object-teaching. They are as follows:

- Subtractive
- Additive
- Transference
- Emphasis
- Symmetry/asymmetry
- Consolidation
- Animation
- Superimposition
- Dimensional change/size
- Substitution
- Fragmentation
- Segmentation
- Isolation
- Distortion
- Remote associations.

In architecture, landscape architecture, urban design and other related fields the subtractive, additive and dimensional change/size transformations are or have been reliable conventions of composing form. We will play with others to experiment with their spatial ramifications as activators in object-learning.

Additive/Subtractive

Additive and subtractive transformational actions are especially useful when dealing with larger masses or volumes, or dense urban built form. They may be at the scale of a plaza in basic two dimensions, and in three dimensions as a building or an urban block. Working on a two-dimensional grid or a three-dimensional grid matrix can assist in beginning a composition.

Transference

Transference may be used to convey an object, symbol, etc. from one surface or object to another as in an impression. Transference is used extensively in environmental art design where symbols and images can be imprinted onto glass, metal and other surfaces to convey a message.

Emphasis

Emphasis is the process of calling attention to something, making it important. In art this can be accomplished through value contrast, placing the lightest next to the darkest value for maximum contrast: *emphasis.* In three-dimensional art and design, size contrast, clustering and positive/negative play-actions to mention a few can accomplish the same effect.

Symmetry/Asymmetry

Asymmetry is the activator which requires any composition that is symmetrical to be made asymmetrical; and any that is asymmetrical to be made even more asymmetrical. A part of this activator strategy is to reverse and break out of a given pattern to explore the polarity for alternate and/or complementary ideas. In its application, I identify key principles within the initial or "before" composition and retain them in the new "after" composition.

Consolidation

Consolidation has a number of activator potentials: uniting objects, shapes, etc. into a whole system; combining components into a single entity; bringing together objects, shapes and patterns into a dense or compact mass.

Animation

The broader definition of animation (*American Dictionary*) is the act or process of imparting life, spirit, motion and action to objects or an idea through objects, drawing, movement as in film, etc.

Superimposition

Superimposition is to lay or place something over something else (*American Dictionary*). It is an excellent way to begin a play-activity at many levels. Primary shapes can be superimposed over one another as well as compositional structures (essentially derivatives of the primary shapes with structuring capabilities). It adds a level of complexity to compositions and can be a means of responding to complex spatial contexts as a starting point for design.

Dimensional Change/Size

Changing the dimension of an object can affect its size, proportions and other characteristics—a square to a rectangle, a circle to an oval, etc.

Substitution

Substitution is the replacing of one element, object, etc. for another. A construction is used in place of another—replacing a circle within a grid for variety, or substituting one housing typology for another to alter a larger pattern.

Fragmentation

Fragmentation means to break or separate something into pieces. This is an interesting challenge for object-learning in that it goes against most conventions of putting something together. Fragmentation can serve as a testing mechanism for a design composition, or as a departure point.

Segmentation

A segment is the portion of a shape or object that still retains characteristics of the larger or parent shape, i.e., a portion of a circle defined by an arc and a chord; or a part of a line extending between two points as in a dashed line—a series of segments.

Isolation

Isolation is the act of making something stand apart, insulated; or to identify or distinguish something like an object or shape as being different, standing alone.

Distortion

Distortion is to deviate from what is normal, to misshapen. This may have applications in relation to emphasis in order to draw attention to some object or pattern.

Remote Associations

Remote associations are unexpected links that combine to form a new and distinctly different outcome. These are best discovered during the play process as they present themselves in various compositions.

Experiments in Object-learning Play

Principles for Experimentation

In the following exercises and examples, a number of key principles guide the process:

1. Play as a free-activity (no failure, uncertain outcome)
2. Initial rule(s) subject to constant change
3. Play initiated with an object-learning activator
4. A pluralistic use of play-tools, each with a skill variant based on the physical characteristics of the tool
5. The emergent design is influenced by the individual tool assembly characteristics within the plurality of play-tools.

In the Adult Playfulness Trait Scale (APTS) (Shen et al., 2014) the ability to play does not stem from an individual, non-reducible quality; instead, "a trait can be more appropriately considered a unique combination of interrelated cognitive qualities, qualities that often function together to drive a particular type of behavior . . . multifaceted yet remain itself distinctively a trait" (Shen et al., 2014, p. 346).

In the APTS, adult playfulness emanates from three traits: fun-seeking motivation, uninhibitedness and spontaneity. In the fun-seeking aspect, fun belief (believing in the value of fun in life), initiative (actively creating fun activities) and reactivity (being responsive to fun stimuli) are critical. Given these trait characteristics, let us explore the key principles with which they interact and are guided. Under cognitive qualities, I add the joy of thinking with the senses through physical manipulation of objects and tools.

Key principles in these activities include the following:

1. Whole mind–body thinking: cognitive pluralism, with the senses using manual dexterity
2. Play in a specific domain: in a specific context (that can change as play progresses)
3. Uncertainty: no goals or predetermined outcomes
4. Playthings: select tools that are enjoyable, challenging, sensual, fun (it's allowed!)
5. Begin with basic rules and be prepared to change them as play progresses
6. Begin with limits and boundaries: limits and boundaries can change as play progresses
7. Stuck? Move anywhere or anything in any direction: just move!
8. Include transformation principles as experiments (changing dimensions, adding or subtracting elements, defining polarities, merging, reversal, inside/outside, etc.)—any activity to prevent premature decision-making on a solution
9. Arousal motivation: be aware of your enjoyable stimulations and follow their lead
10. Utilize the elements and principles of design composition, i.e., structural principles (see Kasprisin, 2011).

EXPERIMENT 1: DO ANYTHING

EXERCISE 7.1: DO ANYTHING (SEE FIGURE 7.32)

- *Intent*. To evolve a drawing image that has an underlying story component with no predetermined structure or outline; this is a fun exercise to loosen students up or for office staff to relax with on a Friday afternoon.
- *Rules*. Each participant (or instructor) selects a broad category, such as science fiction, without any other hints, clues or advancements; participants are then asked to begin a drawing process with a simple shape and perceive a next step from the results of the first.
- *Play-tools*. Drawing materials (paper, mylar, vellum, etc. and pen/ink tools)—no erasures.

The only initial activator used in this experiment is a simple shape drawn with the pen as a first step.

EXPERIMENT 2: MANIPULATION OF PRIMARY SHAPES

EXERCISE 7.2: PRIMARY SHAPE MANIPULATION (SEE FIGURES 7.33 THROUGH 7.38B)

- *Intent*. For each of the primary shapes, experiment with how they can be made more complex without losing their primary characteristics.
- *Rules*. Begin to play within those shapes as cut-outs, making changes as emerging factors indicate. Don't hesitate to change the primary shape frameworks.
- *Play-tools*. Poster board, construction paper, scissors and glue or tape.

I start the students off with two-dimensional construction paper cut-outs, asking them to push the characteristics of the shapes without losing them. The circle, square and line/axis are represented in the example and there are hundreds of variations. This can guide students in pursuing complexity without

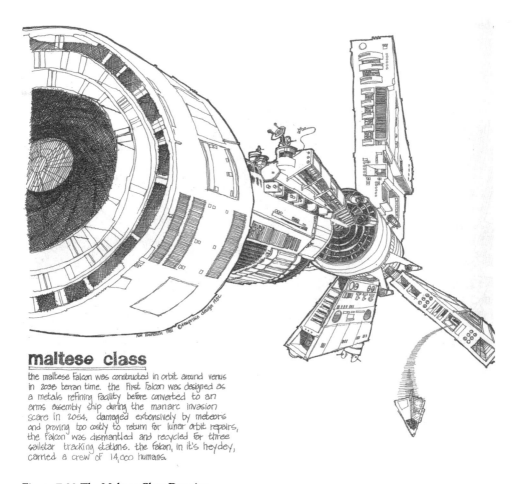

maltese class

the maltese Falcon was constructed in orbit around venus
in 2038 terran time. the first Falcon was designed as
a metals refining facility before converted to an
arms assembly ship during the manarc invasion
scare in 2054, damaged extensively by meteors
and proving too costly to return for lunar orbit repairs,
the Falcon was dismantled and recycled for three
sailstar tracking stations. the falcon, in it's heydey,
carried a crew of 14,000 humans.

Figure 7.32 The Maltese Class Drawing

*This example is similar to "The Phu Surrender" in Urban Design (2011) wherein the drawing is
evolutionary and not preconceived in any manner except to construct a science fiction image/story element,
beginning only with a simple shape. It is an experiment with a progressive play-activity, activated in this case
by a simple notion and begun with a simple circle shape.*

losing the principles of the primary shapes. Let us start with simple two- and three-dimensional
manipulations of the circle, square and line/axis.

Remember that the sequence of semi-abstract to semi-real is an important step in working with
discovery models as clues and new directions are opened up through the process of construction and
observation. A colleague asked me why I did not have students make the models. I replied that I did
not wish to dictate an outcome for myself or a student and wanted to experience how the process model
leads to discovery. This is not about over-focus or perfection; it is about openness, flow and following
the discovery of ideas within the model construction. Do not be precious about your products!

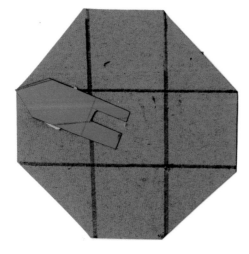

Figure 7.33 Primary Shape Composition: Circle (Two Dimensions)

The circle is first represented in two dimensions, with a center and an arrow with an implied arc and center. This is a simplified version of what can be done by the students as they extend the boundaries of "circle."

Figure 7.34 Primary Shape Composition: Circle (Three Dimensions)

I used Halsam's Building Bricks, right-angled fractals, to construct a three-dimensional circle primary shape, adding variety in heights and implying arc configurations with an obvious center point (square).

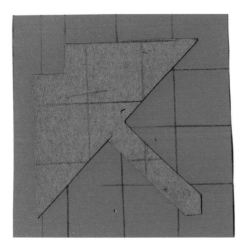

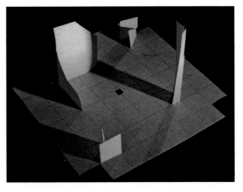

Figure 7.35 Primary Shape Composition: Square (Two Dimensions)

In this experiment the two-dimensional cut-outs highlight three corners with a diagonal and a voided corner. A simple example again that has many diverse variations, limited only by the imagination of the student. Notice the color complements or opposites used to increase the contrast between the two main shapes: arrow and circle.

Figure 7.36 Primary Shape Composition: Square (Three Dimensions)

In the three-dimensional paper cut-outs five squares are represented: (1) the void in the middle; (2) the basic grid; (3) the larger grid with voids as corners; (4) in red, a square represented by two corners with variety; and (5) in orange, a square defined by an implied diagonal. The square geometry may not be obvious to the observer or participant within the spatial construct and the mathematics is the underlying framework for composition.

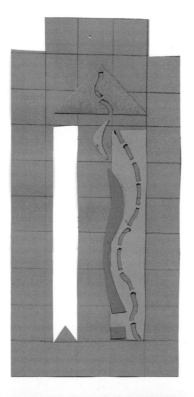

Figure 7.37 Primary Shape Composition: Line (Two Dimensions)

There are at least six lines represented in the construction paper composition: from the larger arrow composite to the smaller, dashed void: straight, curved, implied, dashed, composite, etc. The "line" is a powerful compositional structure, as is indicated and experimented with later in the chapter.

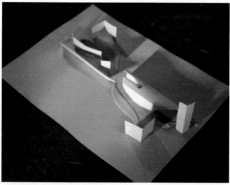

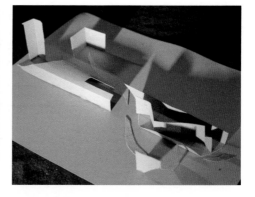

Figure 7.38a Primary Shape Composition: Line (Three Dimensions)

The three-dimensional version is a segmented channel void with an implied axis superimposed by a curvilinear vertical plane. To dramatize the axis and create an intersect point or place, a curvilinear serpentine form crosses the main axis with closed and semi-closed termini at each end—complexity within a simple axial configuration concept.

Figure 7.38b Primary Shape Composition: Line

This is a second view from a different angle of the axial catalyst.

EXERCISE 7.3: COMPOSITIONAL STRUCTURES

- *Intent.* Within a given spatial context—an urban block pattern—use the compositional structures as object-learning activators to begin a play session with initial rules (structure), adding other activators as the play and discovery model progresses. For example, establish a center for a radial burst, two corners and a diagonal for the square structure, etc. as starting points.

- *Rules.* Within the influences of need and space programming (fictional in this example), use the compositional structure on a spatial reference plane as a starting point, making changes as emerging factors indicate.

- *Play-tools.* Poster board, scissors, construction paper, railroad or tag board, corrugated cardboard and glue or tape; Halsam's and Playskool Blocks followed by Legos.

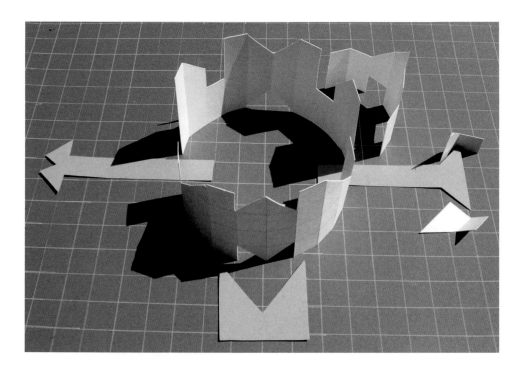

Figure 7.39 Primary Shape Compositional Structure: Circle

Working on a one-inch grid, using poster board for the main model, I began with a simple circular shape consisting of two curved vertical planes, adding repetition with variety to the cut-outs. I added complexity to the composition with a radial burst superimposition and construction paper directional axis. The radial burst structure gives an added directional movement to the composition. I subtracted portions of the circle to add additional complexity while retaining the circle's principles.

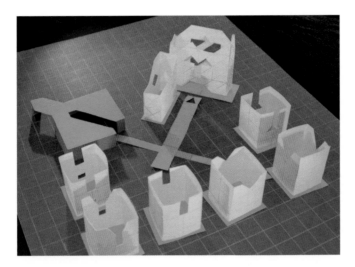

Figure 7.40 Primary Shape with Square as Urban Complex

I enjoyed working with the colors of the construction paper and proceeded to use the same for the square compositional structure. Remember: the square in this exercise is more than a shape—it is a composing structure or rule of assembly. As in the line/axial structure exercise, I began with the simple semi-abstract paper model as part of the activator—a point to get me started on manipulating shapes. The square is defined by two or three corners and a simple outline of building forms, as well as a diagonal vector (all options and not all necessary in the same composition). A grid pattern was used for both horizontal and vertical planes with an added diagonal grid on the verticals for variety. I also utilized directional movement principles with circulation paths and repetition with variety in the building forms. This discovery model represents an added step from semi-abstract to specific development configuration. Red represents commercial and yellow represents residential uses.

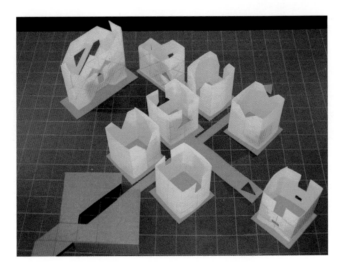

Figure 7.41 Primary Shape with Square Consolidation as Urban Complex

Building from the previous experiment, I used similar objects to "consolidate" or compress the square compositional structure, the activator being the consolidation. The square structure remains as the building forms are moved to the interior of the block.

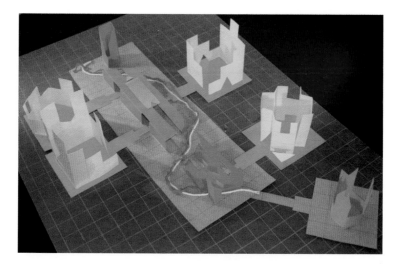

Figure 7.42a Primary Shape with Line/Axis as Urban Complex 1

Increasing the complexity of the exercise, I started with a basic notion of a mixed-use complex, residential and commercial. The activator is the line or axis represented by the open and semi-enclosed arcade (red construct). I used a semi-abstract exercise done previously as a starting point due to its variety of forms and positive/negative shapes. This is constructed on green paper with a one-inch grid as a spatial reference. Based on four serendipity "portals," I cut into the arcade axis and constructed four varying residential blocks, each connecting to a portal. As a conceptual discovery model, it offers opportunities for further specification and directions. I used a grid frame both in the plan and elevations. On two of the building blocks I changed the grid and added diagonals for variety and as a demonstration on how that spatial reference can influence design ideas.

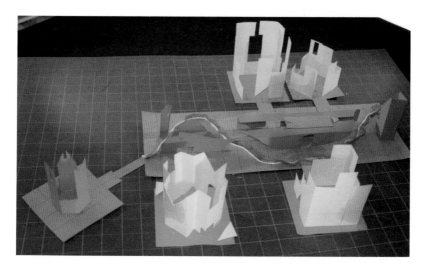

Figure 7.42b Primary Shape with Line/Axis

This is a second view from a different angle of the assemblage of an urban complex using the axial catalyst as framework.

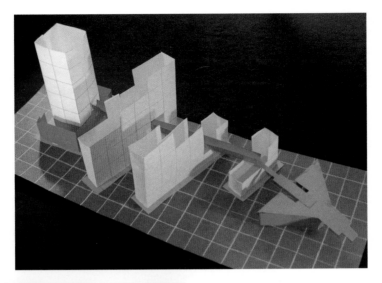

Figure 7.43a *(above)* **Primary Shape with Line/Axis as Urban Complex 2**

I actually returned to a previous experiment that I was not satisfied with and, after working with the square compositional structure, decided to engage it again, learning from previous attempts. In this example, I used a series of separate buildings aligned to form a linear composition using gradation, angular placement of the buildings, dimensional changes, and a connecting linear axis to dramatize the axial structure. Other components may then be attached as appropriate to the space program.

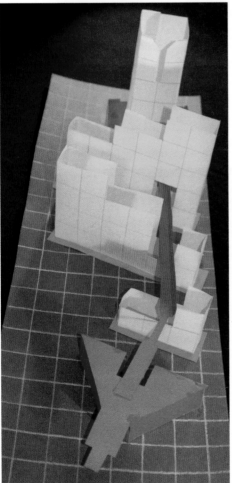

Figure 7.43b *(left)* **Primary Shape with Line/Axis**

This is a second view from a different angle of the assemblage of an urban complex using the axial catalyst as framework.

Figure 7.44a Lake City Gateway: Grid Framework

This exercise uses Playskool blocks (Milton Bradley) for a Gateway building complex in the Lake City neighborhood of Seattle. Based on a program for housing types and related retail facilities I chose Playskool wood blocks because of their variation in size and shape, appropriate scale applications that provided more flexibility in building configurations. The context is angular and low scale with streets coming in at varying degrees. As a starting point I oriented all the buildings to the southwest and repeated a set typology of medium-height building with low-rise building—essentially a repetition with minor variety.

Figure 7.44b Lake City Gateway: Grid Framework

This is a second view from a different angle of the assemblage of an urban gateway to a Seattle urban village complex.

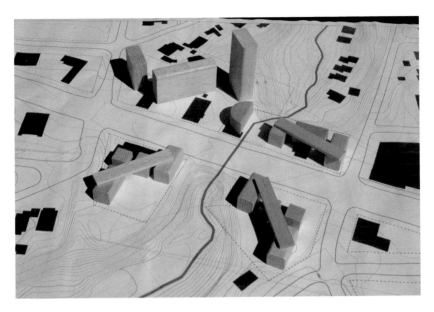

Figure 7.45a Lake City Gateway: Radial Burst Activator

Focusing on the creek ravine and a new community center, I played with a radial burst activator to connect the various parcels. With the center established, the burst emanated outward with four radii, repeating a basic pattern in three- and increasing dimensional changes with larger buildings in the final radius.

Figure 7.45b Lake City Gateway: Radial Burst Activator

This is a second view from a different angle of the assemblage of an urban gateway to a Seattle urban village complex using a radial burst to unify the various obtuse street angles.

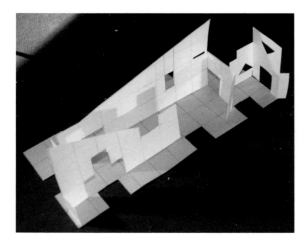

Figure 7.46 The L-shape in an Urban Grid (A)

Using poster board, this series begins with linear vertical plane constructs. I conducted a number of quick explorations until I found some harmony in the shape. The initial versions were busy and distracting with the angular top pieces, and were informative. I used a vertical grid to guide the experiment where it provided places to cut void shapes and places to bend the construct. The L-shape began to emerge as I repeated the planar constructs with variations that eliminated the angular top pieces and limited them to the interior of the plane (A).

Figure 7.47 *(right)* **The L-shape Expanded (B)**

The previous composition was expanded by working with multiple vertical plane segments for the long end of the "L," enabling them to be moved around, reversed, etc., eventually leading to the completed L-shape composition. I decided to keep the short length of the "L" simple and, in contrast to the more complex, longer length, including a simple diagonal highlighting the joint of the two segments; this was then augmented through contrast with a reverse direction angular shape.

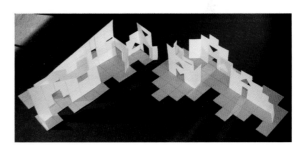

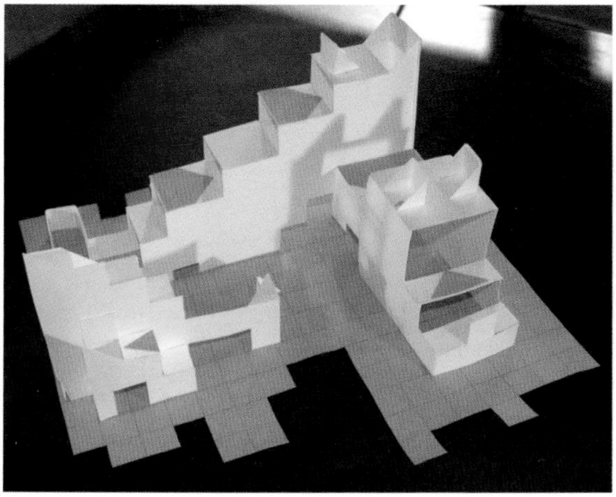

Figure 7.48 The L-shape with Additional Massing

The initial vertical plane concept is expanded in this experiment, adding massing and articulation to the previous experiment and playing with added shapes to highlight the main mass (and reduce its mass impact).

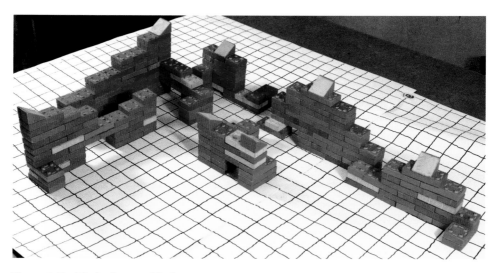

Figure 7.49a The L-shape in Blocks

I then used the paper construct exercises to experiment with the same compositional structure in Halsam's Wood Building Bricks (blocks), adding complexity with the different material represented by individual pieces or fractals. This process can continue through the evolution of the building or block complex, adding more detail and refinement to the design composition.

Figure 7.49b The L-shape in Blocks

A second view of the L-shape manipulation.

Figure 7.50 The Bridge

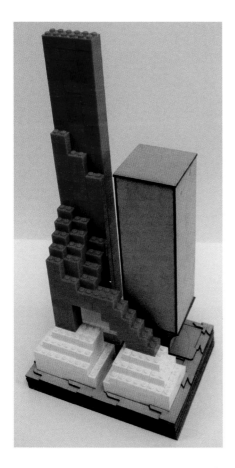

I enjoyed watching graduate student Tiernan Martin evolve his design composition in our urban design studio, working back and forth from process models (both chipboard and Lego Blocks) to digital graphic (BIM) as he replicated the model design digitally and "tested" the various model experiments. The outcome was unexpected and novel in that he arrived at a hybrid building typology for high-rise structures: the classic tower, the transparent and pedestrian-oriented base arcade, and the bridging device that connects and relates the two normative typologies. The bridging device contains residential uses as a separate and yet integral building component.
Model source: Tiernan Martin.

This series of experiments represent an evolutionary expansion of a semi-abstract beginning to a more sophisticated or developed design composition. The series begins with a playful experimentation in tag board of an L-shaped compositional structure, a derivative of the square. From the initial paper construct I added massing to the emerging design concept. Parts of this second phase were satisfactory and others were somewhat bulky in my perception, while others provided ideas for another direction and experiment. From the second phase I used Halsam's Building Bricks to play with another fractal (the wood blocks), adding more detail and texture to the massing. This process can continue through even more sophisticated explorations of the first design notions, changing materials and play-tools as the design composition matures.

EXERCISE 7.4: TRANSFORMATIONAL ACTIONS

- *Intent.* Within a given spatial context—an urban block grid pattern, for example, or other spatial reference system—begin a play-activity for each of the following transformational actions: additive/subtractive, emphasizing and superimposition.
- *Rules.* See the examples and discussions below for guides to exercises.
- *Play-tools.* Poster board, scissors, corrugated cardboard and glue or tape, Halsam's Bricks, Playskool Blocks followed by Legos.

Figure 7.51 Transforming Compositions through Additive/Subtractive Actions Original

This is always an enjoyable exercise for students as they observe through playfulness how a solid mass (composed of fractal parts—cubes and rectangular volumes augmented by half-cubes) can be transformed by taking parts away and adding them in other locations in the composition. All parts are used in the "after" composition. I used grid construction paper to provide a foreground for the two masses and as an organizing horizontal plane to connect them. This exercise was assembled and manipulated quickly (in a matter of minutes). Caution: large Labrador Retrievers like to bump into table legs!

Figure 7.52 Transforming Compositions through Additive/Subtractive Actions Modified

The subtractive pieces are rearranged into new configurations in relationship to the original massing and connected with surface patterns in construction paper.

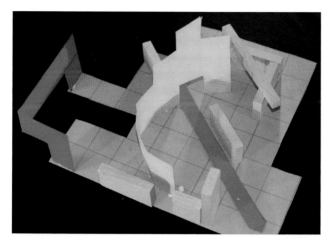

Figure 7.53 Superimposition

In this experiment I superimposed all three primary shapes: circle, square and line/axis. I mixed the play-tools to add variety and to investigate the nature of the varying tools. The first element placed in the grid was the semicircle followed by the red axis. I used a piece of construction paper left over from a previous construct and let that determine the extent of the exercise; leading to the red vertical plane corner— just letting the composition flow without forcing it into a predetermined design.

Figure 7.54 Symmetry to Asymmetry (A)

This begins with a square compositional structure in a symmetrical configuration, emanating out from the center augmented by repetition with variety—repeated squares in progressively higher planes with repeated and varying sized portals. The initial play-activities immediately resulted in changes to the concept plan diagram regarding a reduction in the heights of the squares as they moved away from the center. The symmetrical composition was placed on a color grid that was also manipulated following the construction of the vertical plane square composition— another opportunity. As I began the asymmetrical composition (B), I had a number of starting points—height variations, rotation options, all under the basic rule of equal "weight."

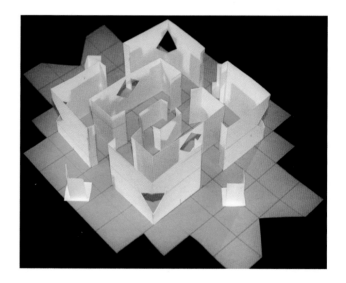

Figure 7.55 Asymmetrical Response (B)

Since the concept of symmetry to asymmetry implies that the major compositional principles of the initial pattern need to be reflected in the altered composition, I maintained the footprint of (A) as a beginning point. From there, I altered heights of the vertical planes to generate an asymmetrical version of (A).

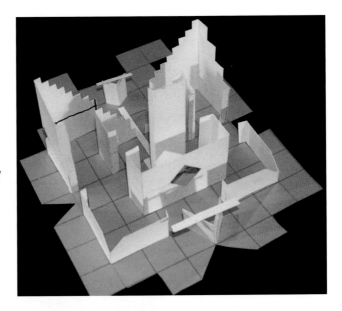

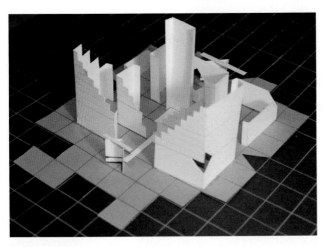

Figure 7.56 Asymmetrical Design Composition

Second view of asymmetrical design.

Mixed Symbolic Object Compositions

In the following play explorations, the cardboard and paper discovery or process model pieces are combined with other symbolic objects (wood blocks, string, wood slats, yarn, etc.) to add complexity as well as discover how the different pieces contributed to the larger composition.

As I was working on the book's play explorations I found myself bouncing around from single-shape compositions to combinations of shapes. In hindsight this helped reduce or avoid "packaging" or formulizing the play-activities. The exercises I gravitated toward with the most energy and excitement were those which began combining the various symbolic objects into urban design compositions.

The following scenarios represent ways of playing in the specific domains of community planning and design. The principles may be applied to other fields. I hesitate to use the term "exercise." In many ways this is an extension of *Urban Design* (Kasprisin, 2011). Due to the time constraint on constructing

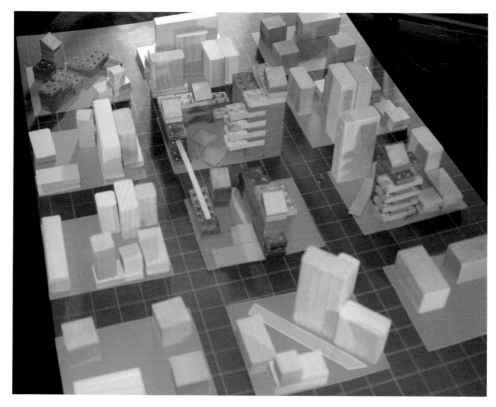

Figure 7.57 Mixed Object Composition Downtown Infill 1

I used the Playskool blocks and Halsam's Building Bricks in this experiment, working with a downtown block base. Again, due to time constraints, the block/street pattern is semi-abstract. The existing buildings are in Playskool blocks and the proposed infill is in Halsam's Building Bricks. As in most of the experiments, I began with a loosely defined problem, an aspiration with ambiguities. I played with basic shapes using activators, and let the design composition evolve and mature. In a real process, breaks to evaluate and test the compositions are interwoven into the play process. This is the first in a series, so I use it as a starting point for other subsequent experiments.

Figure 7.58 Mixed Object Composition Downtown Infill 2

A second view of the downtown infill discovery model oriented toward an historic church building in the lower left corner.

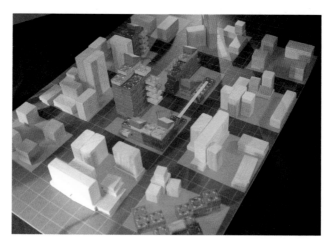

189

Figure 7.59 Hi-density Downtown Infill

This option was simple to execute as I increased the dimensions of the Halsam towers, using yellow bricks as highlights and protruding components. I also reused construction paper pieces from other models. Too many different play-tool types can lose harmony and lead to a cluttered or busy outcome.

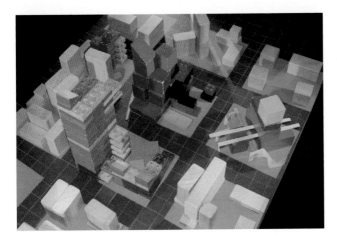

Figure 7.60 High-rise Complex

The experiment is with color wood blocks, the origin of which I am not sure, since I purchased them out of the original package. They are basic and suitable for quick studies, and are smooth and shiny so that they do not interlock and can fall apart easily. I used them with construction paper and wood slats to experiment with an urban block office tower complex.

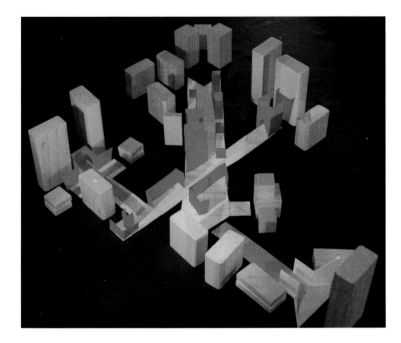

Figure 7.61a Axis Experiment with Wood Blocks A

I reused the line/axis example for a number of experiments that follow. The axis is the activator for the entire complex, framing the buildings and open space components. In play are wood blocks, construction paper and other materials. Each material changes the nature of the composition.

Figure 7.61b Axis Experiment with Wood Blocks A

Another version with wood blocks as the material used can vary and change outcomes.

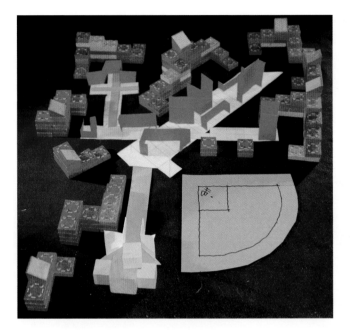

Figure 7.62a Axis Experiment with Halsam's Building Bricks

This quick and enjoyable experiment used the axis as a structuring device to arrange various housing configurations using Halsam's Building Bricks.

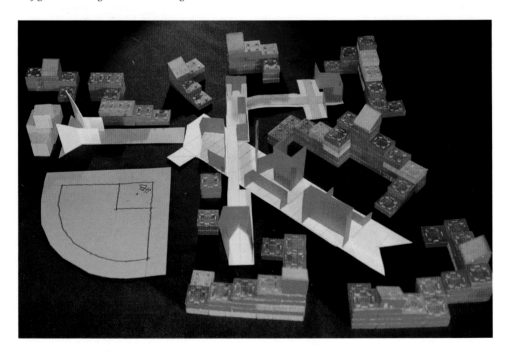

Figure 7.62b Axis Experiment with Halsam's Building Bricks

Additional fast manipulations of objects.

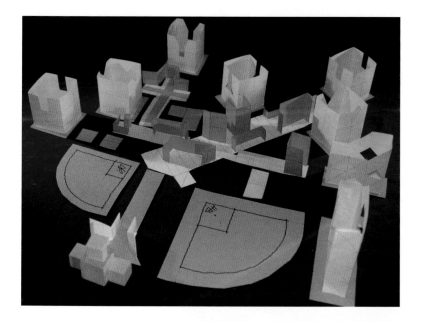

Figure 7.63 *(above)*
**Axis Experiment with
Construction Paper Volumes**

*This experiment used objects that I
constructed for other exercises and
they fit into the axial composition.
Red is commercial, yellow is
residential, etc. This took about
ten minutes or less to complete.*

**Figure 7.64 Urban Complex
Tower 1**

*This is an exercise I developed for
students to understand the force of
vertical axial elements (towers,
office buildings, etc.). I began the
exercise with a notion and not an
expectation, allowing ideas to
develop as I constructed the
various shapes, first of construction
paper. I began with a simple
vertical axis (orange volume) and
added a secondary skirt to
represent other, smaller building
parts that wrapped around the
tower to form a base.*

193

Figure 7.65 Urban Complex Tower 1 with Commercial

I added a red commercial component to the first construction for interest, color and directional movement (highlighting the corner and strengthening the base).

Figure 7.66 Urban Complex Tower Cluster

I added a second vertical axis component as a cluster of three narrow towers for an adjacent urban block. Here I used the concept of polarity or opposites (even symmetry to asymmetry) by breaking the larger original mass into three smaller components of varying heights (repetition with variety).

Figure 7.67 Urban Complex Initial Composition

I assembled the two blocks as an initial composition to see how they fitted and related to one another. I was satisfied based on the polarity between the two blocks and the balance achieved in both compositions together.

Figure 7.68a Urban Complex Tower 1 with Halsam's Bricks

I wanted to integrate a second major material or fractal into the composition, so I chose the interlocking Halsam's Building Bricks to represent housing forms around the base of the towers. I arranged them in a stepped fashion around the base with many possible variations. I did not want to overpower either the larger tower or the yellow skirt form.

Figure 7.68b Urban Complex Tower 1 with Halsam's Bricks

A second view from a different direction.

Figure 7.69 Urban Complex Tower Cluster with Halsam's Bricks

As in the tower 1 complex, I added Halsam's Building Bricks around the bases and through the center of the cluster to form a housing complex. The dispersed three towers presented more of a challenge at crafting a base with the bricks and essentially dictated the arrangement of the bricks.

**Figure 7.70 Final Tower
Composition**

*I put all components together for
the two block configuration as the
near-final composition. After doing
this I decided that the corners
needed articulation to complete a
square compositional structure
using smaller elements such as
lower buildings and open space.*

Figure 7.71 Corner Gestures

*I quickly put together vertical
planes with green horizontal
pieces for open space as the
corner gestures to complete the
square. I found them a little
loose and was not pleased with
the added foam material (trees)
but learned from the effort for a
later rendition.*

Figure 7.72 Last Enjoyable Experiment View A

One more experiment for class: I wanted to quickly demonstrate to my design composition students a last fast experiment using key object-learning activators to reinforce the importance of a spatial language. The larger yellow cube has elements subtracted, as do the smaller cubes. I then added the smaller cubes in a gradation arrangement to the larger cube, interlocking the smaller cubes. All this constitutes repetition with variety, dimensional change, interlocking and additive/ subtractive. I then used the red horizontal axis to establish a diagonal orientation along with another medium-sized cube at the same angle as the axis with subtractive elements. I then finished the composition with a small corner gesture with a yellow vertical plane. Fun—and a language in practice.

Figure 7.73 *(below)* Last Enjoyable Experiment View B

Another view of the spatial language experiment.

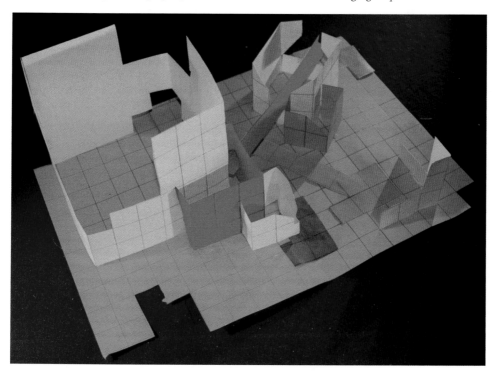

numerous models, I do not add extensive context materials—again a time constraint. In a studio or office, these contextual elements can easily be constructed by a team of students or professionals in a relatively short period of time. See the Urban Design Studio (UW, 2014) student models at the end of this section.

Once a base model is developed there are many variations and versions of concepts that can be played and articulated by a class, community group or office staff. The final two experiments build from the initial infill model, one at the same scale and one at an enlarged scale using different play-tools. The scale of the model affects the selection of play-tools and vice versa. I did not use Lego Plastic Bricks due to the scale; I found them more useful at a district-wide urban scale as the bricks are smaller than Halsam's.

This last section can go on and on and on into the night, producing one idea after another. I found myself visualizing ideas in my sleep at three o'clock in the morning. The creative aspect is the visualizations, not words or formulas. Once embedded in the discovery modeling process the flow is exhilarating. And generate the ideas; do not judge them prematurely.

All of these concept discovery and process models can be expanded into sophisticated designs. That is the next step. But I will end the object-learning play aspect at this point and close the chapter with urban design visualizations of both design composition quality and the quality of crafted skill: the work of Professor James Pettinari, Emeritus, University of Oregon.

Drawing as Object-learning

The majority of illustrations in this book comprise discovery models and diagrams contrary to the many drawings in *Urban Design* (Kasprisin, 2011). Drawing has been and remains a powerful play-tool in creative problem-solving for design and planning. I readily admit that drawing has always been a pleasurable activity and more than a design and communication tool. It requires, like painting, a direct connection and interaction between and among the senses, the pen, ink and paper. It is a personal signature wherein every person's renditions are unique; and each time I do a sketch it changes and evolves.

As examples of the power of drawing in design and planning, with a sense of play and funktionlust, I am using the work of my friend, colleague and business partner James Pettinari, Professor Emeritus, former Director of the Urban Architecture Program (Portland), University of Oregon. Professor Pettinari studied under Louis Kahn at the University of Pennsylvania and Dean Ralph Rapson at the University of Minnesota, wherein both universities placed a high value on drawing as a thinking process. James and I have practiced together since 1972 and we continue to engage drawing (and painting) as a passion of life.

The following drawings combine play, object-learning through drawing, design thinking and skill developed over years of effort and pleasure. They represent an extensive series of aerial oblique drawings by Professor Pettinari on the joy of drawing spatial geographies as means to communicate the larger urban and rural contexts.

Regional Aerial Oblique Perspective Drawings in Pen and Ink

Please note in his drawings the appreciation for and understanding of value with line density that highlights and dramatizes the key components of the drawings. In particular, note his treatment of edges that define the major shapes of the spatial geographies. These drawings go well beyond the technical drawing: they are crafted, not simulated. The drawings are executed with Rapidograph fine-point pens and India ink on mylar for permanence and durability.

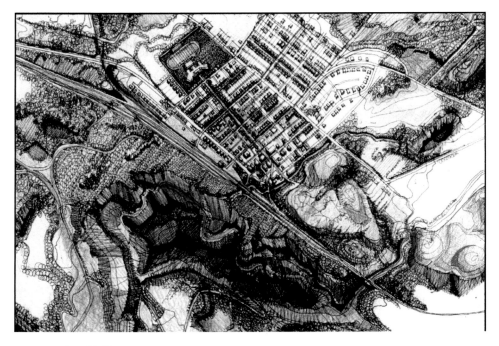

Figure 7.74 Buhl Close-up

This aerial illustrates the relationship of the town of Buhl, MN to the iron range excavations. The art of drawing is evident in these aerial oblique perspectives and serves as a reminder of the visual communication function of drawing and the interpretive and playful aspect in representing that function.
Source: Professor James Pettinari.

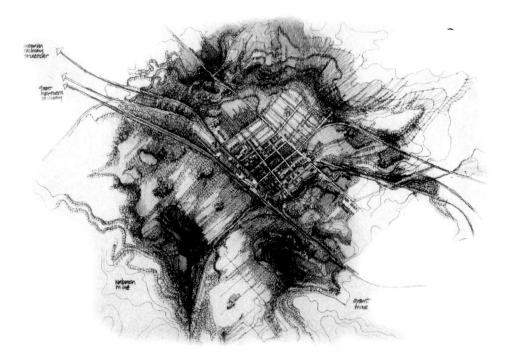

Figure 7.75 Buhl from Afar

The town of Buhl, Minnesota in the center of the Mesabi Iron Range is shown in its larger context.

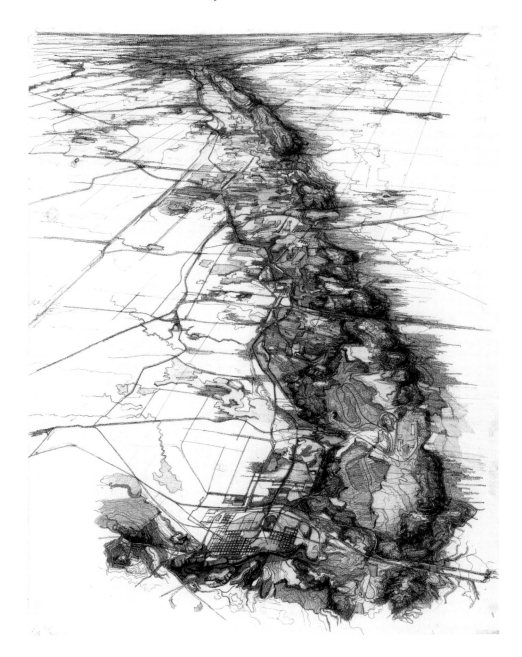

Figure 7.76 Buhl, Minnesota Mesabi Iron Range

This aerial oblique portrays the extent of the Mesabi Iron Range excavations and is a part of the geographical visual analysis prepared by Professor James Pettinari. Professor Pettinari grew up in the range and has had a lifelong fascination with both the range and its working mining towns and the railroads that serviced the industry.
Source: Professor James Pettinari.

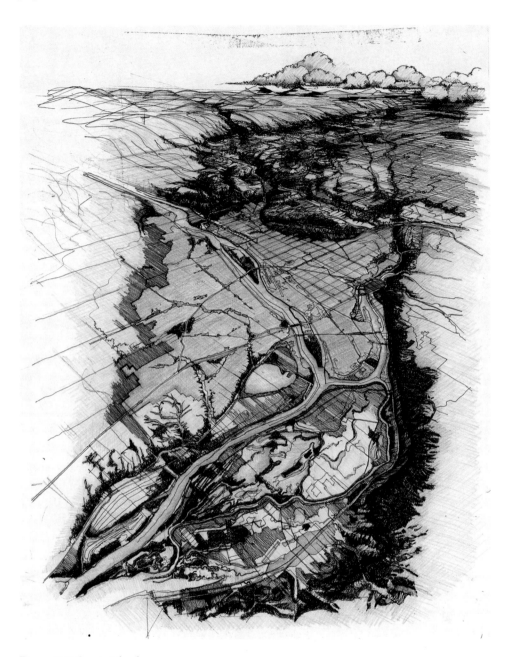

Figure 7.77 Sauvie Island

This aerial oblique perspective portrays the confluence of the Columbia and Willamette Rivers northwest of Portland Oregon highlighting Sauvie Island, an area of controversy regarding growth and rural areas. The aerial captures the context and relationships of community and rural agricultural lands. Professor Pettinari again demonstrates the use of line density to highlight important spaces via their edges and adds local color with color pencils. The power of visual communication and the joy of drawing are again exhibited in this perspective.
Source: Professor James Pettinari.

Chapter 8

INTEGRATION OF DIGITAL TECHNOLOGIES AND CRAFTING PROCESSES

When I began this book project I decided to do all of the experiments by myself with a few exceptions in order to experience the benefits (or not) of the physical manipulation of symbolic objects in the design/planning process, using manual dexterity with hands, tools, materials, etc. Based on an extensive involvement with approximately 150 illustrations, many of them symbolic object composition constructions, I experienced an overwhelming flow of ideas and directions from the process of *direct engagement*—working through the senses, trying and redoing constructions as I progressed through an idea. It is an artful process, something that has been an integral part of design for centuries. And it is one critical component of a larger process of making creative things; at arriving at creative or novel solutions to problems. I did not get precious about the products, treating them instead as fragile and temporary expressions in a larger design and planning process. They are symbolic, imaginal, and hopefully novel—what Cropley and Cropley refer to as *divergent: to branch out in different directions (from a common point), to deviate.*

The other part of the larger process is the analytical component of processing information, testing ideas and evaluating outcomes. Cropley and Cropley refer to this side of the creative problem-solving process as *convergent: to bring together, to come together to achieve a common result.*

The sensory or cognitive perception (divergent) and the intellectual mental components (convergent) do not sit side by side, adjacent; nor do they interact at the same level together. It is more akin to a dance of two people with a give-and-take, leading/following and following/leading in a relationship. They constantly interlock and integrate on all levels of thought and do so differently. In addition, similar to the concept of horizontal leadership, each takes the lead in certain situations with certain challenges that benefit from the aspects and attributes inherent within them. In other words, there is an appropriate use or application associated with each thinking component. This is where I observe a disconnect occurring in the design and planning fields, a separation of the two components of thought into competing and even antagonistic viewpoints with students and young professionals attempting to use one for all tasks in design and planning—a road to compromise.

Given the notion of horizontal leadership in thinking, sensory and intellectual, the argument for a pluralistic approach to (creative) problem-solving has a strong rationale: appropriate application and leadership.

There are some key distinctions in methodology that are critical to this pluralistic approach.

Creativity may occur at all levels of design and planning, from data-gathering to concept discovery to implementation. Those creative activities are different, just as the creative capacity is different for every individual involved in the process. And they benefit from the use of tools and methods that effectively facilitate creative actions. The point being that one tool does not fit all tasks.

Creative problem-solving uses both the intellect and the senses, both different, both utilizing different means and methods, and both integral to overall thought and creative actions. Let us take a look at those differences in more detail as they enable different approaches to creative thought. They both produce ideas with differing characteristics.

Divergent Thinking

> Divergent thinking . . . involves producing multiple answers through processes like *shifting perspective* on existing information (seeing it in a new way) or *transforming* it (i.e. through unexpected combinations of elements usually not regarded as belonging together). The answers arrived at via divergent thinking may never have existed before.
>
> (Cropley and Cropley, 2009, p. 48)

This is critical to the key components of creative problem-solving: the discovery of novel ideas that can lead to innovation. In my experience it is actually more than discovery in that the discovery may imply the uncovering of something hidden or buried rather than the creation of something that did not exist before and emerged from the act of object-learning and play.

Convergent Thinking

> Convergent thinking is oriented toward deriving the single best (or correct) answer to a given question. It emphasizes accuracy, correctness, and . . . focuses on *recognizing* the familiar, *reapplying* set techniques, and *preserving* the already known. It is based on familiarity with what is already known (i.e. conventional knowledge) and is not aimed at production of novelty, although it may sometimes have this result. It is most effective in situations where the answer already exists and needs simply to be recalled from what is already known by conventional and logical search, recognition, and decision-making strategies. IQ scores mainly reflect skill in convergent thinking.
>
> (Cropley and Cropley, 2009, p. 47)

Information processing and simulation fall under this aspect of thinking.

The plurality of approach in CPS is on the one hand generating novelty through discovery by divergent thinking, and evaluating that novelty by convergent thinking on the other. Characteristics of divergent and convergent thinking include the following:

Convergent	*Divergent*
Being logical	Being unconventional
Recognizing the familiar	Seeing the known in a new light
Combining what "belongs together"	Combining the disparate
Homing in on the single best answer	Producing multiple answers
Reapplying set techniques	Shifting perspective
Preserving the already known	Transforming the known
Being accurate and correct	Seeing new possibilities

In the processing, testing and evaluation of information and ideas, quantitative analytical methods dominate regarding means and methods and are well served by computational design and digital technologies. The generation of imaginal, symbolic spatial metaphors and the pursuit of novel ideas is well served by the crafting methods using a fuller range of senses through object-learning and play. Yes, I can do many tasks with only one side of the equation, and are my approach and methods appropriate? Am I simulating a design or generating novelty through discovery?

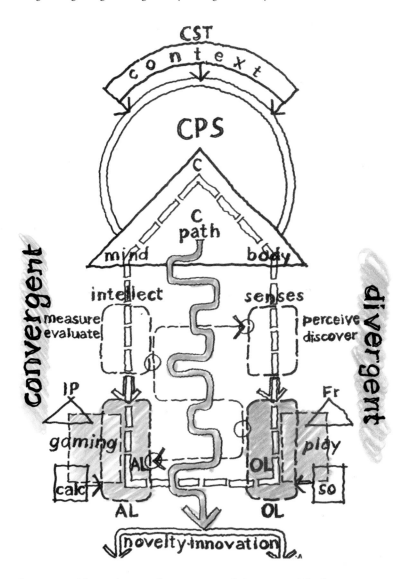

Figure 8.1 Creative Problem-solving with Divergent and Convergent Thinking

The key diagram illustrates the interchangeable use of divergent and convergent thinking, sensory and evaluative, in the larger design and planning process. This does not act as a committee with constant equal roles; instead they interchange the leadership in thought methodologies as is appropriate for the activities at hand.

The intellect via the mind identifies information and data, processes information including sensory experiences, intellectual thought and measures, and evaluates through various explorations their meaning and implications. Information-processing involves the calculation of probabilities, and is aided by digital learning technologies and methods from comparative analysis, graphic information system analytics; modeling and gaming as options are explored—a semi-abstract connection to reality. Cognitive perception is the act of learning (thinking) through the senses, a direct connection to hands-on reality.

My recent experiences (over the past five years or more) with undergraduate and graduate students in planning and design who have not used any methodology or tool except those related to the computer (digital technologies) have strengthened my resolve to bring back the other half, the sensual half, of the creative process. Infatuation with a tool or method (including drawing) does not justify that tool as being universal in CPS. For example, new digital three-dimensional printers present a challenge to the concept of discovery models. The construction of a model using the programmed laser cutter or modeling tool implies that all of the design discovery has been achieved in the programming, or will be evaluated after the model is complete. There is a disconnect here that needs to be addressed before the discovery process is diluted or lost.

In *Drawing for Urban Design* (Farrelly, 2011), the author states that the introduction of digital fabrication techniques for physical models, created from CAD images, is an important development which is stimulating new ways of thinking and designing. Of course they are, but in what aspect of design and planning? In discovery? In simulation, I agree with her conclusions that "In the journey from concept to realization, it is important to have the right tools and methods of representation and use them in an intelligent and skilful way" (Farrelly, 2011, p. 160). The issue here for me is the use of representation as a thought and discovery process—it is neither. As the use of computer-aided visualization methods continue their domination in design studios, this representation/simulation process becomes confused with the discovery process.

With computational design comes simulation—the representation of an operation of features of one process or system through the use of another: computer simulation . . . to make an imitation (*American Heritage Dictionary*). Again, representation is mistaken for discovery. Scheer (2014) discusses the challenges of bodily engagement with the processes of architectural design and the lack thereof with computational design. Efforts are underway, says Scheer, to improve the visual dimension of simulations . . . but (still) deny the designers direct experience with the qualities of physical media, and "the direct experience of planning and constructing a physical object" (Scheer, 2014, p. 162). I will go further: the direct experience of constructing a physical object through play releases ideas and concepts not yet awakened or named, as their existence is totally dependent upon that object manipulation.

Where does this leave us as architects and planners? Anti-technology? Anti-computational design? Hardly, and the reverse is the point: the creative solving process requires both and both are different, with different applications, timing and methods; and that principle is the responsibility of educators to identify and clarify. It is also the responsibility (to design quality) of designers and planners to recognize and apply.

In the work of Cropley and Cropley (2009), they conclude with the "Relationship Between Problem solving and the Phases of Creativity" (Table 11.1, p. 250).

As we look at the integration of the mind/intellect and the body/senses components of CPS, there are academic and professional fields that benefit by a leadership of one over the other, not to the exclusion of the other. From Cropley and Cropley (Table 9.1, p. 210, par.1).

Differences among Academic Fields

Investigative		Artistic	
Characteristics	Examples	Characteristics	Examples
Impersonal	Mathematics	Emotive	Art History
Objective	Engineering	Subjective	Writing
Structured	Biology	Unstructured	Composing
Formal	Medicine	Informal	Visual Arts

For architecture, landscape architecture, urban design and planning this is less clear, as the overall nature of the fields requires both artistic and investigative (or at least historically) processes. The artistic component is disappearing, overshadowed by simulation rather than by generation.

CLOSE TO HOME   **BY JOHN McPHERSON**

Figure 8.2 Close at home

Source: © 2015 John McPherson. Reprinted with permission of UniversalUClick.

*

I hope that the work exhibited in this book can inspire a new generation of designers and planners to embrace this pluralism in approach, this whole mind–body thought process that uses our senses and our technologies in the pursuit of creative solutions to the myriad problems of our cities and towns. Our new technologies are intoxicating with their stimuli and fast-paced processing. There is, I argue, a greater intoxification in the integration of the artful and the intellectual in how we design and plan, not only stimulating but interlaced with passion for the making of things beyond a three-dimensional printer. Play is an adult activity—free and with little or no fear—where failure is a learning tool not a punishment.

Some Final Thoughts . . .

Play is an inherent and necessary ingredient in creative processes—*playing as distinguished from gaming, generation as opposed to simulation.* The psychological studies of creative problem-solving referred to in this book deal extensively with attitude, behavior and environment that enable creative activities. There is a spark within those activities and it is embodied or stimulated by three key principles found in "living" or creative systems (Johnston, 1991) and adapted for this application:

1.   Creative actions are relational, composed of interlocking "parts" as smaller whole systems, experiencing existence in their relationships in a larger whole. There are no relationships without difference; and the difference(s) is experimented through free and uncertain activities referred to here as "play."
2.   Creative actions are evolutionary, with change as an intrinsic ingredient, where the creativity is self-organizing, where form and free activity interconnect in the dance of design. In play, the enjoyment is in the ever-changing nature of the activity, beginning with a set of starting points or rules and changing as the activity progresses into unknown space—emerging into what Soja (1996) portrays as *thirdspace: a third and distinctly different outcome emanating from the essential differences of basic ingredients of the problem.*
3.   Creative actions are meta-determinant, where uncertainty is inherent within the process at all levels, enabling the "design" to organize and assemble from the dynamics of the process, not the simulation or security of an unchanging final order—represented through simulation as established (often corporate) models. Play is not an act of simulation; it is a constant dynamic generation of openness through playfulness: divergent.

The McPherson cartoon (Figure 8.2) represents a comparison of two main approaches to design and planning: the sophisticated gym set serves as the view of design as *design science and technology—where a theoretical knowledge exists prior to any practical application, applied in a methodically prescribed manner;* and the empty boxes serve as the view of design where design rules are not objective and are efficacious and appropriate (only) to the degree that they are capable of giving rise to inexhaustible possibilities of interpretation and action (Snodgrass and Coyne, 2006). The boxes do have a preliminary set of rules characterized by their size and shape as a beginning, and become flexible and manipulable as holes are cut into sides, and parts are bent and formed into spatial metaphors.

These principles of creativity and play may be further extended into the making of cities, as interactions of smaller systems or "parts" (e.g., blocks, neighborhoods, districts) into a larger *creative urbanism.* This creative urbanism has a measure of coherence (a continuing functionality related to meaning that is carried forward until the creative capacitance begins to alter the rules), and can exhibit novel and innovative spatial outcomes due to a significant meta-determinant that is intentionally honored throughout the design and planning processes. Quite a challenge.

As we all grapple with the powerful influences of digital technologies in our design and planning domains, the responsibility of fostering creativity is an ongoing challenge within the overall process and within the means and methods of everyday actions. As emphasized and articulated by Tom and David Kelley (2013), creativity is in all of us; and the task at hand for educators, mentors, supervisors and managers in all domains is to assist in the release of that creativity. And the glue in the larger creative problem-solving process is play—a free activity without failure, uncertain, open and filled with passion—no matter what the domain.

Go play!

Appendix

SUGGESTED EXERCISES IN OBJECT-LEARNING PLAY

Exercises are dispersed throughout the book as suggestions for educators and emerging professionals. They are guides, not established rules. I suggest they be used as a base for complex and challenging exercises and experiments in design studios and studio preparation courses. They can even be used, as did the Bettisworth North (Fairbanks) staff, as fun Friday afternoon adventures in design-play.

I am including additional exercises from my Urban Design Composition course (University of Washington, Department of Urban Design and Planning, College of Built Environments). After experimenting with various exercises from week-long assignments to weekly "sketch" problems, I personally prefer a series of one-week "construct sketches" for the students so that they can learn to quickly put compositions together with specific object-learning activators (repetition with variety, gradation, symmetry/asymmetry, etc.); limiting their problem-solving objectives. In the past I assigned larger scale and longer time event projects. Both have value and the shorter intensives showed excellent advancement among the students.

These exercises utilize the object-learning activators as guides for each composition. All of this is done with the understanding that under real circumstances the spatial-cultural-historic contexts and space programming factors are integrated into the design process. These exercises focus on the elements and principles of composition.

At the end of this Appendix I provide a final example of complex constructs using these exercises.

EXERCISE A.1: THREE-DIMENSIONAL WARM-UP COMPOSITIONAL STRUCTURES

Intent

Three exercises:

1. Identify three axes with a hierarchy (primary, secondary and tertiary); using the axis, assemble three-dimensional constructions from construction paper per the instructor's examples and arrange in a principled fashion (i.e., using one or more of the transformational activators); horizontal and vertical shapes and elements are available (i.e., a green park area is horizontal; a secondary plaza or courtyard is horizontal (and structural)); buildings can be both horizontal and vertical.
2. Using a circle or square as a compositional structure, construct a semi-abstract composition with three-dimensional constructs in construction paper; the same principles apply as for (1).
3. Superimpose two compositional structures, do the same again as above (1 and 2).

APPENDIX

Notes:

- Do this on a piece of illustration board for a stiff base; put a grid on the base with color pencil.
- Play with the vertical planes (roofs are not necessary unless you so desire), put a grid on the construction paper and have fun with vertical plane designs as a part of your larger composition; remember that the "grid" has many derivatives and does not necessarily have to remain a series of squares (triangles, diamonds, rectangles and circles).
- Appreciate and play with the color aspects of the paper (color opposites, etc.).

EXERCISE A.2: TWO ONE-WEEK CONSTRUCT SKETCHES

These examples consisted of the final quarter assignments and students were asked to apply a variety of object-learning activators in their constructs. Again, they are a guide and example, and may be used to establish any relative context base.

Final Project Set-up

Prepare the following context paper construction base to work on in class (group effort); work as a team on the first part of this exercise.

1. On a 20 inch × 30 inch piece of brown or terracotta illustration board, draw in a one-inch grid with a light color pencil such as white or cream on the entire board. I suggest using a T-square or straight edge.
2. Center two 400-feet square urban blocks on the board at 1″ = 40 feet with a mid-block street at 80 feet in width, including surrounding streets. Have surrounding streets go off board in north–south and east–west directions with north at the top of the board.
3. On the north and south, across the street from the northern site boundary, construct a vertical plane "U" building façade 100 feet high; do the same on the south side across the street.
4. On northwest and southeast adjacent blocks, construct vertical "U" façade planes 200 feet in height (play with street-level story using red paper or façade cut-outs if desired).
5. On a northeast adjacent block construct a 40-feet-high vertical "U" façade plane that is set back 30 feet from the street.
6. On a southwest block leave blank as a park (add green construction paper base).
7. Suggestions: use a different color base to outline the blocks; you can use color tape (white or gray) to lay down for streets—one inch is a 40-feet cartway leaving sidewalks between the cartway and the block boundary. Make adjacent buildings out of construction paper or tag or railroad paper (white, inexpensive). Grids on these papers can help establish visual scale and dimensions. Assume 10 feet per floor for office and residential, and 15 feet for commercial uses (it is actually 13 but use 15). If you want to get fancy (not required), you can put a 15-feet-high red paper strip at the bottom of each context vertical plane for the retail ground floor.
8. There is a 90-feet-square vacant historic building located on the site on the southeast corner of the northern block that is set back 20 feet from the street on both streets.

Do two different assignments (see below) using the same contextual project area. The intent of the exercises is as follows.

Due (one week): Use your object-learning activators to prepare a high-density new town (residential, commercial, civic, open space) within the two blocks—develop a basic storyline if you wish or as you work through the exercise (i.e., do not necessarily establish a set storyline before you start—let it evolve).

Due (One Week): Repeat as above and prepare an urban campus that contains high-density dormitories, a student center and library, and associated academic buildings. Use your imagination and don't get hung up in detail on any of these facilities.

Use existing downtown zoning envelopes and, in place of a hardened space program, build out or maximize the site parameters.

Have fun.

EXERCISE EXAMPLE

The following illustrations are the last play exercise I composed for the book. They are a beginning, not an end. As I worked on the constructs many other variations and hybrids surfaced for future iterations, some of which are illustrated regarding a rearrangement of the pods. The construct shown here is busy with a lot of forms and shapes, and provides the base for hybrids, instead of trying to get the first composition "perfect." Working with the individual pods as a starting point aided in flexibility, I was able to move and turn each to develop connections between and among them. I also constructed other pods to drop in for variety and new directions.

I kept small remnant pieces of paper to add to the emerging composition for emphasis. Again, these represent a beginning, not an end in the design process. Let the ideas flow, and evaluate and assess at a later time.

Figure A.1 New Town in Town

This play exercise began with an idea for three interconnected pods of shapes using a variety of object-learning activators: repetition with variety, diagonality, gradation, movement and direction, etc. I intentionally let the composition and the storyline evolve rather than setting a predetermined image and outcome.

Figure A.2 Pod View One

I used construction paper, yarn and illustration board in the constructs for ease of assembly and flexibility. Again, these constructs can be the early stages of a developing design concept that progressively becomes more complex and detailed, changing the materials of the symbolic objects.

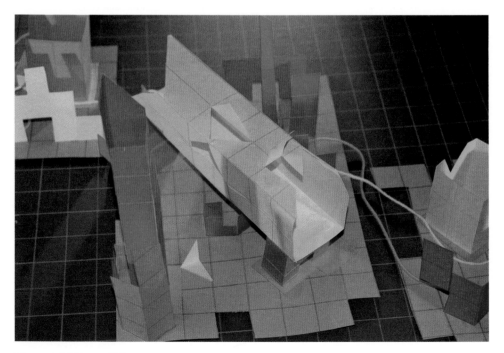

Figure A.3 Diagonal View

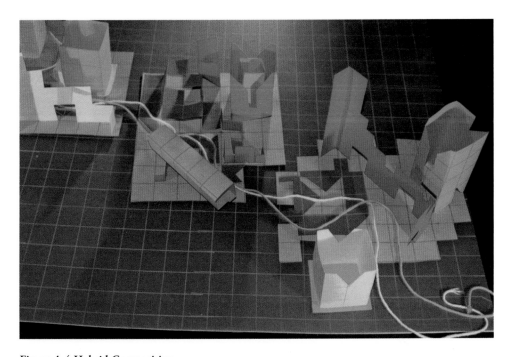

Figure A.4 Hybrid Composition

In this iteration, I reoriented the pods to compose a different axial movement pattern for the composition.

Figure A.5 Pod View Two

Working with flexible materials such as construction paper allowed me to quickly assemble hybrids and drop them into the original composition. The next step can be a change of materials and an additional level of detail both for site as well as building type and massing.

NOTES

1   *The League of Ancient Youth* is a humorous label concocted by friend and colleague Jack Adams, actor/director and wine-maker, to describe a group of us who are in our later stages of life and still irascible and engaged with creative actions.

2   William Hook is an architectural illustrator in the Seattle, Washington area and is featured in Thomas Schaller's book, *Architecture in Watercolor*.

3   "A Community of Learners: Opportunities for the Redmond Elementary School Site," prepared by the University of Washington *Center for Architecture and Education*, April, 1996. Participants on the Design/Planning Team included College of Education: Jerry Bamburg, Director, Center for Effective Schools; Fran Hunkins, Ph.D. Chair, Curriculum and Instruction; College of Architecture and Urban Planning: Ron Kasprisin (Facilitator) URBDP, Julie Johnson, LA, Dale Lang, Ed Maasse, and Maya Wahyudharma (graduate students); and Lake Washington School District, City of Redmond: Architect John Bennett, AIA (Meng Associates), Community and Business participants.

4   A design charrette or intensive as developed by the American Institute of Architects requires a three- to five-day period (preferred) for the execution of the event, including the preparation and presentation of the final product. A one- to three-day charrette, to be executed with any validity, requires significant preparation time and actions, including issue workshops, graphic preparation and stakeholder contacts prior to the actual event. The event must result in a completed product for presentation to the community client as part of the charrette for it to be classified as a charrette or intensive. In the New Westminster Downtown League Design Charrette (New Westminster British Columbia Downtown Association), City staff conducted many issue and idea meetings prior to the event; and the design team prepared base plan and perspective graphics prior to the event to facilitate the design team efforts during the charrette.

BIBLIOGRAPHY

Akhtar, Monish, 2011. *Play and Playfulness: Developmental, Cultural, and Clinical Aspects.* Jason Aronson, Lanham, MD.

Arnheim, Rudolph, 1969. *Visual Thinking.* University of California Press, Berkeley.

Brooks, J.G. and Brooks, M.G., 1993. *In Search of Understanding: The Case for Constructivist Classrooms.* Association of Supervision and Curriculum Development, Alexandria, VA.

Brosterman, Norman, 1997. *Inventing Kindergarten.* Harry N. Abrams, Inc., New York.

Brown, Stuart, 2009. *Play: How it Shapes the Brain, Opens the Imagination, and Invigorates the Soul.* Penguin Group, New York.

Bruner, J., 1966. *Toward a Theory of Instruction.* Harvard University Press, Cambridge, MA.

Bruner, J., 1990. *Acts of Meaning.* Harvard University Press, Cambridge, MA.

Bruner, J., 1996. *The Culture of Education.* Harvard University Press, Cambridge, MA.

Buhler, Karl, 1930. *Die geistige Entwicklung des Kindes [The Mental Development of Children].* G. Fisher, Jena, Germany.

Child, Lydia, 1831. *The Mothers Book.* Carter and Hendee, Boston.

Ching, Francis D.K., 1990. *Drawing: a Creative Process.* John Wiley & Sons, New York.

Cohen, David, 2006 (3rd edn). *The Development of Play.* Routledge, London and New York.

Connery, M.C., John-Steiner, V.P. and Marjanovic-Shane, A., 2010. *Vygotsky and Creativity.* Peter Lang, New York.

Creevy, Bill, 1991. *The Pastel Book: Materials and Techniques for Today's Artist.* Watson-Guptill Publications, New York.

Cropley, Arthur and Cropley, David, 2009. *Fostering Creativity: A Diagnostic Approach for Higher Education and Organizations.* Hampton Press, Inc., Cresskill, NJ.

Csikszentmihalyi, Mihaly, 1990. *Flow: The Psychology of Optimal Experience.* Harper & Row, New York.

Cuthbert, Alexander (ed.), 2003. *Designing Cities: Critical Readings in Urban Design.* Blackwell, Oxford.

Dewey, J., 1910/1933. *How We Think: A restatement of the reflective thinking to the educative process.* Heath, Boston.

Dow, G.T. and Mayer, R.E., 2004. *Creativity Research Journal,* 16, 389–402.

Doyle, Michael E., 1999. *Color Drawing.* John Wiley & Sons, New York.

Eberle, Scott G., 2014. "The Elements of Play: Toward a Philosophy and a Definition of Play." *American Journal of Play, The Strong,* 6(2), 214–233.

Farrelly, Lorraine, 2011. *Drawing for Urban Design.* Laurence King Publishing, London.

Froebel, Friedrich, 1898 [1926]. *The Education of Man.* Translated from the German and annotated by W.N. Hailmann, A.M., Superintendent of Public Schools at La Porte, Indiana. D. Appleton and Company, New York. Reprinted in 2005 by Dover Publications, Mineola, NY.

Gaillois, Roger, 1961. *Man, Play and Games.* Translated by Meyer Barash. The Free Press of Glencoe, New York.

BIBLIOGRAPHY

Garvey, Catherine, 1977. *Play.* Harvard University Press, Cambridge, MA.

Glover, J.A., Ronning, R.R. and Reynolds, C.R. (eds.), 1989. *Handful of Creativity.* Plenum Press, New York.

Goldstein, Nathan, 1989. *Design and Composition.* Prentice Hall Inc., New Jersey.

Henricks, Thomas S., 2014. "Play as Self-realization: Toward a General Theory of Play." *American Journal of Play, The Strong,* 6(2), 190–213.

Huizinga, Johan, 1955. *Homo Ludens: A Study of the Play Elements in Culture.* Beacon Press, Boston, MA.

Itten, Joseph, 1970. *The Elements of Color: A Treatise on the Color System of Johannes Itten,* based on his book *The Art of Color.* Van Nostrand Reinhold, New York.

Johnston, Charles M., MD, 1984/1986. *The Creative Imperative.* Celestial Arts, Berkeley, CA.

Johnston, Charles M., MD, 1991. *Necessary Wisdom: Meeting the Challenge of a New Cultural Maturity.* ICD Press, Seattle, Washington, DC, and Celestial Arts, Berkeley, CA.

Johnston, Charles M., MD, 1994. *The Power of Diversity: A Brief Introduction to the Creative Systems Personality Typology.* ICD Press, Seattle, Washington, DC.

Jones, David, 2012. *The Aha! Moment.* The Johns Hopkins University Press, Baltimore, MD.

Kasprisin, Ron, 1989. *Watercolor in Architectural Design.* Van Nostrand Reinhold, New York.

Kasprisin, Ron, 1999. *Design Media.* John Wiley & Sons, New York.

Kasprisin, Ron, 2011. *Urban Design: The Composition of Complexity.* Routledge, Oxfordshire.

Kasprisin, Ron and Pettinari, James, 1995. *Visual Thinking for Architects and Designers.* John Wiley & Sons, New York.

Kelley, Tom and Kelley, David, 2013. *Creative Confidence.* Crown Business (Crown Publishing Group), New York.

Krasny, Elke, 2008. *The Force is in the Mind: The Making of Architecture.* Architekturzentrum Wien, Basel/Boston/Berlin.

Krysa, Dannielle, 2014. *Creative Block: Advice and Projects.* Chronicle Books LLC, San Francisco, CA.

L'Abate, Luciano, 2009. *The Praeger Handbook of Play across the Life Cycle: From Infancy to Old Age.* ABC-CLO, LLC, Santa Barbara, CA.

Lefebvre, Henri, 1991. *The Production of Space.* Blackwell, Oxford, and Cambridge, MA.

Lehrer, Jonah, 2012. *Imagine: How Creativity Works.* Canongate Books, Edinburgh/London.

Lieberman, Nina J., 1977. *Playfulness: Its Relationship to Imagination and Creativity.* Academic Press, New York.

Linn, Susan, 2008. *The Case for Make Believe: Saving Play in a Commercialized World.* The New Press, New York.

Ludwig, A.M., 1998. "Method and Madness in the Arts and Sciences." *Creativity Research Journal, 11,* 93–101.

McLaughlin, Maureen and Vogt, MaryEllen (eds.), 2000. *Creativity and Innovation in Content Area Teaching.* Christopher-Gordon Publishers, Inc., Norwood, MA.

Morris, Mark, 2006. *Models: Architecture and the Miniature.* Wiley-Academy, London.

Mudede, Charles. "The Art Animal." *Arcade* 31.3, Tuesday August 6, 2013.

National Museum of Play, A Component of The Strong (educational center), 1 Manhattan Square, Rochester, New York.

Pestalozzi, Heinrich, 1951. *The Education of Man,* translated by Heinz and Ruth Norden. Philosophical Society, New York.

Prager, Phillip, 2014. "Making Sense of the Modernist Muse: Creative Cognition and Play at the Bauhaus." *American Journal of Play*, 7(1), 27–49.

Reid, Charles, 1991. *Painting by Design.* Watson-Guptill Publications, New York.

Reid, Charles, 1994. *The Natural Way to Paint.* Watson-Guptill Publications, New York.

Rubin, Jeanne Spielman, 2002. *Intimate Triangle: Architecture of Crystals, Frank Lloyd Wright, and the Froebel Kindergarten.* Polycrystal Book Service, Huntsville, AL.

Schaller, Thomas W., 1990. *Architecture in Watercolor.* Van Nostrand Reinhold, New York.

Scheer, David Ross, 2014. *The Death of Drawing: Architecture in the Age of Simulation.* Routledge, Oxfordshire.

Shapiro, Michael Steven, 1983. *Child's Garden: The Kindergarten Movement from Froebel to Dewey.* Pennsylvania State University Press, University Park, Pennsylvania, PA.

Shen, Xiangyou Sharo, Chick, Garry and Zinn, Harry Spring, 2014, "Validating the Adult Playfulness Trait Scale (APTS)." *American Journal of Play*, 6(3), 345–369.

Shepard, Benjamin, 2011. *Play, Creativity, and Social Movements: If I Can't Dance, It's Not My Revolution.* Routledge, Taylor and Francis Group, New York.

Snodgrass, Adrian and Coyne, Richard, 2006. *Interpretation in Architecture: Design as a Way of Thinking.* Routledge, London and New York.

Soja, Edward, 1996. *Thirdspace.* Blackwell, Oxford.

Solnit, Albert J., MD, Cohen, Donald J., MD and Neubauer, Peter B., MD (eds.), 1993. *The Many Meanings of Play: A Psychoanalytic Perspective.* Yale University Press, New Haven, CT, and London.

Steen, Lynn Arthur (ed.), 1990. *On the Shoulders of Giants: New Approaches to Numeracy.* National Academy Press, Washington, DC.

Sternberg, Robert J. and Lubart, Todd I., 1995. *Defying the Crowd: Cultivating Creativity in a Culture of Conformity.* The Free Press, New York and London.

Stevens, Victoria, 2014. "To Think Without Thinking: The Implications of Combinatory Play and the Creative Process for Neuroaesthetics." *American Journal of Play*, 7(1), 99–119.

Strauss, Anselm and Corbin, Juliet, 1998. *Basics of Qualitative Research*, 2nd edn. Sage Publications, Thousand Oaks, CA/London/New Delhi.

Sylvia, Kathy (ed.) with Bruner, Jerome S. and Jolly, Alison, 1976. *Play: Its Role in Development and Evolution.* Basic Books, New York.

Talbot, John & Associates, 2009. *Visions for Sechelt BC.* District of Sechelt, BC, Canada.

Tomporowski, Phillip, 2003. *The Psychology of Skill: A Life-span Approach.* Praeger Publishers, Westport, CT.

Tufte, Edward, 1990. *Envisioning Information.* Graphics Press LLC, Cheshire, CT.

21st Century Production District, 1989. Produced by the Department of Architecture, University of Oregon, Eugene, OR, through a grant from the National Endowment for the Arts to the Southeast Uplift Neighborhood Program of Portland, Professor James Pettinari, faculty advisor.

Verger, Morris, 1994. *Connective Planning.* McGraw Hill, New York.

Vygotsky, L.S., 1978. *Men in Society: The Development of Higher Psychological Processes*, ed. M. Cole, V. John-Steiner, S. Scribner and E. Souberman. Harvard University Press, Cambridge, MA.

Weigardt, Eric, 2002. American Impressionist Painter (Watercolors), Ocean Park, Washington, DC. Watercolor workshop demonstration.

Weissman, Harold, 1990. *Serious Play: Creativity and Innovation in Social Work.* NASW Press, Silver Springs, MD.

BIBLIOGRAPHY

Wenner, Melinda, 2009. "Smile! It Could Make You Happier." *Scientific American Mind,* September/October.

Wiebe, Edward and Bradley, Milton, 1906. *Paradise of Childhood: A Practical Guide to Kindergarten.* Milton Bradley & Company, Springfield MA (reprint).

Wu, Kingsley K., 1990. *Freehand Sketching.* Van Nostrand Reinhold, New York.

INDEX

Activators, *see also* object-learning activators
Additive/subtractive 170
Animation 171
Arnheim, Rudolph 24
Arousal modification theory 7, 41

Bauhaus 46
Bettisworth North Architects 53
Brainstorming 146–150
Bridging polarities 22, 41
Brosterman, Norman 41–42

Charrettes 67, 150–160
Cognitive pluralism 74
Computational design 206
Consolidation 171
Constructivism 24–26: principles 25;
    characteristics 25; environment 25–26
Context 20
Convergent thinking 203–204
Crafting processes 203–204
Creative Problem-solving: defined 1–3, 9;
    characteristics of 17; components 14;
    guidelines 18; principles 16
Creative Urbanism 208
Creativity 3, 10: assessing 11–13; blockages 35;
    training for 11
CST matrix 13, 20–22

Diagram 128: as doodle 105; *see also* Semiotic and
    semiotic diagramming
Digital technologies 203
Dimensional change/size 171
Distortion 171
Divergent thinking 203

Emerging complexity 107
Emotion 7

Emphasis 170
Environment 8, 16, 18, 59: as studio 60–70

Failure, as success 64
Fear 36, 40
Fragmentation 171
Froebel, Friedrich 4, 41: the gifts of 42–46

Gameboard 125
Gaming 123–126
Generation 208
Gignac, David 53
Goal-oriented thinking, *see* normative problem-
    solving

Halsam's American Wood Building Bricks 91
Horizontal leadership 203
Horizontal thinking 203

Innovation 63–64
Insight 8
Intensive, *see* charrettes
Isolation 172

Johnston, Charles MD 41

Kindergarten 41: and US Public Education
    System 48

Le Corbusier 47–48
Lefebvre, Henri 6, 13
Legos 100
Lloyd Wright, Frank 47
Luebtow, John 4, 52

McPherson, John 207–208
Meaning-making 6, 21
Meta-creativity 3

Meta-play 3, 30, 74
M.J. Approach 127
Models, process and discovery 118–121:
        gaming 119

Neoteny 8
Normative Problem-solving 2
Novelty 12

Object-learning 2, 8, 15, 23: functions of 30
Object-learning activators 168
Object-play 26
Object-Teaching 24

Panpsychism 8
Pestalozzi, Johann 24
Pettinari, James 110, 140, 142–143, 198–202
Play 4, 6, 27–29: attributes of 29; cathartic
        function 7, 34; combinatory 31;
        descriptions 29; emergent system 7;
        functions 30; social-unit 33; motivational
        aspects 31; sensory process 5
Playfulness 28
Play-objects 7
Play-skills 7
Playskool wood blocks 97
Play-tools 19: as fractal geometries 38
Proprioception 8

Remote associations 172

Segmentation 172
Semiotic and semiotic diagramming 129
Simulation 208
Soja, Edward 6, 13
Spatial metaphors 6
Spatial reference guide 78
Studio: as integral education process 64;
        as uncertainty process 65; *see also*
        environment
Substitution 171
Symbolic objects 72, 75–78
Symmetry/asymmetry 171

Thinking, *see* whole mind-body thinking;
        horizontal thinking; divergent thinking;
        convergent thinking
Thirdspace 208
Toys 75
Transference 170
Transformational actions 170

Vygotsky, L.S. 6

Whole mind-body thinking 10